C000180688

WALKING
TOWARDS
OURSELVES

WALKING TOWARDS OURSELVES

INDIAN WOMEN TELL THEIR STORIES

Edited by Catriona Mitchell

hardie grant books

Published in 2016 by Hardie Grant Books

Hardie Grant Books (Australia)
Ground Floor, Building 1
658 Church Street
Richmond, Victoria 3121
www.hardiegrant.com.au

Hardie Grant Books (UK)
5th & 6th Floor
52–54 Southwark Street
London SE1 1UN
www.hardiegrant.co.uk

All rights reserved. No part of this publication may be reproduced, stored in a retrieval system or transmitted in any form by any means, electronic, mechanical, photocopying, recording or otherwise, without the prior written permission of the publishers and copyright holders.

The moral rights of the author have been asserted.

Individual essays © retained by the authors 2016
Collection © Hardie Grant Books 2016

A Cataloguing-in-Publication entry is available from the catalogue of the National Library of Australia at www.nla.gov.au
Walking Towards Ourselves: Indian Women Tell Their Stories
ISBN 978 1 74379 112 7

Cover design by Mark Campbell

Text design and typesetting by Patrick Cannon

pp. 57–56: Some sections of 'Black' by Rosalyn D'Mello were originally published in 'Dark and Prejudice', *The Hindu Business Line*, 2015

pp. 193–207: Some sections of 'Cast Away' by Tisca Chopra were originally published in *Acting Smart*, HarperCollins India, 2014

The publishers wish to acknowledge the Australia–India Council for their generous financial support.

Australian Government | **Australia-India Council**

Printed by McPherson's Printing Group, Maryborough, Victoria

FSC
www.fsc.org
MIX
Paper from
responsible sources
FSC® C001695

The paper this book is printed on is certified against the Forest Stewardship Council® Standards. FSC promotes environmentally responsible, socially beneficial and economically viable management of the world's forests.

CONTENTS

FOREWORD: WOMEN IN SEARCH OF THEMSELVES   1
Namita Gokhale

INTRODUCTION   7
Catriona Mitchell

PROLOGUE: BREAKING THE SILENCE   25
Leila Seth

REARRANGED MARRIAGE   39
Ira Trivedi

BLACK   58
Rosalyn D'Mello

SQUARE PEG, ROUND HOLE   68
Mitali Saran

OXYGEN   78
Urvashi Butalia

OVER MY SHOULDER   88
Annie Zaidi

HOME GIRL: A DAY IN THE LIFE OF
A SMALL-TOWN SOCIAL WORKER   104
Anjum Hasan

BEYOND MEMORIES   119
Salma

CONTENTS

THE VILLAGE WITHOUT MEN   131
Anita Agnihotri

TICK TOCK   141
Tishani Doshi

SCENES FROM A MARRIAGE   154
Anonymous

LOVE IN THE TIME OF THE INTERNET   159
Ira Trivedi

S/HE GENERIS: SHAPE-SHIFTING OUR WAY
ACROSS THE RIVER OF DESIRE   166
Margaret Mascarenhas

KARAIKAL AMMAIYAR AND HER CLOSET
OF ADORNMENTS   181
Sharanya Manivannan

CAST AWAY   193
Tisca Chopra

MATAJI   208
Deepti Kapoor

BAMBOO BASKETS AND BROCADE SARIS:
LIFE AND STORIES OF DALIT WOMEN   222
C.S. Lakshmi

TWO SISTERS, TWO LIVES   235
Nirupama Dutt

THE SCIMITAR OF WORDS   247
Chitra Banerjee Divakaruni

ABOUT THE AUTHORS   256

ACKNOWLEDGEMENTS   264

ABOUT THE EDITOR   266

FOREWORD
WOMEN IN SEARCH
OF THEMSELVES

NAMITA GOKHALE

As a writer, publisher and festival director, there are various journeys I have made across my life. Through *yatras*[1] and *parikramas*[2] and pilgrimages, I have tried to make sense of my world and find patterns of meaning within it. Through writing and publishing books, through literary events, through the lived life which is the raw material of it all, it has taken me some time to accept that I am woman writer.

When my debut novel *Paro: Dreams of Passion* was published in 1984, it subjected me to the shocked outrage of Indian readers who could not believe that a bona-fide Indian woman had so flagrantly crossed the line of propriety. I had thought of it as a comic novel and was surprised by the outrage; it's a relief that different generations of readers have found it funny for over thirty years now.

---

1. Sacred journeys
2. Circumambulations

It's been a long journey, a stumbling quest across twelve books, and another I am currently working on. I have at last come to terms with being a woman – an Indian woman – whatever that might imply.

I am a writer, I am a woman. Yet, as writers, we are more than the sum of our sex, gender and biology. As writers we are constantly trying to enter the minds and skins and situations of all the people we write about, be they men, women, both, or neither. And yet there is a critical mass of womanhood inside many of us – an aggregate of hurts, rejections and assertions – that we don't want to leave behind; that we do, in fact, wish to address as writers.

The life of a woman is an interior life; it is spent in daily tasks, it follows the rhythm of the seasons, and, usually, it ends and passes without record.

One of my books, *Mountain Echoes: Reminiscences of Kumaoni Women,* compiled oral biographies of my grandmother and three grand-aunts, all four highly individualistic, vibrant and feisty women. My family roots are in Uttarakhand, in the mountains around Nainital and Almora. In the dedication I observed, 'In our mountains women are rarely afraid. They are strong, direct, loyal, and in most situations they are free to speak their minds. You see them roaming the forests for fodder, strong-footed as goats, fearless as lions. They are not afraid of the dark and they brave the cold, they ford the swift mountain streams sure-footedly and when they are surprised by an attacking tiger, they have been known to raise their scythes and give chase to save a savaged sister from a man-eating predator.'

When I began recording the lives of my grandmother and grand-aunts, and the lives of their mothers before them, I encountered a moving personal strength and a disturbing social vulnerability. I observed, 'The history of women is left to us in folklore and tradition, in faintly remembered lullabies and the half-forgotten touch of a grandmother's hand; in recipes, ancestral jewellery, and cautionary tales about the limits of a woman's empowerment.'

♦ ♦ ♦

As a writer, my interests moved to mythology and its living manifestations in India. Four books, *The Book of Shiva*, *The Mahabharata for Young Readers*, *Shakuntala: The Play of Memory* and *In Search of Sita: Revisiting Mythology*, emerged from this quest. I learnt a lot from *The Mahabharata*. Unlike in *The Ramayana*, the women of this vast epic negotiated their lives outside as well as inside domestic spaces. Be it Kunti, Draupadi or Hidimba, Amba, Ambika or Ambilika, queen, demoness or transgender, these women demanded agency and lived life resolutely on their own terms. As a child, I had been told that *The Mahabharata* was not to be kept at home, or read by women, as this would cause discord. I realise now that this injunction was born of patriarchal caution, that the self-willed strength of these epic women was not a role model the men wanted emulated. The mythological figure of Sita stands as an archetype for most Indian women. Mythology is not an academic area of study in India but a part of a living cultural continuity. The gods and goddesses are alive here and we encounter them at every stage and step of daily life.

Indian women fill up a large space in the map of humankind. There are approximately 623 million of us – approximately 8.6 per cent of the human species. The stories of our lives, and the contexts and circumstances within which we negotiate our womanhood and selfhood, are as diverse and varied as India herself. As a nation and a culture, India remains a paradox and an enigma, replete with contradictions. India is a land where women are worshipped as goddesses, yet barbaric practices such as *sati*[3] and child marriage continue to exert their hold into the twenty-first century. It has had a woman prime minister and president, and women excel and exert influence

---

3. The (now illegal) practice of a Hindu widow cremating herself on her husband's funeral pyre in order to fulfill her true role as wife.

in professions such as politics and law, the administrative services, media, literature, medicine and banking. But the real strength of Indian women, those unsung heroines who hold up more than half the sky, comes from the disadvantaged, the indigent and marginalised, the often-silenced majority who till the soil, graze their cattle, work in menial domestic jobs, and look after and sustain their immediate and extended families.

Although the sheer size, scale and gradations of Indian culture and society make any form of generalisation untenable, its *Stree Shakti* or feminine strength, and the resilience and spirit of its women, are manifest at every turn and encounter. This individual strength is at odds with their social vulnerability, with both rising to the fore at a time of intense, liminal change. The upheavals of modernity and the indelible imprints of an ancient and enduring civilisation combine to create fresh opportunities, and also new fractures and faultlines.

Walking Towards Ourselves has contributions from writers with a range of distinct and strongly individual voices. Many of them are friends, others are writers I have read and admired. Resisting easy stereotypes, they tell their stories, or those of women around them, with direct and compelling truth telling. Somewhere between these stories of women in search of themselves, one glimpses tangled strands of narrative, shared vulnerabilities, common strengths.

Leila Seth's measured yet passionate plea in support of the rights of women, calling for an end to the wrongs done to them by a feudal patriarchy, is echoed with personal anguish in 'Scenes from a Marriage' – a disturbing testimonial by one writer who has chosen to remain anonymous. Leila's thoughtful and wise examination of legal redress puts autonomy and violation of bodily space into perspective.

In a society where women's minds as well as their bodies are perceived as belonging to their fathers, their brothers and their husbands, women write about sexuality to test the limits of autonomy, to take charge of their intellect and creativity. Skin, flesh and outrage merge

4

into powerful protest and acceptance in the direct, unblinking pieces by Rosalyn D'Mello, Margaret Mascarenhas, Mitali Saran, and the anonymous writer. 'Autonomy is the most powerful drug in the world,' declares Mitali Saran, as she tells of how she manages an open and individualist lifestyle while living with a 'madly brave and madly fearful' mother.

The essays and musings in this collection – wise, anguished or rebellious as they may be – are drawn from across India, some in translation from Bangla, Tamil and Punjabi. Writer, essayist and retired civil servant Anita Agnihotri writes in Bangla, one of India's most evocative literary languages, and the sixth-most spoken language in the world. Her piece 'The Village Without Men' is set in the fragile and threatened eco-system of the Sundarbans, where one woman's battle for dignity and survival becomes the story of 'each and every woman of the Sundarbans.'

Novelist and critic Anjum Hasan's powerful and moving documentation of the dreams, responsibilities and duties of a young social worker in Southern India carries the resonance of many lives and many hopes, 'and most of all, just this: a roof over her head, a warm blanket, the life that she and her family have built, which is very precious and very hard won.'

On a very different note – tongue in cheek but deadly serious – Annie Zaidi walks us through the personal journey of a woman writer and journalist negotiating the hazardous contours of urban Indian landscapes.

Deepti Kapoor writes an interrogative piece about her grandmother, her mother and herself, examining the continuum of women's narratives, and the many contradictions in their entwined stories and disparate worldviews.

Ira Trivedi's poised yet poignant foray into the frenzied world of the Indian matrimonial industry reveals the dark truths of the bridal market.

Sharanya Manivannan employs clothes and the wardrobe as a metaphor for identity and adventure.

While Tishani Doshi writes of children and progeny and the idea of motherhood, Salma chronicles her rebellions against tradition and modernity using the weapons of words and poetry.

C.S. Lakshmi, 'Ambai' to her devoted readers and fans, writes of SPARROW – the Sound and Picture Archives for Research on Women – and her groundbreaking work on documenting oral histories and narratives.

Chitra Banerjee Divakaruni's piece picks up the strands of childhood memories to stress the abiding centrality of women, education, literacy and learning. Nirupama Dutt's memoir of her sister, Devi, twenty-eight years her senior, and her tragic and wasted life, ends with the question 'where does your story end and mine begin?'

For me, the emblematic piece in this anthology is Urvashi Butalia's recount of her journey from being a 'newly minted young feminist' to founding the now-iconic feminist presses Kali for Women and Zubaan. As she concludes, her story converges, as many in this anthology do, with that of her mother, who dies, a week short of her ninetieth birthday, in her arms. 'As happens in life, by the time she was into her eighties, our roles were somewhat reversed, she the "child", I the "mother", both of us feminist, both of us working women, both of us Indian.'

These are transformative tales and they carry the texture and nuance of being Indian, and of being women, within them. They bring alive a revelatory panorama of struggle and survival, sorority and resistance, and remind us that we are each other's stories.

INTRODUCTION

CATRIONA MITCHELL

Last time I was leaving Delhi, my flight home to Australia was scheduled for 2 am. Being someone who travels a lot and at odd hours, it didn't occur to me that this might be a problem until the date arrived and I realised I would need to cross the city at midnight. Lack of safety for women in Delhi had been a focus in the international press for at least two years. In the absence of a driver with whom I was familiar, and with the safety of Uber under question at the time because of a sexual assault by one of its Delhi drivers the previous month, I felt a growing sense of vulnerability – especially as darkness descended and a night fog started to envelop the neighbourhood.

Then I remembered an article I had come across a few days earlier, which was about an N.G.O. that had set up an all-female taxi company. It sought out unemployed women from the city's poorest parts, taught them to drive and to read maps, gave them training in assertiveness, self-defence and communication skills, put them in uniform, and paid them a wage so decent that even the most resistant in their community were supportive of their employ.

I made the phone call.

The taxi arrived just after midnight, making its way slowly down the laneway to where I stood waiting with my suitcase in the dark. I could barely see the driver above the steering wheel, she was so slight. She was young, too: barely over twenty. She smiled as I clambered in with my case and introduced herself as Deepali. It seemed to me her smile carried enough voltage to light up the whole city.

There were few other cars on the road, but a stream of trucks passed us at speed down the Aurobindo Marg and the night air was thick with dust in their wake. There was no one else outside at this hour. At the lights, the truck drivers were able to stare from their cabins into our car. On seeing the two of us alone in the taxi, there was leering, and jeering. I pulled a scarf over my blonde hair and glanced at the safety lock of the car to see that it was pushed down. Deepali focused her attention on the road ahead, giving no indication that she was even aware of their presence; she started to peel some of the burgundy varnish off her chipped fingernails.

A barrage of questions was forming in my mind: Does this happen often? When you're alone, too? Do you feel protected, with just the safety lock of the car standing between you and them? What happens if someone attacks you? Whom can you call? What happens when you need to refuel the car? Where do you go to the toilet? What does your father think about your being out on these streets through the night? How old *are* you, anyway?

In the end, I settled for: 'Do you like your job?'

To which Deepali replied: 'I don't know.'

She drove on in a focused, pensive way to the airport, as if the force of her concentration alone would keep her safe.

From the reassuringly bright lights at the airport's drop-off point, I watched Deepali's taxi edge back into the stream of traffic, re-entering the dark and smog and fog of that winter night. I feared for what lay ahead of her until the dawn broke, and marvelled at her youth and courage. I felt ashamed that this journey would stand out in memory for me – an Australian visitor to India – for being subversive and a little frightening, something I wouldn't repeat if I could help it, whereas for Deepali, this was her daily, or rather nightly, reality.

◆ ◆ ◆

The international press regularly tells us that India is one of the most dangerous places on the planet to be a woman.

When at home in Australia, I am vocal about my love for India to the point of obsession, and this sparks what has become a rather predictable pattern of conversation. Women in my country are constantly telling me that they're eager to visit India, but don't dare, for fear that they might be attacked. The question they want me to answer for them is: *If I go there, will I be safe?*

Meanwhile, Indians from Jaipur to Bangalore to Cochin to Pondicherry have asked me the same question about visiting Australia. This was true particularly in the wake of the shocking murder of an Indian student in Melbourne in 2010, and other race-motivated crimes against young Indians in Australia around that time, but the questioning continues to this day: *If I go there, will I be safe?*

◆ ◆ ◆

In December 2012, when a young medical student was returning home after an evening screening of *Life of Pi* in a mall in South Delhi, she and her male companion boarded a bus that was not, contrary to appearances, a public transport vehicle. Rather, a group of young men had commandeered a bus and were cruising the streets looking for some entertainment. They had been drinking. A fight broke out when one of the men admonished the young woman's companion for being out with her at night, when the two weren't married. The others pitched in – into an argument motivated by the men's perceived need for 'moral shaming'[1]. The ensuing attack left the boy injured and the girl near-dead after being violently gang raped and thrown from the bus; she later died in a Singapore hospital when her doctors, who had never seen such unspeakable damage to a woman's body, were unable to save her.

This tragic and horrifying incident sparked a furore across Delhi, and then across India, and then across the world. By stepping into that bus that night, that young woman, who came to be known as Nirbhaya ('Fearless') inadvertently changed the course of India's history.

◆ ◆ ◆

At the time of Nirbhaya's death, I was in the emergency ward of an Australian hospital. I had been leading a group of Australian and Indian authors through South India by train for a month in a 'roving writers festival' called Bookwallah. I had contracted typhoid, salmonella and dengue fever during that trip, but not found the time while on the trains for the appropriate medical care. On my return to Australia, my mother found me collapsed in her bathroom; she thought I had died.

It's for this reason that I missed the protests in India – the unbridled outrage that poured out into the city streets. I wanted to be there. I wanted to join my Indian 'sisters', to add my voice to their

---

1. In an interview with the BBC, Mukesh Singh, the driver of the bus, said from jail, 'Women who go out at night have only themselves to blame in case they attract attention of male molesters ... Housework and housekeeping is for girls, not roaming in discos and bars at night or wearing wrong clothes.'

emboldened chorus, to share in this pivotal moment, a kindling of India's gender revolution.

The heated demonstrations in the streets put such pressure on the government that sexual assault laws in India were changed as a result. I am deeply honoured that this book features a prologue by Leila Seth, the first woman judge of the Delhi High Court and first female Chief Justice of a state High Court in India. She was one of only three members – and the only female member – of the anti-rape commission assembled in direct response to the Nirbhaya case. In her essay here, Leila highlights exactly how those new laws were negotiated and drawn up, as well as the challenges and obstacles faced by the commission along the way. The information imparted in Leila's contribution underpins, in a sense, all of the stories in this book.

◆ ◆ ◆

One cannot speak of India's women without speaking of her men, and certainly many men are stepping forward to support women's safety and empowerment – for example, with organisations such as M.A.R.D. (Men Against Rape and Discrimination).

This collection in no way intends to cast aspersions on India's male population, nor does it seek to portray Indian men as misogynists. Such a generalisation would be not only wildly inaccurate, but absurd. Certainly, if numbers of India's men are disenfranchised, brutalised and desensitised, then that desensitisation will affect women also, and this was a factor in the Nirbhaya case: her attackers were from impoverished backgrounds and several were labelled as 'vagabond' in the court records. The youngest of them had been living without family on the city streets since the age of six.

Violence needs to end on both sides of the equation.

It is true, however, that the all-too-common incidents of violence and depravity exercised against women in India, and the Nirbhaya case in particular, provided the impetus for this book. I found myself thinking about Nirbhaya, day after day after day. I could not get her out of my mind. I was not alone – her story came to epitomise the story of any young woman, in any country, innocently on her way home from a movie after dark – and it touched many people very deeply around the world.

I followed the debate about safety for women while convalescing in hospital in Australia. At some point I wished to hear the voices of India's women directly, freed from the hype and sensationalism of the media. It was, and still is, my experience that India is a source of greater inspiration, vibrancy, colour and enchantment; of more profound political, intellectual and spiritual enquiry; of more deeply felt and meaningful conversation; of more frequent displays of kindness from strangers and friends alike, than anywhere else in the world. Although addressing an all-important issue, the international press seemed to be overlooking India's stunning diversity and cultural richness in its focus on the dangers.

I wanted to hear first-hand from Indian women about the challenges, big and small, that they faced on a daily basis, and to share these with readers. I wanted to hear about the joys, rewards, opportunities and great *range* of experiences of being a woman in India too, in addition to the challenges. I wanted to hear from those who were bucking the gender stereotypes. I wanted to know what the country's women made of the burgeoning gender revolution, and what it meant to them personally to be an Indian woman living through this time of incredible transition and intense confusion. I wanted to hear stories of love and hope, beyond the negative coverage: I wanted a balanced view.

I was familiar with the writing of many female Indian authors and journalists, having got to know them over years of engagement with literary projects and festivals in different parts of the country. However, I hadn't read many personal narratives – narratives that articulated the real-life experiences of India's women in a subjective, candid, and intimate way. It was time for those experiences to be delved into, given a voice and shared.

Seeking out these stories from established women writers was a logical leap. The idea for this book was born.

I asked the authors to mine their own lives and experiences for their pieces; or, if they preferred, they could write about a woman in their immediate acquaintance whose daily reality offered a window onto a fascinating and telling world. The aim was to share the intimate details of real lives, and create a diverse, wide-ranging collection of stories that would say: 'This is what our lives look like.'

The title of the collection, *Walking Towards Ourselves*, comes from renowned dancer and choreographer Chandralekha[2]. In an exploration of that which connects art with life, Chandralekha said, 'we are simply walking towards ourselves.' So too, in this volume of 'mini memoirs', each contributing writer is walking the edge between her art and life. Each one is walking, one word at a time, towards the expression of a subjective reality, towards having a voice: a voice that rings out clear and untrammelled and original and vulnerable and strong and personal and true. Each one is using words as a means to find her way home, when home is a land that doesn't always make her feel welcome, or cherished, or free.

◆ ◆ ◆

Free speech is sometimes brutally suppressed in India, as indeed in other parts of the world. In August 2015, in one such instance, the nation was shocked when a college professor and scholar from

---

2. An artist, feminist and environmentalist who was considered in her later years to be something of a national treasure, Chandralekha believed that a woman must have her own politics and sexuality – as Tishani Doshi explains in her contribution 'Tick Tock'.

Karnataka, who openly questioned idol worship in the Hindu religion, was killed by a shot to the head at point-blank range at the front door of his home.

For India's women, speaking out is an act of courage. For India's women writers, articulating the female experience and putting it in print for all to see – in other words, the expression and exercise of freedom of speech – can be perceived as an act of defiance or rebellion, a refusal to conform, a flying in the face of patriarchy that invites criticism, shame, recrimination, intimidation, or worse.

Salma, the Tamil poet and fiction writer featured in this anthology, who shot to fame with her novel *The Hour Past Midnight*, became a writer in a closeted Muslim environment: she was locked inside her family home on reaching puberty, then married off, and later wrote to maintain her sanity but had to hide her writing from her husband and his family in order to preserve her life. When her first book was launched, it was under a pseudonym. Another contributor to this collection, who has written with outstanding courage and candour about her experiences of marital rape, has had to safeguard her identity in order to stay out of harm's way.

There is no doubt that in many instances, in choosing to share their stories, these women are staring down real fears.

◆ ◆ ◆

For centuries an Indian woman was the 'property' of her father and then her husband, subjected to an arranged marriage and then to the responsibilities of maintaining her family home. The honour of the entire family rested upon her shoulders, and her moral piety was seen a core contributor to social harmony on a broader scale as well. Since the opening up of India's economy in 1991, however, women have been exposed to new opportunities for education and for joining the workforce. The impact of this cannot be underestimated. It is only this recently that women have really started to find economic independence, and have therefore been able to withstand social pressures towards marriage and other duties.

Why have India's women been traditionally subjected to such an extreme expression of patriarchy? This has deeply entrenched religious as well as socio-economic roots. According to the Hindu religion, parents cannot achieve liberation or 'moksha' after death unless there is a son to perform the cremation rites; and largely because of the dowry system, daughters have traditionally been seen as a financial burden on a family, while sons were considered to build upon a family's wealth. Put simply, boy children are wanted and girl children are not: this has been true down the ages and holds true, for the most part, today.

Although sex determination is illegal in hospitals (I was taken aback on a visit to an Indian hospital to see a huge sign at the entrance, declaring that the sex of foetuses would not be identified there) it is not uncommon even nowadays for female foetuses to be aborted and dumped, and for baby girls to be left at orphanages simply because the parents can't afford to raise them, and see them married off, and be expected to provide a dowry or a fancy wedding, which has become the modern, more acceptable (and legal) form of dowry. There's a higher infant mortality rate amongst girls too, because medical care for girls is seen as less of a priority than it is for boys. As a result of this, there is a staggering gender imbalance in today's India, and it's a source of alarming and ever-increasing frictions. Ira Trivedi writes in her bestselling book *India in Love* that in 2011, India had 37 million more men than women, and about 17 million excess men in the age group that commits most crimes. Ira asserts: 'Violent crime increases as the deficit of women increases.'[3]

♦ ♦ ♦

---

3. *India in Love*, p.155

More of India's women are choosing to speak up than ever before. This is true across the board, but most overtly in the arena of sexual violence. It's unknown if the number of sexual assaults against women in the country is on the rise. What is true is that taboos have broken open and sexual violence and sexual matters more broadly are being discussed in a way that was previously unthinkable; as a result the sense of a victim's shame is diminishing.

A few brave young women are breaking the way open for others to follow, by making themselves heard in the public sphere. I flew back to Delhi recently to participate in a live event on women and gender. One of the speakers was a young Dalit woman from Uttar Pradesh who in 2012 (when she was thirteen years old) was set upon by four men of a higher caste on her way to school. The men gagged her, and raped her, and filmed the attack. They later sold this recording in a local market.

The courage it must have taken for this young woman (now known as 'Bitiya') to report this is unfathomable – she who had no power at all was speaking out against those who did. Her family accompanied her to the talk she gave in Delhi. 'I was thrown out of the school ...' Bitiya told the audience. 'The school teachers treated me as an accused. The villagers pressured me to take the complaint back.' Her mother said, 'We don't care what happens to us anymore. I will not let this happen to any more daughters again.' Bitiya's aged grandfather also came to the event; despite being startled by finding himself on stage, in front of spotlights and cameras, he stood in solidarity with the women of his family.

Acts of speaking up, of demonstrating courage of this kind, by men and women across different generations and castes, bespeak inestimable social change.

Nita Ambani, wife of business magnate Mukesh Ambani (India's wealthiest man), made a speech at the same women's event in Delhi where Bitiya and her mother spoke. Nita was born into a (combined) family of eleven girls and one boy, but crucially the family was completely free of gender bias. She highlighted the fact that education was made available to her, making all the difference to her future.

Nita's was a view of hope: 'When I see the people in this room, and their commitment to women's empowerment, I know the future looks bright.' Indeed there has been improvement for women and girls in recent years: economic growth and technological developments have been massive contributors to India's social and cultural change, leading the country to such rapid modernisation that countless lives have morphed beyond all recognition within the space of a decade. This is spectacularly true for India's young women, who are coming into new opportunities for education and employment.

Deepti Kapoor captures this sense of radical change for the young in her contribution to this anthology. 'In India it was an exciting time. The India I knew was going through a great upheaval. The economy was flourishing, people were no longer fleeing abroad for a life, jobs were abundant, the arts were vibrant. Social relations were changing too; life was loosening in the cities ... I had many potential futures – TV newsreader, human rights advocate, wife to a wealthy banker, post-grad student at an Ivy League college. It was my decision to make. It was a time of optimism and opportunity and hope. I couldn't wait to get on in the world.'

Today's India is characterised by a giant melting pot of roles for women, a veritable mix of tradition-meets-innovation. One woman's life is bound by social mores that extend back centuries, with rules that are frozen in time, while another's is defined by an all-new autonomy, a sparklingly modern sense of identity, like Deepti's.

These discrepancies are captured in the range of lives described in this collection. Contrast Anita Agnihotri's protagonist Taramoni, who is fighting for her life amid post-cyclone catastrophe, with only a makeshift bamboo home for shelter from tigers and other threats, with hip urbane Indians preoccupied with an online dating app, as described in Ira Trivedi's 'Love in the Time of the Internet'. Contrast Salma's story of being kept inside her husband's home in Tamil Nadu, where her in-laws' reputation is measured by the extent of her chastity, with Margaret Mascarenhas's unique and daring exploration of gender fluidity in her home in Goa.

Contrasting realities, indeed.

India is so vast and diverse as to be more like a series of different countries than a unified whole; multiple voices are needed to shed light on her ways. For this reason, *Walking Towards Ourselves* seeks to give authentic voice to a range of women writers from different parts of the country. These women are of varying ages, religions, castes, socio-economic backgrounds, political orientations and sexual pro-clivities. And some of the contributors have different mother tongues. While the majority of the pieces were written in English by writers already in my acquaintance (owing to my own linguistic limitations), I'm delighted to say that in researching this project, my attention was brought to some authors working in regional languages who were hitherto unknown to me.

They have been beautiful discoveries.

Anita Agnihotri is one such example: her contribution 'The Village Without Men' was originally written in her native Bengali. Salma's 'Beyond Memories' was translated from Tamil. In 'Bamboo Baskets and Brocade Saris,' C.S. Lakshmi documents the riveting life details of a Dalit writer by the name of Urmila – their discussions were originally conducted in Marathi. Nirupama Dutt's moving depiction of the contrasting lives she and her sister led – born twenty-eight years apart to different mothers, and with entirely different access to education opportunities – is a story that was lived out in Punjabi.

Despite the obvious diversity in the stories, one of the joys in editing this book was witnessing the common themes that emerged across the contributions, reflecting back at one another like jewels in a net. Different Indias intersect here, at times in startling and surprising ways. Rosalyn D'Mello's account of being dark-skinned, and how this inestimably affected her sense of self-worth and desirability, is a theme explored in an entirely different way in Ira Trivedi's 'Rearranged Marriage'. Mitali Saran's irreverent choice to lead a bohemian life with neither husband nor children in Delhi, is twinned in Tishani Doshi's more reflective piece on why she has decided not to become a mother in Tamil Nadu. The legal issues addressed in Leila Seth's piece – and more specifically her disappointment that marital rape is still not recognised as a crime in India – are directly mirrored by the author who has chosen to remain anonymous: 'Within a marriage, fighting back comes with its consequences. The man who rapes me is not a stranger who runs away ... He is the husband for whom I have to make the morning coffee.'

Above all, the ways in which women inspire and help each other through the generations, is a theme that crisscrosses the contributions. For example, Urvashi Butalia describes the powerfully positive influence of her mother upon her own trajectory as a feminist publisher: 'my mother ... persuaded him to let me try. "She'll find her feet," she said, and I did.'

Education stands out as an essential thematic strand, particularly when it comes to this legacy from older generations. The mothers (and fathers, and grandmothers) mentioned here step in most forcefully when it comes to education and career opportunity for their girls, and without this guiding light the writers might never have discovered their literary talents. As a blossoming young poet, Salma can only be published when her mother sneaks her poems out of the house, wrapped in a cloth bundle, to find someone to post them. Chitra Banerjee Divakaruni, who has received a dazzling number of literary awards and whose books have been translated into twenty-nine languages, states, 'Thanks to the power of education, and to a mother who would not compromise on my schooling, no matter how much people pressured her – I did it. Words became my scimitar.'

Although only twenty-five per cent of India's women are employed, this collection frequently features women at work. Anjum Hasan's protagonist, a plucky young social worker in Karnataka, cares for girls who have been abandoned by their families, and who are 'ravenous for affection'. C. S. Lakshmi offers a window into her world at SPARROW, an initiative that records and archives the stories of women from around the country, thereby providing a sense of 'herstory' as well as 'history'. Also based in Mumbai – but on a different note altogether – Tisca Chopra offers humorous insight into life as a Bollywood actress, and the challenges of being on the casting couch and in the hotel room of a scurrilous director who hopes to take liberties with her.

There are moments of humour and moments of women at play. Mitali Saran, for example, is 'an Indian woman in her mid-forties, single, childless, jobless, who dresses like an uncool teenager, wraps presents in newspaper, drinks, smokes, occasionally pops into a bar or a movie theatre alone, drives around in the middle of the night, has no ambition, dances tango, has taken to the guitar ...'

Beauty is a theme that repeats – both the pursuit of it and, interestingly, the active avoidance of it. Ira Trivedi, a former finalist in the Miss India pageant, talks to young women whose experiences tell them that only fairer skin will lead them to a suitable matrimony. Sharanya Manivannan explores what different forms of adornment signify; she masterfully interweaves a love of sartorial splendour and feminine expression with the inherently political. 'If a red lipstick is wonderful anywhere in the world, it is most wonderful of all on the mouth of a woman who has claimed her own voice.' Both Sharanya and Annie Zaidi dress in dowdy clothing in order to feel safer in the workplace. Out and about at odd hours as a reporter on Mumbai's streets, Annie writes: 'I remember looking down at myself – at my loose, long, chequered *kurta* and *salwar*, no make-up, flat slippers. I used to try to dress down for work, afraid that taking pains with my appearance would be held against me somehow ...'

And then there are women claiming autonomy over their bodies and their sexuality. Tishani Doshi reflects upon ready access to contraception, and the new life-choices this brings. 'To be a man who decides not to have children barely registers on the seismograph. To be a woman who says "Actually, babies aren't for me" is to unleash a minor tsunami.' Rosalyn D'Mello discusses the complexities of having a lover almost twice her age: '... my lust wantonly waxing while his own wanes with age; my spirit and flesh eternally willing, his increasingly in a predicament.' Margaret Mascarenhas tells the story of her unexpected love affair with a woman: 'Early in the morning Mohini reached out, kissed her hands, and said, "I've never met anyone like you. May I touch you?" It was not the first time a woman had asked, but it was the first time she had said yes.'

◆ ◆ ◆

It is worth mentioning that the stories in this collection claim to be nothing more than the expression of the authors' highly individual and subjective points of view. And, obviously, *Walking Towards Ourselves* represents but a handful of lives among millions. Yes, there are essential voices missing; yes, there are gaps that could not be plugged. The subject of this book is simply too vast to be fully plumbed in one book.

Despite this, it is my hope that this anthology performs the simple but essential role of putting women's stories in the spotlight, and contributing to a vigorous and much-needed discussion about the multitude of ways Indian women experience daily life, in both public and domestic spheres. Why this discussion matters so deeply is perhaps best summarised by Nobel laureate Amartya Sen, who has said that empowering women and girls with more choices and more freedoms is crucial to achieving a better future for all.

May these stories raise awareness and encourage debate around the gender revolution taking place in India today. And may the revolution grow in momentum until such time as India's women truly can make their own choices, and experience sexual liberty, and be shown professional equality, and count on safety in spaces both public and private, and have the freedom to say and do and dress and write as they please, by day and by night, in urban centres and in the more remote areas across the land.

This journey towards gender equality is certainly in process in India, but conflict is also there, and it's showing no sign of abating soon. It's arising because of the speed at which this gender shift is happening: there simply hasn't been time for methodical, gradual, step-by-step readjustment. New values and old are bumping up against each other. Sparks are flying. Many men and women (particularly those moving in large numbers from rural areas to urban centres for economic reasons) are reeling, unsure of which values to adhere to or believe in, unsure of where they can position themselves in the maelstrom. They are caught somewhere between yesterday and tomorrow.

And so, India's gender revolution is characterised by both progress and backlash. A fiery clash of values lies at the very core of contemporary Indian society, across the country and across all strata of society … and yet, the impetus towards female empowerment has become so strong that despite the inevitable setbacks, it is hard to imagine it can be stopped.

This push-pull-push is what *Walking Towards Ourselves* attempts to capture and explore.

◆ ◆ ◆

In Delhi recently, I was once again challenged by having to cross the city after dark. This time, however, it was only a matter of getting back to my accommodation from Khan Market: a fifteen-minute ride at most. I hailed an auto-rickshaw. En route, the driver told me his name was Pandit then went out of his way to assure me that I was safe: 'We respect woman. Because woman respect is very important for every-one. Woman is our mother, sister and daughter. In my tuc-tuc, woman customers are always very happy, because they know my service is safe and respectful.' He said this with such obvious pride and sincerity that any anxiety on my part was assuaged.

A taxi passed as we pulled up at my gate, and a large sticker on the back windscreen flashed momentarily under the street-lamp. I had just enough time to take in the words: 'This taxi respects women'.

It was the first time I had heard, and the first time I had seen, this idea publicly expressed.

In India, safety for women is interlinked with economics and also with the issue of public infrastructure. Had Nirbhaya had a personal driver, or the money to pay for an auto-rickshaw to take her across the city after the movie that night, her life might have been spared. An increase in safe public transport options (such as the ladies' carriage in the Delhi Metro, and the number of taxis driven by women), and an increase in the numbers of public toilets for women, would already make a world of difference. These would permit women to come out in the streets in greater numbers, rather than being relegated to their homes. And there is safety in numbers.

◆ ◆ ◆

In around ten years' time, India will have more women than any other country in the world. And yet, when I asked about non-fiction books on India's women recently in my favourite Delhi bookstore, pitching the request at booksellers I both like and respect, I was met with blank stares.

In reading *Walking Towards Ourselves*, may you enjoy walking in the shoes of this diverse range of talented and courageous women writers, as they share, with generosity and pathos, some of the ordi-nary and extraordinary details of their lives. They write here in order to add their voices to a debate that is much larger than themselves. They write here in order to interrogate a question that is essential for our times, not just in India but across the world. This question was posed with great dignity by Nirbhaya's father in Leslee Udwin's documentary film *India's Daughter*: 'What is the meaning of a woman?'

PROLOGUE:
BREAKING THE SILENCE

LEILA SETH

The year was 1942. I was almost twelve years old and travelling by train. I went to the toilet and came back ashen faced. I told my mother that I was going to bleed to death. She smiled and told me not to worry and that I was menstruating. She explained that it was a natural phenomenon for girls of my age. She also said that I was not to discuss it with others, especially with boys and men. It was a woman's secret and all through the ages it had been like that. I kept silent.

When I was fifteen I went for a drive in a car with my uncle (my mother's sister's husband), who asked me whether I was a lipstick girl. I did not know what it meant and asked him. He tried to pass it off and said, 'A girl who likes to be kissed on her lips.' He then tried to touch my breast. I quickly shrank away. I felt awful. He told me I should not tell anyone about it. I kept silent.

On my eighteenth birthday a young male friend suddenly kissed me on my lips. I was pleasantly surprised but terrified as I thought I might have a baby. I felt guilty and ashamed. I kept silent.

I got married when I was twenty and my husband presented me with a book called *Ideal Marriage* by van de Velde. That's when I really learned about the facts of life and my own body.

• • •

Why are women and young girls terrified into silence? There are many reasons. One is that they are blamed and shamed, as if it is their fault. It is often said, 'She deserved it – look at the way she dresses and conducts herself.' The dress and conduct of the man are not commented on; instead, a remark such as 'Boys will be boys' is often made, even by senior political leaders. The trauma the woman has suffered is not considered. Indian society is conservative and patriarchal.

Families often want victims to remain silent since the publicity could ruin not only the victim's chances of having a good arranged marriage, but also those of their siblings. Marriage is the be-all and end-all of life in a traditional society. Women are expected to stay at home and be subservient to men and make all the adjustments themselves. If the perpetrator of a rape or sexual assault is a relative or a friend of the family, again, in order not to embarrass the perpetrator, the woman or girl is expected to remain silent.

Even when the victim came from a less tradition-bound family, very few rape or sexual assault cases used to be filed. This is because it would become, in effect, a multiple rape for the victim. First, there was the actual rape; then the lurid questioning by the insensitive male police when she made an effort to try to get a First Information Report[1] registered; then the explicit, agonising cross-examination in court during a tardy trial, with very little prospect of a conviction. Added to all this was the media glare, with all its sensational reports. This whole process, and attitude, was and is extremely traumatic for a woman.

---

1. This is a document prepared by police when they receive information about an alleged criminal offence.

A woman's status in a hierarchical, patriarchal, caste-ridden society is low, and judges quite often fail to convict even when faced with clear evidence. For example, in the well-known gang-rape case of Bhanwari Devi[2], the accused were acquitted on the ground that they were middle-aged, respectable men of a higher caste and therefore could not possibly have wished to rape a lower-caste woman. Such acts – and such attitudes – are extremely humiliating for a woman, especially as rape is often used as an extension of power rather than for the fulfilment of lust.

Laws and education are trying to bring about a change in society. Women in India are being given equal property and other rights, and the education of girls is being encouraged. Empowerment is the buzz word. The middle class is growing. The Internet is bringing about a knowledge-based society and an effective social media. India is changing in many respects, but the change in mindsets is slow. Equality of opportunity for the poor is still a distant dream. Equality between men and women is taking its time.

♦ ♦ ♦

It was in this atmosphere that on 16 December 2012, a 23-year-old paramedical student, returning home with a male friend after watching a movie, was gang-raped in a bus in Delhi. They had boarded an off-duty charter bus at about 9.30 pm after being told that it was going towards their destination. There were only six other people, including the driver, on the bus; one of them was a juvenile. When the friend noticed that the bus was taking a different route, he objected. Instead of asking the driver to change course, the other occupants taunted

---

2. The way in which Dalit social worker Bhanwari Devi was treated by the police when she reported the rape – and the court acquittal of the accused – attracted widespread media attention in 1992, in India and abroad. It subsequently became a landmark episode in India's women's rights movement.

the couple for being out so late at night. They then raped the woman. When her friend tried to intervene, he was beaten and gagged. The woman struggled, but was sexually brutalised in a horrific manner, including with an iron rod. They were then thrown out, almost naked, onto the road. The media reported the matter and gave the young woman various names, including 'Brave Heart', but eventually she came to be known as Nirbhaya, the fearless one, as the law did not allow her real name to be disclosed.

The incident triggered huge but peaceful protests by young people, both men and women. They were angry, anguished and frustrated at the rapes and sexual molestations that they and their friends had faced for years without any stringent action being taken against the molesters and rapists. They wanted sterner laws and speedier justice. It was perhaps the first time that young people had come to protest without a call from a leader. It was the issue that mattered, and people who did not know each other were discussing it openly. They were contacting each other on social media, and the electronic media as well as the print media were giving them huge coverage. Sex was now out in the open – a subject which did not get discussed earlier, either in educational institutions or with one's parents. The police tried aggressively to disperse the crowds, even using water cannons in the cold December weather, but they returned again and again, day after day, until the government was forced to make a commitment to do something to stop sexual violence. The crowds were holding up placards demanding, among other things, enhanced punishments for the rapists, some of them insisting on castration or even death. 'Enough is Enough!' is what they were shouting, breaking a barrier of long silence. These powerful protests spread rapidly to other cities in India and abroad. It was a game changer in that the stigma attached to having been raped was being wiped out.

The 23rd of December 2012 was a Sunday, and a few friends had come over to our home for a quiet lunch. The discussion quite naturally turned to the horrendous gang-rape case. Since I belonged to the legal fraternity, my friends were asking me what the government would do, and I replied cynically that it would appoint a committee or commission to look into the matter and thus postpone the decision for six months or more, so that the momentum of the protest would be lost.

Little did I know that just a few minutes later the finance minister at the time, Mr Chidambaram, who also happened to be a senior lawyer, would telephone me and request that I be a member of such a committee. I was not sure how effective the committee would be, and asked him the names of the other members.

He told me that it would be headed by Justice J.S. Verma and that the third member would be a senior advocate. I knew that Justice Verma, who had been Chief Justice of India, was a fiercely independent and courageous judge, and I considered it a privilege to be invited to work with him.

I felt very strongly about the issue of sexual violence against women, and had wanted to contribute suggestions and ideas that might help to curb it. I realised that I had just been offered a rare opportunity to do so.

I asked the finance minister about the period within which this report was expected to be presented. In India, commissions like this could sit for years. He replied, to my astonishment, 'Within thirty days.'

I agreed to join the committee, even though it would mean working ceaselessly to complete the work in time.

The third member of the committee was Mr Gopal Subramanium, who was an eminent jurist and former solicitor-general of India. He was a fireball of energy, compassion and learning. He put his extremely lucrative practice on hold for a month in order to give his full attention to a social cause – trying to ensure justice for women.

Though the ostensible terms of reference of the committee seemed limited, we knew that we had to present a holistic report for it to be meaningful. We also knew that to achieve this within thirty days was going to be difficult.

The Justice J.S. Verma Committee: How events unfolded

The establishment of the committee was finalised that very day and published in the *Gazette of India* on 24 December 2012. On Christmas Day we issued a Public Notice in a number of newspapers, including the *Times of India*, addressed to eminent jurists, legal professionals, non-governmental organisations, women's groups, civil society members and indeed all members of the public who felt they could contribute to our efforts. We requested they share their ideas, knowledge and experience with us, and suggest possible amendments in the criminal laws and other relevant laws that might provide for quicker trials of persons accused, and enhanced punishments for criminals convicted of committing sexual assault of an extreme nature against women. It was further added that since the committee was hard-pressed for time, their valuable suggestions should come in at the latest by 5 January 2013, so that the committee could complete its report and submit its recommendations within a month.

We discussed our strategy and how to complete the task within the allotted time, knowing that if we waited for the government to provide us with all the necessary facilities, or even rudimentary ones, the job could not possibly be completed in time. Gopal offered his entire office infrastructure, and his juniors volunteered to work for us as well. They brought in other volunteers: law students, young lawyers and even a law professor. The group of about sixteen members, including four women, worked relentlessly, researching and collecting relevant material from all over the world. They also collated the overwhelming number of suggestions (about 80,000) that poured in from the public, academics in India and abroad, eminent jurists, social activists, women's organisations, national commissions and from political parties as well.

Despite the fact that there were so many written suggestions, we also felt it was necessary to listen – face to face – to the viewpoints of women's groups, feminists, academics, the lesbian-gay-bisexual-transgender community and others so that they could share with us their apprehensions and fears, ideas and proposals. We also wanted to hear the explanations and suggestions of the administration and police. So we held two days of public hearings, where we listened to various voices from Kashmir to Kerala, from Maharashtra to Manipur.

The discussion, though it was emotionally charged and, for the most part, imbued with compassion and understanding, was of a high order intellectually. While there had been a great outcry at the time of the protests and some of the general public had demanded castration and the death penalty as punishment for rapists, most of the participants were against such measures. We were especially moved by the stories we heard of rapes in conflict zones and by the army.

Meanwhile, although we had given a deadline for suggestions, views just kept pouring in.

During the final days, we worked from morning to midnight every day. After coming home, the day's work was still not done; two nights before the report was due, I remember sleeping for only a couple of hours. Some of the volunteers worked right though the night.

The day before the report was due, we were still debating whether the crime of rape should be gender neutral or gender specific. When I had helped draft the bill for the 172nd Report of the Law Commission, we had made it gender neutral, which meant that the perpetrator could be 'any person' and the victim could also be 'any person'. This was the more modern – and reasoned – approach to the question, and was based on the principle of equality. But women's groups and many others were pressing that it be made gender specific: that is, that we specify that the perpetrator be a man and the victim a woman.

After a great deal of brainstorming, we arrived at a consensus, and recommended that though the perpetrator should only be a man, the victim could be 'any person', thus bringing in males, females and transgender persons as possible victims under the law. We raced to rework the proposed bill. The commitment of the young volunteers was very strong, as they too were eager to help bring about change.

On 22 January 2013, Justice Verma and I left at midnight, but Gopal and the young team worked through the night to incorporate all the corrections and changes. It was only a few minutes before 7 am on the 23rd that they telephoned Justice Verma to tell him the work was complete.

It was then sent to the printer; a hard-bound copy was produced by 12.30 pm. The three of us signed and immediately dispatched it to the Prime Minister together with a covering letter, which expressed our hope that there would be speedy implementation of our recommendations 'to retain public confidence in good governance'. Prime Minister Manmohan Singh thanked us for our labour of love and assured us that the government would 'be prompt in pursuing the recommendations of the committee'.

Our recommendations and the outcomes

It is not possible to discuss all our recommendations here, but, generally speaking, we enlarged the definition of rape and sexual assault, introduced clarity regarding consent, and dealt with the sexual harassment of women in the workplace.

We recommended fast-track courts without endless adjournments, so that trials could be completed in a short time. We also recommended gender sensitisation of the police and the judiciary.

The gender of a rape victim

The government did not accept our recommendation that the victim should be 'any person', which would have protected males and transgender persons, and others. Instead, they passed a law making the offence entirely gender specific. In the government's view, rape victims could only be women and rape perpetrators could only be men.

I am of the view that this was a very serious mistake and that Parliament failed to realise the injustice done to many people who are and who have been brutalised.

Minors

Since one of the main offenders in the Nirbhaya case was a seventeen-year-old minor, who would be tried by the Juvenile Justice Board without undergoing the rigours of trial and punishment by the court, there was also a great deal of debate as to whether the age of the minor who commits rape should be reduced from eighteen to sixteen. Though a criminal offence cannot be given retrospective effect and it would not have affected the particular minor accused in Nirbhaya's case, it was argued that a large number of rapes were committed by persons between the ages of sixteen and eighteen and that they should be brought within the ambit of the regular criminal law and punished accordingly. We examined this aspect carefully, but certain factors, both scientific and sociological, led us to the conclusion that no change in this aspect of the law should be recommended.

An important factor, to our mind, was the neurological state of an adolescent brain, which undergoes significant changes in structure and function and whose 'culpability or blameworthiness is diminished, to a substantial degree, by reason of youth and immaturity'[3].

We also considered the United Nations Convention on the Rights of the Child, and the fact that transformation was hardly likely to take place if juveniles were put into jails with hardened criminals. Further,

---

3. Roper v Simmons 543 US 551, U.S. Supreme Court (2005)

we considered the fact that recidivism had declined over the years and that children deprived of parental guidance and education had some chance of being rehabilitated if the reformatory system in juvenile institutions was drastically improved.

The government accepted this position and the age of the accused was not reduced. Unfortunately, there is now once again a move to rethink this matter.

Castration and the death penalty

We were against castration and death as punishments; however, our view that even the most grievous offence of rape did not require the imposition of the death penalty was not accepted by the government. We stated that punishment for life, meaning a full life term, would be sufficient and that the punishment of death already existed in the Indian Penal Code in the case of murder. (Nirbhaya had since died in Singapore, where she had been sent by the government for better medical treatment.)

Marital rape

We examined marital rape in the light of the historical perspective and the principle of patriarchy, and this matter in particular was hotly debated. The offence of rape was originally based on the idea of theft of a man's property. A woman belonged first to her father and after marriage to her husband. So if anyone had sexual intercourse with her before marriage, the father's right and honour were affected, and after marriage the husband's.

According to the English common law of coverture, a woman was deemed to have consented at the time of marriage to having intercourse with her husband at his whim. In 1736 Sir Matthew Hale declared that a husband could not be guilty of rape on 'his lawful wife, for by their mutual matrimonial consent and contract' she had agreed to sexual intercourse and this consent 'she cannot retract'.

The situation has changed drastically since then. A woman's autonomy and bodily integrity are concepts that have developed over the years, making rape an offence against an individual in which consent is an essential concept.

In England in 1991, Lord Keith, speaking for the House of Lords, declared, 'Marriage is in modern times regarded as a partnership of equals, and no longer one in which the wife must be the subservient chattel of the husband.' The European Commission of Human Rights also endorsed the conclusion that a rapist remains a rapist regardless of his legal or marital relationship with the victim. The very essence of the Convention on Human Rights is the respect for human rights, dignity and freedom.

In South Africa marital rape was criminalised in 1993. In Canada too it is a crime to rape your wife. In 1991, the Australian High Court had no doubt that 'if it was ever the common law that by marriage a wife gave irrevocable consent to sexual intercourse by her husband, it is no longer the common law'. These jurisdictions roundly rejected the fiction of irrevocable consent as being offensive to human dignity and incompatible with the legal status of a spouse. They have also recognised that consent is most important and cannot be implied and that marital rape cannot be considered a lesser crime meriting a more lenient sentence.

We were aware of the countless married women who suffered without recourse under Indian law from the sexual violence of their husbands. Consequently, we strongly recommended that the exception for marital rape be removed.

Despite our strong recommendation, the government did not agree to make marital rape a crime. Many voices were raised against the recommendation, including those of patriarchal insensitivity and those who believed that such a law would be misused. Some people raised the bogey that it would result in the unnecessary break-up of marriages. But the reality is that it would have been an enabling provision where a woman would have had a choice to lodge a First Information Report against her husband if she was sexually victimised. (Under the provisions of the criminal law, the police would have been duty-bound to register such a report.)

The marital exemption referred to above is contained in Exception 2 in Section 375 of the Indian Penal Code, which reads: 'Sexual intercourse or sexual acts by a man with his own wife, the wife not being under fifteen years of age, is not rape.'

I am of the view that the non-removal of this exception, despite our very strong recommendation, is unjust to women and violates their dignity and bodily integrity.

It is against the spirit of human rights and the Convention for the Elimination of All Forms of Discrimination Against Women. Is a woman to be bound by the feudal fiction of irrevocable consent the moment she takes her marriage vows? Can she never thereafter maintain her own self-respect and individuality?

With one breath the government talks of encouraging women, empowering them and enhancing their rights, and with the next it takes away their right to refuse to have sex if they do not wish to. The government has been overpowered by a patriarchal mentality and has failed to do the right thing by women.

However, I do not believe that women should lose heart. Change will come in time; I hope sooner rather than later. We need to educate people about the constitutional right of equality. Awareness programs are essential for ordinary people so that, as Professor Sandra Fredman observed, 'Marriage should not be regarded as extinguishing the legal or sexual autonomy of the wife.'

In fact, many of our recommendations were not incorporated in Act 13 of 2013 (which followed on from the committee's report), although some, such as those relating to voyeurism and stalking, were.

Disfigurement

We were glad to note that an acid attack (throwing or administering acid) was being included as a specific crime. We had heard horrible stories in which a man stalked a woman and, if she objected or turned down his advances, threw acid on her face, thus disfiguring her, destroying her self-worth, causing permanent psychological damage, and completely ruining her life. We felt that this might have been averted if stalking were clearly an offence and the matter was nipped in the bud. It would also ensure the security and safety of women. We are happy that this recommendation (imposing a punishment of up to three years in jail and a fine) was accepted.

Slow to change

Although first an Ordinance and then the Act mentioned above were passed promptly, many of the other suggestions in our 631-page report, which aimed to make both the law and its implementation effective and to truly empower women, have not been dealt with. These include police reforms; changes to *The Representation of the People Act* 1951; changes to the *Armed Forces (Special Powers) Act* 1958; the establishment of a Women's Charter; improvements in infrastructure and safety measures of various kinds; improvements in living standards, sanitation, health and educational facilities; and increased awareness in order to help change our patriarchal mindset. We were consistently of the opinion that equity and respect for the girl child and woman had to be of paramount consideration.

◆ ◆ ◆

I wonder if Nirbhaya's case and our report have changed anything substantial. I do believe the report has helped to break the silence regarding sexual violence against women. It has brought about an awareness of this deeply troubling matter, and has reduced the stigma attached to the victims of these offences. It has made men and women more willing to report cases and to speak about their trauma. The discussion of gender crimes is now not confined to women's groups; many men are also now involved with the issue. As I think of my own youth and my ignorance about sex, I realise the importance of sex education in schools, and hope it will become a reality throughout the country.

The movement for change has to continue and, in time, bear fruit. It is for the youth to take it forward and to build a more equal society. I am confident that they will.

REARRANGED MARRIAGE

IRA TRIVEDI

For centuries, India has had a complicated relationship with skin colour, but at no other time in history has the obsession with fair skin been so extreme as now. An estimated 65 per cent of Indian women use fairness creams; the Indian fairness cream market generates annual revenue of more than US$400 million and has been growing by close to 20 per cent annually.

This obsession with fair skin is nowhere more visible than in India's burgeoning matrimony industry. Marriage remains the cornerstone of Indian society and is widely thought of as the most important step in a woman's life. Beauty comes into play as women strive to make the best possible match in a highly competitive arranged-marriage market, where eligibility is based on a few select factors such as wealth, looks, education and family status.

So many girls are rejected as brides by boys and their families, only because of the colour of their skin. When dark-skinned girls finally do manage to find a match, their families have to pay out larger dowries, which take the form of throwing grand weddings and giving expensive gifts to their prospective sons-in-law.

It is through the prism of marriage that I decided to explore how the beauty epidemic – and, more specifically, an obsession with skin colour – manifests in India. This journey is a deeply personal one because I too am part of India's beauty epidemic. I have used skin-lightening creams extensively. I have been a finalist in the Miss India pageant, and I have spent an inordinate amount of time in marriage bureaus, not only in the guise of research but also looking for a husband. At the marriage bureaus, I have personally experienced how a decision of a lifetime can be made in a matter of hours, and how important, through all of this, skin colour is.

Part 1: GROOM WANTED – for beautiful girl. Slim. Wheatish. Family income Rs 50 lakh+ Works in M.N.C. Religious. Homely. Family-oriented.

'Please find her a husband,' beseeches Mrs Mehta, her chapatti-round face solid and sincere. Lines of silver fleck her thick, oiled plait – her lumpy, generous body is draped in a peony pink chiffon sari, and clunky golden bangles jangle around her chubby wrists. Mrs Mehta is the classic Indian matron known universally as 'Aunty-ji'. She takes a quick look at her daughter, Sakshi, the subject of the matrimonial advertisement above: slumped in a chair, staring languidly at her Blackberry, visibly distraught to be present at this meeting. In stark contrast to her mother, the office-going Sakshi is dressed drably in a loose black pantsuit with a pair of dusty flats, on their last legs. Despite her unbecoming clothing, Sakshi is a comely girl – she's got the lithe frame of an athlete, a pretty, heart-shaped face with well-proportioned features, and, perhaps her best asset, passed down from her mother, thick, shiny, serpent-like hair.

Mr Gopal Suri, the proprietor of South Delhi's most successful marriage bureau, *A to Z Matrimonial,* gives Sakshi a sceptical look and then turns back to her mother.

'Madam, at the moment we are very busy. It is difficult for me to take on any more clients.'

'But Gopal-ji, Sakshi is twenty-five years old! If we don't find her a husband now then it will be *toooo* late. And her papa – he is willing to pay a *very* high price for this,' squeals Mrs Mehta.

At the end, an avaricious Mr Suri simply can't resist, and he signs on the Mehtas, with a 30 per cent hike in his usual fee on account of the difficulty of the job that lies ahead of him.

Prima facie, Sakshi is the perfect client – an attractive, twenty-five-year-old, educated girl with well-to-do parents who are desperate to get her married and ready to pay any price for it. But for Mr Suri, who assesses clients day in, day out on their marriageability, Sakshi has low marks. Sakshi is considered highly ineligible on India's matrimony market on account of the colour of her skin. Though the matrimonial advertisement that her parents published in the papers markets her as 'wheatish' – a uniquely Indian term as common as black or white, used to describe a dark-ish complexion – the reality is that Sakshi is not the colour of wheat but the colour of dark chocolate. With over fifteen years of experience in the matrimony department, during which he has brokered close to a thousand arranged marriages, Mr Suri has found that there are few takers for girls as dark as Sakshi.

◆ ◆ ◆

'We want pretty, fair girls only,' asserts Mrs Gupta, an aunty who arrives shortly after Mrs Mehta.

Mr Suri is at his obsequious best. He pulls out all stops – endless cups of lemon tea, snacks both savoury and sweet from the local market, and, to appear as if he has abundant resources, his entire team of six sit in on the meeting. Mrs Gupta has a coveted asset – an eligible son whom she is desperate to find a bride for.

A true salesman, Gopal Suri pulls out his knock-off iPad to show Mrs Gupta biodata of prospective daughters-in-law.

Mrs Gupta is unimpressed by the *A to Z* inventory.

'Gopal-ji, these girls are not fair or lovely enough for my Rohan,' she complains.

Mrs Gupta is not particularly fair-skinned herself, nor is her son. But she, unlike Sakshi, might be described as 'wheatish'. It appears that most of Rohan's friends are Punjabi and Mrs Gupta tells us that if she finds a bride as fair as cow's milk, then her son would marry her in a heartbeat. Propelled by Indian mass media, the 'Punjabi' notion of beauty – fair skin, big eyes, long thick hair – has become hugely popular. Punjabis are typically tall, fair and more 'Western'-looking than most other Indians. There was a time, not so long ago, when a woman like Mrs Gupta – from the Marwari community, known to be conservative and reserved – would be appalled at the thought of nuptial ties with the Punjabis – known to be brash, loud, colourful and a bit flashy.

After spending weeks at the marriage bureau I have developed some matchmaking expertise myself. It isn't exactly rocket science; rather, the way that Mr Suri matches two people is so simplistic that I am often left flabbergasted. Relationships, especially finding 'the One', feel like the most complicated things in the world to me. Here at *A to Z*, though, they are decided practically every day.

Mr Suri creates biodata for all his clients. This biodata lists height, the date of birth, caste, education, family income and family details: parents' professions, siblings, grandparents, uncles, aunts and whomever else the client chose to include. The biodata always comes with a few photographs.

The most important criteria for matching are age, family income – both the families should be in similar wealth brackets – and the photograph. For boys the most important criterion is looks – they all want to marry pretty girls, and in this case 'pretty' means 'fair';

only colour photos are circulated, so the fairness of a girl's skin can be assessed.

And these days nothing happens without 'chemistry'. This new factor has significantly complicated Mr Suri's simplistic model, and he can never understand why two people who match so well on paper don't seem to get along in real life. This is where my expertise lies – I am good at gauging chemistry – whether two young people will get along and be attractive to each other. After all, most of the clients at *A to Z* are close to my age, and many of them are more open with me than with Mr Suri about what they hope to find in their future husband/wife. I have made four matches over the past six months.

Rohan is twenty-seven years old, of medium height, and undeniably average-looking. He has lived in Delhi all his life and he loves sports, especially tennis. I immediately think of the sporty Sakshi, a local tennis champ. It turns out that Sakshi and Rohan live a few blocks away from each other, studied a few years apart at the same high school and even went to neighbouring colleges. Both families are in similar wealth brackets and also from the same caste. It is quite literally a match made in heaven – especially when the in-house astrologer at the marriage bureau confirms that their birth charts match perfectly.

I share my discovery with Mr Suri, who immediately slams the match.

'I think they'll get along like a house on fire.'

'Yes, they will set the house on fire and then Mrs Gupta will blame me only,' grumbles Mr Suri. 'Mrs Gupta wants beautiful girls only.'

♦ ♦ ♦

Over the past few weeks I have come to know Sakshi well and have become fond of her. She regularly visits the bureau with her mother, who frantically scours the *A to Z* database for potential sons-in-law. Sakshi is sweet, easygoing, funny and bright – a great girl who works at a respectable consulting firm, and, contrary to how the matrimonial ad has made her seem, she loves going out, drinking, dancing and having a good time. Though Sakshi has had a seemingly modern life, since the day she turned twenty-one her parents have been putting pressure on her to get married. Because their daughter is dark-skinned, the Mehtas have always known that marriage isn't going to be an easy task, and so they have been amassing dowry – jewellery, saris and items of gold and silver that they will give as gifts to Sakshi's future husband's family. They have also started an investment fund through which they will pay for their daughter's wedding. It seems bizarre to me that Sakshi's life could be so modern and yet so regressive at the same time.

One fortuitous afternoon at the marriage bureau, an increasingly desperate Mrs Mehta comes across Rohan's biodata on the database.

'This boy,' she gasps, 'is perfect for my Sakshi.'

Sakshi, too, is taken by Rohan's pictures – professionally shot, one of him posing with his red car, another with a fuzzy white dog, and a third with his tennis racquet.

Under the combined pressure of my enthusiasm, Sakshi's willingness, Mrs Mehta's anxiety and Mr Mehta's fat cheque, Mr Suri begins strategising.

He orders a photo shoot for Sakshi, and then personally supervises the Photoshopping process so that, at the end, Sakshi looks almost fair but also fluorescent in her pictures.

It appears that the marriage broker does know best and the Photoshopping, combined with Mr Suri's waxing eloquent about the Mehta family's many virtues, lands us an invitation from the Guptas for tea – the first and critical step in the courtship between two families.

Mrs Mehta begins preparations for the meeting, organising sufficiently opulent outfits and jewellery for herself and Sakshi, purchasing gift baskets piled with fruit, sweets and nuts for the Guptas, whisking Sakshi from the salon to the dermatologist to have her at her glowing best, and consulting an astrologer to prescribe an auspicious time for the first meeting. Mrs Mehta even asks me what I am going to wear for this meeting, and in her temporary spirit of largesse offers to buy me a new outfit.

After a frenzied week, the day of the meeting is finally here. Mrs Mehta arrives, puffed up like a Pomeranian, draped in an extravagant sari studded with Swarovski crystals, and covered with jewels to show off the family's wealth. Even the usual monochromatic Sakshi has on a glittery *salwaar kameez*. She has had her make-up professionally done and she has a cake of foundation on her face. Although it lightens her up sufficiently, it has also made her look anaemic and tinted with grey. Her hair is set in frothy curls.

The Guptas are welcoming and, much to Mrs Mehta's pleasure, seem impressed by the assortment of gifts – the trays of dried fruits and exotic imported fruits, the containers of sweet *rasgullas*, and the large bouquet of flowers. Sakshi seems equally dazzled by Rohan, who in real life is more handsome than in his photos – he is gym-fit and, with his gelled-back hair, tight pants, big belt buckle and tight shirt, is the perfect picture of a pampered Delhi rake.

Mrs Mehta dominates most of the conversation, braying on about the wealth of the family and the plans they have for throwing Sakshi a grand wedding. The Guptas seem increasingly excited and I notice that Sakshi and Rohan are throwing approving glances at each other. Everything is going according to plan and I notice that a tense Mr Suri, sitting quietly in the corner, is beginning to relax a little.

Then, apropos of nothing, Mrs Gupta leaps up from the sofa, a look of alarm on her face. She motions for her husband to follow her into the kitchen.

Mrs Mehta is not concerned with their departure, taking this time to carefully appraise the room we are sitting in – assessing the clarity of the crystal pieces, the value of the paintings on the wall and the quality of the furniture. I can almost see the math in Mr Mehta's head as he calculates the square footage of the house.

The Guptas return and as Mrs Mehta launches into another spectacular rant, they are unusually quiet. A few minutes later, an embarrassed Mr Gupta mumbles that he has to leave for a meeting. A tight-lipped Mrs Gupta stands up, thanks everyone for coming, and rudely leaves the room. Mrs Mehta's pride is totally deflated, but she is a tough lady and she storms out of the room with gumption, a confused Mr Mehta in tow and Sakshi and me trailing. Mr Suri stays behind to pick up the pieces.

◆ ◆ ◆

'She says that her feet were very dark. They don't want such a dark girl. They were *very* angry,' he says darkly.

Gauging my utter incomprehension, Mr Suri's assistant patiently explains to me that looking at a girl's feet is an age-old trick to determine her 'real' skin colour, since make-up or fairness creams are rarely ever applied to the feet.

I'm in equal measures speechless and disgusted. In so many ways, Rohan and Sakshi are a great fit – I could tell, even by the brief meeting, that they had excellent chemistry. The families, too, are compatible. The only reason they are holding off is the colour of Sakshi's skin. Unbelievable – especially because it isn't so easy anymore to find an appropriate match for two young people. In the olden days, two people were married off if their families approved. But these days the 'chemistry' factor makes it harder. Though Sakshi was on the arranged marriage market, she wouldn't just marry a man her parents chose for her – she would have to like him too.

Seeing me looking so distraught, Mr Suri tells me with unexpected gentleness, 'Ira, this is the way it is only.'

The more time I spend at the marriage bureau, the more I realise how correct Mr Suri is, and how indeed this is the way it is only.

♦ ♦ ♦

The matrimonial search continues for Sakshi with limited success. Sakshi and her parents have several first meetings with families but hardly any second meetings follow. Mr Suri attributes this mostly to the colour of Sakshi's skin.

Meanwhile, without the knowledge of their parents or Mr Suri, Sakshi and Rohan have connected over Facebook and have been meeting clandestinely. Sakshi seems to be over the moon about Rohan, and she comes to the marriage bureau more frequently than ever on the pretext of looking at biodata, though while she is there she either goes to meet Rohan or spends her time locked in one of the cabins chatting to him on the phone.

While is it clear that Sakshi has fallen for Rohan, and would marry him in a heartbeat, Rohan's intentions towards Sakshi remain unclear. He has been meeting girls pre-approved by his mother. And there is one girl, who looks and behaves like an over-indulged poodle, with whom he seems to have hit it off.

I can't stand watching Sakshi fall deeper into the black hole of love, and I confront Rohan and ask him squarely about his intentions, or lack thereof. His leading Sakshi on is unfair.

A few days later, a lacklustre Sakshi walks into the office. She's not her cheery self – her usually glowing face is splotchy, her normally perfect hair is limp and her typically manicured nails are dirty. She is spiritless and, though she is supposed to be perusing biodata, she's staring blankly into space. After three cups of sugary tea, she reveals to me that Rohan has stopped replying to her texts.

I feel horribly guilty. That lily-livered Rohan probably backed off after our confrontation. I confess to Sakshi that I had put Rohan in a corner, and have probably scared him off.

Sakshi is silent and I brace myself for a scolding, but she is too dejected to be angry.

'It's because I'm dark, isn't it?' she says with a whimper. 'That's why he doesn't like me.'

Part 2: Bride-hunting in the Punjab

'*Kaalia*[1], get in the right lane,' yells the hot-blooded young Punjabi, wearing sunglasses, a fluorescent yellow t-shirt and no helmet, his long hair in a greasy ponytail, as he whizzes past us noisily. His horn blasts with an angry wail.

'Welcome to Punjab,' says Tej to me grimly, slowing down and switching to the correct lane. He settles behind a truck emitting a dark cloud of pollution and transporting a dozen terrified, bleating goats.

'I just don't like seeing them being taken to their death,' Tej grumbles, referring to the goats.

'Maybe they're being taken to a farm,' I say, gazing at the picturesque mustard fields and bucolic green fields, flanking us on both sides.

'Wishful thinking,' Tej says, cautiously keeping a safe distance behind the truck.

Tej Bajwa and I are on a road trip in the Punjab. Tej is a marriage broker specialising in acquiring brides for wealthy N.R.I.s (non-resident Indians). His global business, which takes him around the world from Canada, Hong Kong and Kenya to Punjab, is hugely successful, and today we are enjoying the fruits of his success as we drive in his sleek Mercedes Benz, a gift from a client whose divorced son he arrange-remarried.

Our mission today is to track down girls for a special client of his – Ram Kuttuswamy, a technology millionaire who lives in Washington D.C. Originally from Tamil Nadu in South India, Ram has recently divorced the woman he was arrange-married to at the age

---

1. 'Black' in Hindi – a common expletive for a dark-skinned person

of twenty-one. In his second innings, buoyed by his move to America and his newly minted wealth, he is in the market for a new bride.

Ram's only requirement is for a young and beautiful wife. In his case, beautiful means fair, and so we have set off to the Punjab, one of the few pockets of fair-skinned denizens in India.

'What if his fair-skinned bride is not a cultural match for him?' I ask, concerned.

'He'll send her to a finishing school,' says Tej matter-of-factly.

'And the emotional connect?'

'In any marriage, that comes over time.'

I met Ram in Delhi, and he struck me as being a modern, open-minded, progressive sort of guy. But he had internalised the fact that fair skin was beautiful, to the point that it surpassed all rationale.

Our first stop in the quest for Ram's wife is Bathinda, a medium-sized city which until a few years ago was mostly farmland but today sports the ubiquitous trappings of development – traffic, concrete eyesores and shopping malls. We are here to meet Sikh priests at the local Gurudwara or Sikh temples, which double as local marriage bureaus. The Sikh priests form a crucial part of Tej's business. They are the first point of contact for families with marriageable young sons and daughters, whose biodata they pass on to Tej. Over the years, Tej has forged relationships with these priests and created networks at hundreds of Gurudwaras around the world.

The relationship is symbiotic and Tej is helpful to the priests for a number of reasons. First, he gives them money if a successful match is made; second, it is good for the priest's reputation to marry off poor Punjabi girls to rich N.R.I. men. Third, the weddings that the priest brokers typically take place in his Gurudwara, which means more money.

For many families, Ram would be a catch. He neither wants dowry, nor does he expect the bride's parents to throw a lavish wedding. The downside is that Ram is divorced, he has a daughter from his previous marriage, and he is Tamilian (might as well say alien in this part of the woods) and his wife will have to move far away from the innards of Punjab to Washington D.C., with infrequent trips back home because Ram dislikes India and has only been making trips here to secure a bride.

On arriving in Bathinda, we enter a small ramshackle Gurudwara where a wizened, gnome-like priest, with a long flowing grey beard and a baby-blue turban, is delighted to see Tej.

'*Sat Sri Akaal*, Tej-ji,' he bellows in Punjabi.

Tej gives the priest a bright smile, embraces him, and then speaks in fluent Punjabi.

'So good to see you! The blessings of Guru Nanak have brought us together again.'

I am handed a cup of delicious salty buttermilk, and then I am largely ignored as Tej and the priest pore over biodata and photographs of pretty, plump, fair-skinned Punjabi girls.

After Tej shortlists a few girls – the youngest and fairest of the lot – the priest makes a few phone calls and sets up the meetings. Tej has a definite bounce in his step as we leave the Gurudwara to meet three potential wives for Ram.

The first family that we visit is just a few kilometres away from the Gurudwara. We drive through a congested residential colony and arrive at a shanty home – decrepit but clean. When we arrive, we find the whole family, along with a street dog, intently watching television. Despite our fervent protests, they get up from the small cot they were sitting on and offer it to us, making themselves comfortable on the floor.

I hadn't expected grandeur of any kind, but the conditions inside the house surprise me. The entire house consists of two rooms – the one where we sit, the living/dining/TV room, and the other a small bedroom, attached to which is a squalid toilet. Wires hang loosely from the roof, and a few light bulbs sputter from the ceiling. The only decoration is a dusty portrait of a snowy-bearded Guru Nanak on the wall.

We are offered cups of sweet chai, served by a shy, pretty girl who I assume is the bride-to-be.

The father looks proudly at his daughter.

'Cow's milk,' he says proudly, referring to the health of her complexion, patting her on the back so hard that she spills the buttermilk on the floor.

The father looks furious, and the daughter flies out of the room, her fair face beet-red with embarrassment. Seconds later her mother returns with a washcloth and mops up the mess.

Tej does the talking. He explains that his client, Ram, is worth millions of U.S. dollars, lives in a house with seven rooms, taps that spout hot water all day, and electricity that never gets cut. Ram, he gushes, owns three cars (I know for a fact that he owns only two) and he is a loving, caring son to his parents and will be equally loving and caring to his wife and future in-laws.

The father shakes his head approvingly, and with each passing second I can see his growing excitement.

'What's the issue?' he asks politely, for obviously there has to be one for a man so rich to look for a poor bride in the Punjab.

Tej is matter-of-fact.

'He has a daughter. She's ten. But she lives with the mother, Ram's ex-wife.'

'Have you seen the divorce papers?' asks the astute father.

'I have them here with me,' Tej says, pulling a few papers from his briefcase.

The father takes a quick look at them. The paper is upside down, and I realise that he can't read English.

'Can I see a photograph?' asks the father.

For a second Tej hesitates, and he makes a show of shuffling papers around.

'I'm not sure I have one,' he says, sifting through the papers.

I am Facebook friends with Tej, and I know that Tej has about twenty photographs of Ram on his page. I am about to offer to show some pictures on my phone, but I stop, noticing the nervous look on Tej's face.

After his infinitesimal silence, the father says in Punjabi. 'A photo will have to be seen.'

'My phone!' says Tej nervously. 'Of course, I have a picture on my phone.' And with that, Tej taps at his phone, gushing to the father that the expensive iPhone was a gift from Ram, and then hands it over to the father.

It's as if the sun has set over heaven. In a matter of seconds the father's face, which until just a few seconds ago was aglow with expectation, is contorted into a look of fury.

I don't understand most of the expletives, but I see that the cool-as-a-cucumber Tej is frightened. He crouches on the cot, while the father, over six feet tall, stands up, yelling at him.

Tej hops up from the cot, grabs his briefcase and, forgetting all about me, rushes out of the room. I follow him quickly lest he leave me behind, and we hop into his Mercedes, which has a gaggle of admirers floating around it. The screaming father follows us and as Tej drives away I hear a huge bang – someone, I presume the angry father, has thrown something at the car. Tej drives recklessly fast, knocking down two dumpsters in the process and running over some sort of animal, which I pray he hasn't killed.

We find our way out of the crowded neighbourhood onto a large street, and a shaken Tej finally relaxes.

'Does this happen often?' I ask.

'Sometimes,' he says wearily.

'Why did he go crazy?'

'Because Ram is dark and also because he is South Indian,' he replies.

Responding to my shocked silence, Tej says, 'In these parts being dark is like being a leper. Also, South Indians are looked down upon because they are typically dark.'

'Despite all of Ram's money?' I ask.

'They'll marry her off to a wife-beating drunkard. But that's okay, as long as he is fair and Punjabi,' he says.

Tej skips the next two meetings in Bathinda – he doesn't want to stick around these parts, so we begin the three-hour drive to Ludhiana. I too am relieved to be leaving Bathinda. I keep looking over my shoulder, paranoid that a livid Punjabi father will emerge from the shadows to take down poor Tej.

We arrive in Ludhiana, where the local priest, savvier than the last one, has already shortlisted and emailed Tej biodata. We head straight to the homes of potential brides. At the prospect of a potential husband for their daughter, Indian parents are at their obsequious best and, despite the fact that we have informed them only two hours before our arrival, they are happy to welcome us.

On the drive over, Tej is moody and anxious. I suspect that it is because of the recent fractious encounter, but he reveals that something else is on his mind. Tej is worried that he may never find Ram a bride. This is Tej's seventh trip to Punjab, bride-hunting for Ram. He has been inculcating priests for several years, and Ram has paid him over US$100,000 in fees. Tej has never had this much trouble with a client; he attributes the difficulty of finding a bride for Ram to the colour of his skin.

♦ ♦ ♦

In my research of the matrimonial market in India I had seen how important it was for women to be fair, but here in Punjab, the mecca of fair skin, I realise how pervasive the obsession with fair skin is. In every single permutation and combination of India's complicated class equation, Ram qualifies as high class. He belongs to the high-caste Brahmin community and he is rich and well educated. But in the eyes of the father we just encountered, and so many others like him, class rests in the colour of the skin, and he considers it a stain on his family's honour to give his daughter in marriage to such a dark-skinned man. It is also ludicrous that South Indians are looked down upon by Punjabis because they are dark-skinned. As wealth, caste and class lines become increasingly blurred in India, fair skin is more important than ever before, and the beauty epidemic in India has become so pervasive that even men are falling victim to it.

A priest I met in a Gurudwara in Chandigarh with Tej told me that fair skin determined class in a time when nothing else did. Low-caste farmers have become millionaires in months because of booming land prices; caste doesn't hold as much status as before, since high castes are poor and poor castes are rich, so because of the lack of any other metric, people are using skin colour to judge class.

I suggest that maybe we should look for a bride elsewhere for Ram, but Tej tells me dismally that Ram is set on a fair-skinned Punjabi bride. Nothing else is more important to him.

'This,' asserts Tej sadly, 'is the only way.'

In Ludhiana, we cross a busy market place, pass through a few gargantuan structures – malls, which have become all the rage here in Punjab – and make our way to our destination. Our G.P.S. leads us to an apartment building on the outskirts of town. We park and cross through several dank, winding corridors till we finally find ourselves outside apartment 14B, block C, wing E.

The door is opened by an elderly couple, Mr and Mrs Singh, who are friendly and welcoming. Their flat is surprisingly charming – especially after the horror of the Bathinda encounter. They seem to be quite religious: there are pictures of Hindu gods and gurus everywhere.

Pleasantries are exchanged, tea and samosas are served, and then Tej begins his usual sales pitch. Mid-pitch, the doorbell rings and

Mrs Singh leaps up to open the door. A chubby, fresh-faced, smiling girl comes into the apartment.

She greets us in perfect English, and her parents ask her to sit down with us.

Tej has done a quick expert survey, and from the glint in his eye I can see that he approves.

'Tell them about yourself,' urges Mrs Singh in Punjabi.

'My good name is Sheena Singh. I am a Master's in Education and English from Khalsa College for Women. I am twenty-three years old. My dream in life is to become an English teacher,' she recites in a singsong monologue.

Tej seems sufficiently impressed.

'Good to meet you, Sheena,' he says, extending his hand, which she takes shyly with a smile. He seems to be in a glittering mood – so different from before that for a moment I wonder if he wants to marry Sheena himself.

After an hour of banter, Mrs Singh invites us to stay for dinner and soon Mr Singh is telling us all about his family.

Sheena is the third of three children. Her two older brothers, Manmeet and Gurmeet, are out of touch. They are addicted to drugs – apparently a common problem among the Punjabi youth – and have squandered much of the family property holdings to finance their addiction. Sheena is the Singhs' only daughter, and because of the damage their sons have done, they have no money to pay for her wedding and are unable to find a husband for her.

'Now you have! Ram is perfect for her,' extols Tej. 'He wants an educated wife, and Sheena can study further and pursue a career in the U.S.'

Seeing the stunned look on the Singhs' faces, Tej continues with a smile. 'Ram is very open-minded and modern. Now, there are only two problems,' he continues.

All three Singh faces fall.

'Well, three actually,' he says. 'First, he is divorced, which to be honest, nowadays, is not a problem. Second, he has an issue from his first wife. That is also not a problem, because he has plenty of money, and his daughter lives with his first wife. Third,' continues Tej, a slight strain entering his voice, 'Ram is from Tamil Nadu and he is dark.'

I wait to see the look of horror on the Singhs' faces, but thankfully they still seem to be hanging on to Tej's every word.

'In America, dark is considered very beautiful. Their President is black. His wife, also black, is thought to be America's most beautiful woman. In America, where Sheena will live, black people have a lot of respect.'

There is an uncomfortable silence, and Tej and I await their comments with bated breath.

'Is that it?' asks Mr Singh.

'Yes,' says Tej conclusively.

'Can we see a picture?'

Tej passes his phone to Sheena. All three Singhs huddle over the screen, appraising Ram's smiling face.

'He is a little black,' says Mrs Singh quietly.

I brace myself for disaster.

'He is a little tanned in this picture. He was just back from visiting the beach, where there is a lot of sun,' says Tej nervously.

'If our daughter is okay, then we are okay,' says Mr Singh with a gentle smile, looking expectantly at Sheena.

'Is he a nice man?' Sheena asks me, shyly but intently.

I feel as if a mountain of pressure has been placed on me. I am taking too long to reply and I feel a kick underneath the table.

'Yes. Yes, he is,' I say finally, because I do honestly believe that Ram is a nice guy.

Two hours later, at the stroke of midnight, Tej and I head straight to the only bar in Ludhiana. The Singhs have agreed to give their daughter in marriage to Ram on the condition that Sheena can study further in the U.S. and pursue her dream of becoming a teacher. Tej is keen to celebrate in whatever style Ludhiana has to offer.

An ecstatic Tej calls Ram. 'Broooo, we found your woman!' he says joyously. 'She's beautiful, fair as milk, a real beauty, and a very nice girl too.'

'Don't you think Ram should meet her before he agrees to marry her?' I ask, a little bewildered by this turn of events.

'Nope,' says Tej. 'I know this man inside out. He's going to love her.'

'Maybe he should meet her just once.'

'I'm *totally* sure. What's not to like? She's fair, she's sweet, she'll give him fair-ish babies, she'll look great on his arm after he sends her to finishing school. That's all he really cares about.'

'What about her? Will she be fine?'

'A penthouse in D.C. versus a village in India? Which one would any woman prefer?'

I guess the answer to that question is pretty clear.

Driving back to Delhi from Punjab I remember the truck full of goats we had come across on our drive over. In many ways, this matrimonial process reminds me of those poor goats. These girls, like the goats, have no clue where they are being shipped off to – a butcher's hell or a pastoral heaven. But then again, as Tej said, at least they are lucky to have a choice, thanks to the colour of their skin.

BLACK

ROSALYN D'MELLO

Even as I write this, the charred remains of what was once skin is being shed; the thin peel, as black as the carbonised exterior of a roasted eggplant, slips off piecemeal, revealing a narrow strait of pink flesh. The wound is too prominent, poised precisely above the parting of my breasts, calling too much attention to itself. It no longer stings, is no longer raw, but along its periphery is a persistent itch. I need to keep it sufficiently greased.

I've never been as determined to erase a potential scar. I've never before been ashamed of a burn. I'm known to wear all welts like souvenirs. If the circumstances were different, if I were not to blame for the singeing of my own skin, if I'd been a victim of another's callousness, I'd be more at ease. But it was I who was responsible. I was not humble enough: I should have made the required intercessions to the gods that be, as I am usually wont to do.

I'd done this so many times before that I deluded myself into believing the caramel custard had been perfectly steamed. I didn't flinch even once when, holding both dishes too close to my body, I upturned the custard and the liquid concoction of milk, eggs and sugar splattered over the upper region of my chest.

Without letting out so much as a squeal, I walked towards the sink, ran the tap and splashed water over my chest to contain the sting. My lover, who was beside me, salvaged the unsteady custard, making it presentable, quelling my fears about this last course being a disaster. He took the hurriedly made dessert to the table, poured two capfuls of rum over the caramelised top, setting it aflame, allowing it the privilege of a perfect rich glaze.

◆ ◆ ◆

It seems almost narcissistic to have to tend to my body so obsessively. It is not a practice I am accustomed to. I grew up learning to detest my skin. If ever I faltered and administered to it too preciously, the world around me was ever present to remind me of its imperfection. I was never accorded the status of being beautiful.

In a country fixated on fairness, my unsavoury black skin has been a curse. The politically correct 'dusky' is an understatement when it comes to my skin tone. Mocha brown is more accurate. Its denseness makes me stand out wherever I go. If random bystanders do not call me 'blackie', 'nigger', '*kali*', 'black beauty', 'negro' or '*Kali Maa*', they ask me if I'm from Kenya, South India or Sri Lanka, often even when I'm in Goa, the land of my origins. Once, two women who were walking towards me on a street in Mumbai actually found themselves in a quandary: they noticed how my colour resembled a black cat's and spent a fair amount of energy manoeuvring their gait so as to avoid crossing my path. Like these superstitious women, no one knows what to make of a confident, self-aware, dark-skinned woman.

◆ ◆ ◆

When I was twelve and self-conscious, I had a nightly ritual. I'd stand in front of the mirror, comb my hair, brush my teeth, wash my face, dry myself, then stare at my reflection, wondering if this was really me.

Before sleeping, I'd say a little prayer. Always the same words coursed between my lips because there was only one thing I wanted most of all.

Beauty.

I prayed for beauty.

When I woke, I'd walk to the mirror and face my disappointment. Nothing had changed. My skin was still as dark as roasted cocoa. I'd lament the day: my mother's protest at my opposition to fairness creams, my dwindling self-esteem, my battle with choosing clothes whose colour wouldn't contrast so sharply with the black of my skin.

I was the misfit by default. I hated being different. I hated wearing my skin like a cloak of shame. Everywhere I trod I had to bear witness to petty humiliations. I wanted to be invisible. I wanted to be able to camouflage my body, but I seemed fated to stand out like a sore thumb.

I was tired of derision. I wanted to be desired.

This petitioning and the ensuing disappointment continued for two years. Until one night, when I decided to alter the texture of my intercession.

I stopped asking for beauty. I asked for wisdom instead.

It has made all the difference.

◆ ◆ ◆

We all aspire to beauty, without adequately questioning its parameters. What constitutes an object/subject's beauty? Is it its context? Is it Zeitgeist? Is beauty subject to the vagaries of trends and shifting tastes? Is it its transience? Or its apparent translucency or opacity? Is it its relation to truth, as Keats would have it? Is it subterranean, perceivable only to sagacious eyes? Does it lie at the cusp between vanity and humility? Must beauty only be defined by the beholder? Or can it possibly be something more inherent? Can something be beautiful if there is no one to admire its beauty? Can it be lived as well as felt? Is beauty a function of light?

For years I've battled with the aphorism 'beauty is only skin deep'. The world as it exists will not allow us the luxury of entertaining such a profound belief. A perfunctory glance at the matrimonials will show you the fact that all prospective brides, grooms and mothers-in-law in India prefer a fair-skinned alliance to duskier counterparts. For dark-skinned women to stand any chance in the marriage bazaar, they must disguise their darkness. Fair equals beautiful. Dark equals a hefty dowry.

Our biggest misconception is that we see whiteness as synonymous with lightness. What we have lost, in our ignorance, is the metaphysical connotations inherent in the word 'light'. What we have forgotten are the mystical inferences redolent in the word 'black'. In our Aryan-Dravidian hegemony, we have completely suppressed the mythical significance of words like *kali*, referring to the black goddess herself, of time, doomsday, and death. Kali is a figure of defiance, her brazenly black complexion symbolising her transcendental nature, her nude body attesting to her state of being shorn of all that is illusory. I had been derisively called *kali* so many times I never once thought to investigate the nuances behind the word, always processing it as an adjective or a proper noun, rarely as the evocation of a divine, all-powerful entity.

◆ ◆ ◆

Recently, when I was perched on what could easily have substituted as a gynaecologist's chair – legs splayed, hands spread outwards against each arm rest, dress hitched high enough to barely cover my delicates – I re-encountered the extent of my darkness. It wasn't the state of almost nakedness that prompted this; two women, one on each side of my body, made a fair contribution. The one on my right lifted the powder puff from its receptacle and rubbed it over my ankle. The talc contrasted sharply against my skin. 'Arms *pehle karte hain*,' said the woman on my left. *Let's do the arms first.* A firm strategy now in place, both women proceeded to first spread hot wax over my skin, after having powdered it, and then to rip it off with a white paper strip, removing, in the process, all the unwanted hair.

At least two months had passed since I was last deforested, which meant there was a fair amount of hair to pull off. The women performed the procedure simultaneously, and, despite their dexterity, my nerves smarted from each erasure. When the ordeal was finally over, one of them wiped each of my limbs with a wet cloth before baptising me with astringent. My skin gleamed.

It was only later, in the bath, that I realised this was my most pleasant experience to date at a beauty parlour. As I revelled in the silken feel of my waxed body, I actually wore a smile. Apart from my epiphany about the density and extent of my darkness, there was nothing exceptional about this particular session, which is precisely what made it extraordinary. Perhaps the women were too eager to have lunch to be their usual inquisitive selves, or perhaps it was that they had mistaken me for a married woman (I was wearing a sari and a bindi when I had come in an hour before to make an appointment, something they asked me about later). Under normal circumstances, ten minutes into being waxed, I am usually asked one of two things: to either bleach my face or get a fairness-inducing facial. 'Look at your skin, it's all tanned,' one such 'professional' once told me. 'That's the colour of my skin, you idiot,' is what I wanted to say. Instead, I placed one waxed arm against my face to show her the colours matched. 'Your whole body is tanned,' she said, now alarmed. 'We can make it lighter.'

Having put up with this manner of inane observation for most of my life, over time I learned not to let it get to me.

• • •

As a black-skinned feminist I've learned how the conjunctive 'but' can be used as a compensatory word to stinging effect: 'You're beautiful, but dark' or 'You're dark, but you have great features'. The otherwise simple act of accepting a compliment continues to be fraught with anxiety, mostly the consequence of my mother's conditioning.

'You look so dark in this colour,' she often said if I wore anything non-pastel.

'But people have told me I look nice in this [navy blue] dress,' I would say in my defence.

'They're just saying that, they don't really mean it,' she would assure me.

Multiply this conversation by a hundred, and what you're left with is an inherent suspicion about any vocalised admiration – the side effect of a now deep-seated insecurity about my appearance, which can make for highly stunted exchanges. So when a stranger makes the effort to seek me out in a room or a street to tell me I'm 'beautiful', my first instinct is to distrust him and guard my valuables. Beauty is something I cannot seem to take as a given. It seems to lie too disadvantageously in the eyes of beholders.

The entire advertising industry profits from my being not acceptably beautiful, from my being anomalously dark. I'm their target consumer, who refuses to buy into their spiel. Ergo, I presumably deserve all the humiliation I face.

• • •

Long ago I attempted to defend myself against the societal pre-disposition to characterise me first as black by seeking refuge in humour. I did so at my own expense. I laughed at myself. It was the only way I could participate in the joke I was seen to be. If some eager friend wanted to take a photograph of me after sunset, I'd laugh it off and tell them I would be camouflaged by the night sky. 'You need a very strong flash,' I'd say. Or if I'd arranged to meet an acquaintance who was yet to meet me in the flesh, I'd forewarn him or her to look for a tall and dark girl. Or I'd invent a story about how some Goan ancestor of mine must have had an affair with an African slave. Granted, it was self-deprecating, to say the least, but as long as I was in charge of the narrative, it couldn't damage me.

I am yet to forgive myself for being so flippantly self-damning throughout my girlhood. I hadn't realised then how self-destructive self-deprecation can be. As I approached womanhood, as I slowly amassed enough experience of being the object of desire, I realised my only redemption against this deep-seated, nationwide prejudice was to embrace my blackness. That society continued to see the world in shades of black and white was the failure of humanity. And I, too, was implicated, because I had inadvertently subscribed to that hegemony by never questioning it, by allowing it to reduce me, by permitting it to affect my otherwise equanimous state of being. If I embraced my 'unfortunate', 'inferior', 'undesirable' skin tone, I could perhaps let the light in.

◆ ◆ ◆

'Is it difficult to photograph dark skin?' I asked my lover, a photographer by profession.

'It's a question of compensating the exposure,' he told me, an answer that was in sync with the reading I had done about camera settings online. It depends also on the light, he explained: the midday sun, for instance, would be unflattering to a cricketer from the West Indies playing a test match. 'Either you'd bleach out the white of his uniform or you'd darken his face. You have to compensate the exposure,' he reiterated. His advice had all the gravitas of a maxim.

♦ ♦ ♦

I met my lover a few days after I'd turned twenty-three. It was the first time my itinerant body had been offered a sense of home, of being in a place where I didn't feel like I needed to be elsewhere. Soon after that first meeting, I wrote him an epistle informing him that I'd left my heart behind in his white kettle, and that bits of it were probably dissolving with his sugar everyday and entering his bloodstream along with the tea.

'I remember your body so well,' I confessed over the phone the evening after I first met him.

'I do too ... I remember your skin, so dark and taut and beautiful.'

It was the first time he testified to my beauty, an act that would come to be performed increasingly rarely as our relationship progressed from the unexpected comfort of a one-night stand to the underrated humdrum of the everyday. I've never grudged him his reluctance to flatter. I found it refreshing. I had come to be repelled by men who practised repetition, where each sexual encounter would be punctuated by their grateful, charitable moans that attested not so much to my alleged beauty but to the exotic appeal of my black naked body: 'Look at your skin, how it glows in the light.'

Even now I cannot explain how or when I came to be desired. Having spent my girlhood being made to believe that my dark skin would interfere with any such possibility, I was and remain surprised by every instance that proves the contrary.

Sometimes my lover says things that assume the form of epiphanies. For example, once, when I told him about a potential rival, he seemed unfazed that another man should be attracted to me.

'Ah! So you admit I'm beautiful?' I said.

'It depends on how one defines beauty.'

'And what is your conception of beauty?'

'I think of beauty as light. Light that shines through from within … Yes, I think you're beautiful.'

After he said so, I remembered how fortuitous it was that we first met in a virtual room, when my status on Facebook was an audacious one in which I stated that I was reflecting light.

'Nice status,' he typed, initiating what would evolve into a seven-year-long ongoing dialogue.

Considering his profession, I took his comment as a compliment. I knew it wasn't a superficial one based on a profile picture, but had everything to do with my choice of words and what they evoked when I had placed them together in a sentence.

♦ ♦ ♦

They say the body renews itself every seven years. In the span of the last seven years, my lover and I have come full circle. Our love is renewed. I am the same person I was when I met him: fragile, belligerent, yet stronger than I give myself credit for. But I am different. I have become beautiful.

Three weeks ago, an hour before I was to leave for Dubai on an assignment, he came over, his camera in tow. Despite having asked him more than a year earlier, it was only now, in the heat of a deadline, that he finally brought himself to photograph me. Though his portraits of past lovers are renowned for their utter beauty, he never sought to replicate the pattern with me. I have, in these seven years of our togetherness, existed outside the scope of his lens: more companion than muse; more partner than passionate lover. I am his middle-aged love. As I explore the boundaries of thirty, he is inching towards sixty, his body already succumbing to time: my lust wantonly waxing while his own wanes with age; my spirit and flesh eternally willing, his increasingly in a predicament.

He waltzed into my bedroom, drew the blinds to let in the afternoon light, cleared my bed of the many books that had been strewn across the mattress, and motioned at me to take a seat. I saw myself captured in the sphere of his lens, my skin gleaming, my eyes trapping light, my lips eager. He told me to look away from him, to raise my chin ever so slightly, to withhold my smile. Then he pressed the shutter and made a memory of me.

♦ ♦ ♦

I studied myself in the mirror today. I have become leaner, the consequence of regular running and a mindful diet. The three-inch wound from the self-inflicted burn leapt out at me, strawberry pink. I no longer fear that it may never be erased. It has been etched in, almost, and seems permanent. It is a ghastly sight, but less so than when it was first imprinted. I expect no miraculous transformation by which it will be rendered invisible. Coconut oil and Silverex can only do so much. I must make peace with all that it symbolises: a moment of defiance, when I involuntarily allowed myself the luxury of overconfidence. I refuse to be tainted by the scar it will leave behind, which in time will be discoloured to meld with the rest of me. The edges will darken, the fleshy pink will eventually dissolve and my blackness will be almost restored. Until then, and even after, I will continue to write into it.

My body will continue to be my instrument, my blackness my deliverance, my skin my muse.

SQUARE PEG, ROUND HOLE

MITALI SARAN

I have a vivid memory of a train ride, years ago. The third-class compartment in the overnighter from Delhi to Calcutta was packed. It was after 10 pm and I was out of cigarettes. Since we'd exchanged a few sentences, I asked the passenger next to me for one, from the packet outlined in his breast pocket. He glanced nervously at his family – a wife, a couple of teenagers – and fished one out. After a beat he said, 'How old are you?' Twenty-seven, I told him. 'And you aren't married?' he said, flustered. 'You should be married.'

I wandered out to the empty vestibule and lit up. Four seconds later a small phalanx of young men had lined up opposite me in the narrow vestibule to stare in gape-jawed silence. I said, '*Namaste,*' and got nothing back. Were they disapproving? Just curious? Uncertain? I couldn't tell. For lack of ideas, I offered them a drag. They broke into horrified half-smiles, turned around and fled. Uncertain, then.

Uncertainty is the most common reaction I get in India, and it comes from being a hybrid animal in a deeply structured society. Nobody knows what box I belong in.

I'm an Indian woman in her mid-forties, single, childless, jobless, who dresses like an uncool teenager, wraps presents in newspaper, drinks, smokes, occasionally pops into a bar or a movie theatre alone, drives around in the middle of the night, has no ambition, dances tango, has taken to the guitar, is a commitment-phobe and an atheist, and says no a lot. For many people, if there's a box that this fits into, it's got a big 'Handle with care' sign painted on it. People do.

At a nearby petrol station, there's a mechanic who's been topping up my car and checking my tyre pressure since I was twenty-six years old. The first time I ever took my car in for servicing, I jumped down into the filthy pit after him to look up the skirt of my car. To this day, when I pull in to the station, this mechanic asks, 'You're here on holiday?' It's no use telling him, for the ten thousandth time, that I live in Delhi, right around the corner: he decided, eighteen years ago, that I either am not Indian or live abroad. He believes this with unshakable resolve.

India is a famously complicated place. For women, it's doubly complicated – we live with staggering mainstream sexism and both casual and egregious violence at every level of the power pyramid. You can choose not to conform, but only if you're willing to negotiate the crass misogyny and judgement that will come your way, and to risk your physical safety. Driving at night, you might be followed by a car filled with men who try to run you off the road. Walking down the street, you might find people staring and breaking into song, or groping you. People will try to make you aware of your shameful oddness in thousands of little ways.

Shame is key.

India's goddesses are fearsome, beautiful, bare-breasted power-houses who make and break universes. They hold weapons in their many hands, and represent power. India's flesh-and-blood women have vaginas, which make them the very fountainhead of shame. This country worships phalluses, but women are raised to believe in their own shamefulness, and taught that female modesty protects the whole world's honour. There are degrees, of course – perhaps you're a rural woman who allowed an unrelated man to see her face uncovered, or you're a city slicker showing too much cleavage – but shame is the monkey on your back, and when it shows up, it imperils your whole family's reputation. It's been a long historical fall from the erotic celebration of Khajuraho to the prudery of today.

I appear not to have come preloaded with shame. My parents had more of it; they were raised in boarding schools by Irish nuns and Jesuit priests, but they were also great readers, well educated and forward thinking. They didn't make a big deal of shame while we lived outside of India. I did ten formative years of growing up in Switzerland and Indonesia, blissfully unaware of the shit-storm that a bare leg or a public kiss could elicit. When we were home on vacation I had spectacular fights with my parents over things like wearing shorts or going out for a late coffee with a man I had only just met, but they argued for my safety, not against shame. I wore shorts anyway, and I went out for coffee anyway.

There was just one time in my teenage years that I confronted their socialisation – my father walked in on my boyfriend and me necking, and exploded: 'This is not a flophouse!' I remember being not ashamed of myself but shocked that he was calling me a hooker by implication. I yelled at him about it later and got a remorseful apology. I never heard anything like that from him again, whatever his opinions may have been.

I moved back to Delhi after college, living alone in my parents' house while they were abroad. I chose to not choose shame, or the crappy words that come with it – loose, bold, fast, immodest, forward, slut, whore. A neighbour once leaned out of his window, wearing a singlet, and called across to the balcony where I was having a late-night smoke with a male friend: 'You shouldn't do all these wrong things.' You could point to many things about my life that aren't terribly orthodox, but the bottom line is I'm not squeamish about bodies. They sweat, bleed, excrete and get horny. This is, first and foremost, what it means to be human, as much as appreciating opera and writing philosophical treatises. Bodily truth is the frontline of existence in the world. I'm given to potty talk, menstruation talk and sex talk. I use my vagina the way I want to, and I am not ashamed of being a sexual being.

How do you go about being like this in a society that bleeps the word 'arse' out of TV shows? I discovered very early that eight times out of ten, doing the unexpected (or not doing the expected) deliberately, calmly and normally can calm and normalise the situation. Twenty years ago, the first time I walked into the local hole-in-the-wall liquor store, which is also stuffed groin-to-butt exclusively with men, you could hear a pin drop. I made my way in, making eye contact, smiling and saying excuse me, and they shifted scrupulously aside. They stared, but they were courteous.

When you don't fit in, people are much more likely to assume that you don't belong and don't know any better than that you need to be taken down a peg or two. When they know that you do belong, they are very much more uncertain about how to treat you. Uncertainty has two positive points: it is not objectionable; and it makes people hesitate, a breach which you can nimbly fill with deliberate calm and normalcy. When you choose calmness and normalcy, you are often choosing it for the other person too, who didn't know which way to go.

The columns I write for a national newspaper range in subject matter from the conceptual and political to the wildly personal, and they reflect my life as much as my thoughts. I've talked about a chequered love life, about not being built for marriage, about not wanting children. As much as I've received appreciation, I've also received reader mail like, 'I think you are insane ... For God's sake, stop your corrupting writings in a responsible newspaper.' Unhinged Hindu fundamentalist keyboard warriors cry 'Prostitute!' at the drop of a hat, but usually only when a column criticises the government.

Men sometimes write to say that they're fans; those emails are filled with a kind of benign, intense curiosity – 'How does your life work?' 'What sort of creature are you?' 'Do you think we could get a drink sometime?' – forgetting, I guess, that people you like in print are usually disappointing in the flesh. But most of the people who bother to write say something that boils down to 'Exactly!' and 'Me too!' (I think there's a square peg, round hole cohort out there.) Inexplicably, one notable slice of mail comes from readers asking me for a job, or some vaguely worded 'guidance'. I'm constantly writing about how financially and professionally clueless I am, so that always cracks me up.

I left my brief marriage, to an absolutely lovely man, for no good reason other than I'm not built for marriage, which, if you ask me, is a very good reason. I knew that before we got married, and told him so. He said that it would just be easier on everyone than if we lived together. I said that if I got restless or unhappy I would leave. He said we'd cross that bridge when we came to it. When the time came, he said, 'Well, you always said that this might happen, and I will support whatever decision you take.' That makes him a jewel among men, particularly Indian men.

Leaving a jewel of a man is not the sort of thing you do lightly. In a society that is pathologically devoted to marriage, and hates free-range vaginas, you can expect shock and horror. Oddly, other than a few close friends who urged me to think about it, nobody said a single word to me, though I know people talked about it a lot. That's the upside of living in a liberal elite cocoon in which people are too polite to bring up your separation, but love to speculate behind your back about whether maybe you're a lesbo. After we split, my ex-husband used to take special pleasure in making sure we arrived simultaneously at a party, just to confuse the crap out of everyone.

After that breakup, I came back to my mother's house (we had lost my father some years earlier). It was meant to be a stopgap arrangement, but somehow it turned into the default.

My mother is an odd mix of the madly brave and madly fearful. This is a woman who has done many courageous and interesting things in her life. She learned Old Javanese, served as a guide-lecturer on a catamaran sailing around the Indonesian islands, took her kids into volcano craters and overcame the temptation to leave them there, did a postgraduate degree in her forties, has written a very scholarly book, travels the world and still loves a zippy car. She values independence as much as security. She saw to it that I got my driving license in my twenties, and a couple of months after that handed me the keys to her car in a foreign country so that I could drive friends six hours across the peninsula. After my father died, she found the steel she needed to deal with many things she had never had to, and developed spectacular financial acumen. She's no pushover, this lady, but goodness, you can't take the parent out of her. So I choose to ignore the parent in her.

For a while, she sat up every time I went out, waiting for me to come home, and yelled at me for making her worry. For a while she assumed that I would participate in any dinners or teas hosted at home for her friends, and was hurt and disappointed when I refused to on the grounds that they were *her* friends, in *her* life. After a certain amount of bloodletting, however, she and I came to a fairly peaceable understanding that I was not going to mend my ways. Either she's very progressive or I broke her spirit, or an asthmatic person has only so much breath to waste on deaf ears. I realise that she might face some disapproval of my allegedly wild ways from her family and friends, and I appreciate the fact that she never brings it home to me. Maybe she knows it's pointless.

There's a general sense that you shouldn't be living at home as an adult, but I quite like it. It gives me leeway to do what I enjoy – to not work all the time, to have leisure, to see friends, to travel, to devote myself to the study of something. My mother and I sometimes don't meet for three days under the same roof, but a rumpled newspaper here or a pair of shoes left by the front door there will tell us what's up. Sometimes we leave each other notes. She is, de facto, my flatmate.

My relationship with her is the kind of daft domestic relations dance that provides much fodder for my columns. I make fun of her convent-educated breeding, which she displays magnificently by taking it in the right spirit. 'Where am I?' she'll say, if I've left her out of a column, 'I miss me.' She worries about my physical safety ('You drink/smoke too much, you drive too late, you sleep too little'). But she has learned to fully accept my life, if not fully understand it. She's peered at it at close quarters and is reassured that while it is unorthodox, I'm not stealing cars or trafficking drugs – at least not that I admit to – and appear to be reasonably happy.

But there is one thing she cannot seem to overcome, and that is shame – on my behalf. She can't bear the idea that when I come home in the morning in the previous evening's clothes, or when I walk out of the house with a man who's wearing what he had on the previous night, the staff who hang around the gate of the complex – the guards and drivers – might leer knowingly at me and gossip about it. I have no idea why she believes that they do – they're unfailingly polite to me – or that they don't, even when there's no man in sight (which is most often). This is also the view of many other people who employ domestic staff. Do they think that those in the Economically Weaker Section are like kindergartners, innocent of sex and swear words, around whom we must not let on that such a thing is possible? I imagine they have a rich enough sexual life that they might not perish of shock on the spot.

The gentleman who has worked in our family for three generations is a good example. Once in a while I might come down in the morning and take two cups of coffee back up to my room. He and I will look each other in the eye and have a completely deadpan conversation. If he's uncertain how to react, whatever he thinks of me, he keeps it to himself – he's a true professional. Not that I would do it differently if he weren't.

• • •

The real threat is not, of course, gossip. It's violence: chronic, daily, mainstream violence against women. India has always had a dubious fame for being a place where women are harassed, threatened, groped, violated, abused, raped, stabbed, burnt, hanged and melted by acid, but somehow we never got a national conversation going about it until December 2012, when a girl in Delhi was gang-raped and so brutalised that her doctors were shocked. She died of her injuries, but not before setting the country on fire.

Delhi – home to the politically apathetic bourgeoisie – erupted in massive, furious protests against that rape and all the gender crimes it represented. Thousands of women, and men, decided to step up and refuse to continue to ignore or silently accept the gross violations of sexism. They decided to raise hell, and so did the media. Suddenly, the people who shame women for getting raped, for dressing or behaving in certain ways, for having mobile phones and wearing jeans, were getting called out – loudly. Words like patriarchy, sexism and misogyny became TV studio staples. And, as in any cultural tipping point, there was backlash. The patriarchs and misogynists got louder too, and made specious nationalist and traditionalist arguments about Indian culture and how Leslee Udwin's BBC documentary on the story was giving India a bad name.

The listless UPA[1] government of the day typically failed to recognise and seize an opportunity. It could have harnessed public anger to push for the political good for all Indian women. Instead, it tried to dismiss the protests as elitist and insignificant, yet cracked down on them with thousands of police personnel, water cannons and metro shutdowns, and came off as confused and terrified. Today's BJP[2]

1. United Progressive Alliance
2. Bharatiya Janata Party

government under Narendra Modi is, if possible, even more gender tone-deaf than the last, especially since it is rooted in patriarchal Hindu culture. But the conversation has begun, and is slowly beginning to push back, in small but relentless ways, against the mainstream sexism that pervades Indian society.

Women are certainly fighting back harder than ever before – reporting crimes and misdemeanours more, taking cases to court, calling out workplace sexism, wearing what they want to wear, marrying the people they want to marry, or not marrying at all, and increasingly not just refusing to cede space but actively expanding it. Women have just been accepted into combat roles in the Indian Air Force. They are making a name in sport. They're playing in rock bands. They are voting according to their own priorities. They are dissenting loudly in the media. Indian women are an impressively strong lot of human beings, and they only intend to get stronger. Economic compulsions, the mind-altering possibilities of the Internet, and the world beaming in on us from television and phone screens are putting big cracks in the implacable power structures we've always had.

It will be generations before we get anywhere near gender equality. It's an inevitable process, however, because – I'm convinced – the impulse to freedom and self-expression is as fundamentally human as the impulse to live with social acceptance. And women are fighters.

◆ ◆ ◆

Autonomy is the most powerful drug in the world. The ability to govern your own life, your own thoughts, to make the choices you want to make, is a wild high given to too few people around the world.

I'm a lucky woman. The choices I make in Delhi as a member of the freelancing liberal elite, with supportive family and friends, have about a million more insulating layers than the choices of a blue-collar, lower-caste woman who lives in a village or a slum in the middle of an orthodox joint family. There is nothing brave or pioneering about my choices; the only thing I have to worry about, really, is other people's opinions, and I choose not to. I have the liberty to live relatively autonomously. Why, then, wouldn't I?

There is, of course, a dark side to a life singly lived. People often ask me if I'm lonely, if I worry about dying alone, if I will feel the same way about my life-choices in the future as I do now. A cop recently asked me, with a kind of stunned compassion, 'You don't have a husband *and* you don't believe in God?' The answer is: of course there are moments of piercing loneliness. There are bouts of hair-standing-on-end fear, of impossible depression, of feeling lost and alone, of weeping into my bed sheets at 4 am, convinced that I'm dying of a brain tumour – dying being much preferable to malingering, dependence or incapacitation – and moments of wanting nothing more than to crawl into someone's arms and be taken care of. I sometimes go around begging my friends for hugs. There are moments of utter alienation from my environment. But these are the exceptions, not the rule. They constitute the cost of the choices one makes, and on balance those choices make me happy as a potty-mouthed clam.

As for the future, who knows? Perhaps I'll feel differently, perhaps not. For now I'm just a girl, standing in front of one to four guys, asking them to love her in whatever degree is mutually acceptable, for some indeterminate length of time. Or not, and that's fine too. It's also possible that I will one day grow up, settle down, adopt a kid and have a career.

Just kidding.

So yes, there's lots of uncertainty in my life. I choose it. I have an acute sense of mortality and don't plan to waste my brief time on earth being someone else's idea of me. Uncertainty allows space for new and interesting choices. What more can a thinking person with a free-range vagina ask for?

OXYGEN

URVASHI BUTALIA

I was twenty-one when I walked into the offices of a publishing house in Delhi in search of a life and a career. I had little idea what I would find. I knew only this: three decades into independence, Britain and all things English still held sway in India. At university I'd chosen to study literature, which effectively meant English literature. Much though I loved Milton and Spenser (yes, even him), they had nothing to do with the reality I saw around me. I desperately needed to escape the teaching job (English literature!) that awaited me. I needed oxygen.

'We're a little doubtful about giving you a job,' my prospective employers told me. 'We do not normally appoint women in executive positions because they get married and go away.' I felt immediately guilty on behalf of all women – my feminist teeth hadn't become quite as sharp as they are today – and rashly promised I would not do so 'for at least five years'. More than forty years later, I've still kept that promise. I've not married, and I've not gone away from publishing.

At home, my parents – my mother a teacher and my father an editor – talked about my job. My father's worry was how I would come and go – for the offices of the Oxford University Press were quite a distance away, and Delhi transport at the time was nothing to write home about. My mother – I never quite understood how she was so brave on our behalf – persuaded him to let me try. 'She'll find her feet,' she said, and I did.

The year was 1973. I was twenty-one. You'd think twenty-one would be 'old enough' but that wasn't the case in India then. An adult, I still lived at home – though I harboured thoughts of moving out – and for the first few months, did not contribute to the family income. It wasn't the done thing. Parents were meant to 'look after' their 'children'.

◆ ◆ ◆

At university – I'd only just left so the memory was fresh in my mind – we'd begun to think and talk about feminism. We, the 'newly minted' young feminists of India at the time, were reading, furiously. Political turmoil was all around us; in Bengal the Naxalite movement, a violent left-wing group against landlordism, inspired many students to abandon college and join what they thought would be the Revolution. In Delhi, as young women, we fought small battles – better hostels for girls, safe transport and more. The times were heady, exciting, inspiring; every day brought a new campaign. We were confident that we would storm every citadel.

I sort of realised that the days of street protests and slogans and songs and furious shouting would have to be left behind when I stepped into a corporate office. But the question stayed in my mind – could there be a way to combine feminist politics and the workspace? It took a while to find an answer to this question, and in the meanwhile I proceeded to fall deeply and irrevocably in love with publishing.

The feminism didn't go away either. In the evenings, at weekends, on holidays, my young feminist peers and I worked hard on campaigns, battling rampant violence against women. We created a women's magazine, we lobbied for new legislation. One hot summer afternoon, we'd just finished lunch at home. I strolled idly out to our balcony to check something, I'm not sure what, and saw an elderly woman in a white sari standing under a tree, clutching a piece of paper and looking up at our house. The paper turned out to be a leaflet against dowry violence that we'd distributed in a protest march the previous day in another part of town.

Satya Rani Chadda came up into the house and told us her story: her daughter, Kanchan, had been killed by her in-laws for dowry.[1] They'd set her on fire, made it look like an accident, waited till she was badly burnt, and then called her parents. Satya Rani was distraught. My mother listened to her story, fury battling with despair at the injustice of it, and I think that was one of the moments that pushed her into her decision to do something to help women in distress. Karmika, the women's centre my mother subsequently set up, fought cases on behalf of women, helped them file police reports, get custody of their children, battle abusive husbands and more.

Around this time – I'm not sure if it was before or after – we got to hear of these things called 'virginity tests'. It seemed that the U.K. immigration authorities, suspicious that Indian immigrants were importing women from India to marry them (and thereby increasing the numbers of Indians in the U.K.) decided that one way to find out if a woman coming to the U.K. was illegitimate or not was to check if she was a virgin. In other words, if her hymen was intact. The assumption was that Indian men would only import virgins to marry, so any woman who was found to be a virgin was suspect.

---

1. Young women are sometimes murdered or driven to suicide by their husbands and in-laws, via harassment and torture, in their pursuit of an increased dowry.

My mother was infuriated by this, as were large numbers of women, including the younger generation. How dare this country, which called itself 'developed' and 'advanced', violate women's rights in this way? My mother worked with a group of women her age, and together they decided to gather outside the British High Commission, storm the premises and go in and lodge our protest. So off we went. In those days, embassies were not fortresses. You could actually go up to the gates and beat on them and shout. That's what the women did, with women like my mother lifting their saris high and scaling the walls and forcing their way in.

Intoxicated with our 'success' – I'm not sure if we actually stopped the virginity tests but we created a huge noise about them, enough to raise questions and cause embarrassment – groups of feminists decided to take campaigns against violence to the streets. With the help of two friends in theatre, we created two street plays, one on dowry and one on rape. By this time our large umbrella group had a name – Stree Sangharsh, which means women's struggle. We went out and bought ourselves black kurtas, and became a travelling theatre group.

By this time the feminist struggle had caught the imagination of other members of my family. My brother joined in the team for the play. We based the story on the lives of two women, friends, one who'd been killed for dowry and the other who'd survived. We'd arrive at a street corner, start beating our drums, collect a crowd and start performing. The initial noise would die down, and you could sense people's interest. As we performed the scene where the young bride is cruelly killed in her marital home, my mother's beautiful singing voice would soar – clear, sweet, powerful – singing a moving, gooseflesh-making song of farewell, sung as young brides leave their natal homes. The pathos was not lost on anyone, and there were very few dry eyes around.

In many ways our feminism grew together, my mother's and mine. We were very different – she always much angrier, always ready to do battle; I more temperate, sometimes conciliatory, a cold anger my last, but familiar, resort. Perhaps this was why she continued with her women's group and I began to think of something different – of somehow changing the world that I now inhabited, my professional, publishing world.

I can't exactly pinpoint when it was I began to think of feminist publishing, of making books by women, about women. But somewhere along the way, the street-level activism that we'd all been engaged in began to find its way into my professional life. Why was it that when we wanted to understand the battles we were fighting, to figure out why the world was the way it was, we had so little to read that could help us? Was violence against women a new phenomenon? How had patriarchy come to be shaped in India? Women were so central in the battle for independence, why did we hear virtually nothing about them afterwards? Or, for that matter, during colonial times?

The idea to set up a feminist publishing house took seed and grew, slowly. As often happens, life intervened, things happened, the idea lay dormant, but never quite disappeared. I left my job, took up another, less demanding, one, worked on the idea, then took up a scholarship for a doctorate. Halfway to Hawaii, which is where I was headed, I had a change of mind, and plan, and gave up the scholarship and worked instead in a publishing house in London, and two years later, voila, there it was. What had seemed like a pipe dream had become a reality: in 1984, Kali for Women was born.

Throughout, my parents watched and encouraged: 'If this is what you really want to do, go for it.' It couldn't have been easy: they were not rich, just two professionals with no family money, only their salaries. And they must have worried about having to support grown offspring (fortunately they did not have to). I was thirty-two by then. Now and again they also worried about marriage, but then they gave up. Years later – I must have been around fifty – my mother said to me, 'You know, I used to worry about what would happen to you if you didn't marry, but now I worry what will happen to me if you do marry!'

Kali for Women, the feminist publishing house that emerged out of my engagement with the women's movement and my involvement in publishing, was formed with a publishing colleague called Ritu Menon. It was a strange sort of hybrid: part N.G.O., working on a non-profit basis (we had no money so this was the only choice available) and part business, producing books in the business world and selling them to produce more and to stay alive.

It was the women's movement that gave birth to us – I suppose today one would use the term 'incubated' – and it was the movement that sustained us. Female activists wrote for us, they bought our books, they encouraged us and with this we survived, slowly, steadily bringing Indian women's voices to the mainstream.

Looking back now, I can't think of a moment that was not exciting, or challenging. We were so happy – we were doing something we loved and believed in, and we had so much support from other feminists, from family, from friends. Oddly enough, our colleagues in publishing – all men – were not against what we were doing. But they were a bit sceptical. Women? Do they write? Do they read? Who will buy your books? And printers and paper merchants and typesetters and block makers – at the time, all these were individual, separate services – did not know what to make of us.

But the feminists? They bought every book we published, going to bookshops and demanding, 'When is the next Kali book coming out?' And they wrote for us, and pointed us towards possible sources of money. Often, they'd turn up at our office to chat, and ideas for new books would grow out of these informal conversations. Basically, every turn we took, they were there, smiling, nodding, pushing, encouraging. I'm not sure what we would have done without them.

One afternoon, a group of women came to see us. They were village women from Rajasthan, accompanied by four urban activists.

They brought us a book – the kind of book feminist publishers dream about – created by Rajasthani village women in a series of health workshops as part of a government development program. They asked if we would publish it and imposed certain conditions (like having the names of all seventy-five authors on the cover – 'We don't know the concept of individual authorship in rural India,' they said, reminding us of the collective nature of knowledge). Meant for rural women, the book, called *Shareer ki Jaankari* (*Know Your Body*) used illustrations to look at the female body from childhood to old age.

The women told us a wonderful story of how they had tested the first draft of the book in the village: they had been scoffed at for having drawings of naked women and men in it. 'How can you call this realistic,' they were asked. 'You never see naked people in villages.' And so they went back to the drawing board, and worked out a unique way to draw pictures and cover them up with liftable flaps, so that you could see the human anatomy that lay beneath the layers of clothing. To this day, this remains our bestselling book, though we've never sold a single copy through a bookshop. It only ever goes to women's groups.

Many years later Kali transformed into another avatar: Zubaan. Similar in intent, different in name, open to changes in the women's movement, and operating now in a changed publishing environment, Zubaan presented new sorts of challenges. By this time, we had been around some twenty years, so we knew we were doing something right, but for me the challenge now was to see if Zubaan could be turned into a feminist workplace. Could we combine flexi-time, the priorities of single mothers, providing office lunches and more with a professional work ethic? Could we consider how workplace relationships might look if they were viewed not from the point of view of the employer but from that of the employee?

Meanwhile, my mother ran her own organisation, small, contained, but committed to helping women fight their battles. Along the way, she picked up many new 'children' – everyone she helped basically adopted her. I admired her for her commitment, and her ability to take on even those she knew, if she felt they were being unfair. In the upper-middle-class residential area of Delhi, where we lived, she fought cases on behalf of domestic workers who were badly treated by their employers, daughters-in-law who wanted custody of their children. The local police became her friends, and sometimes her enemies.

At some point she was persuaded – not by me but by a publisher friend at Penguin – to write a book about her experiences of working with women. We worked on this book together – she would write, I would edit and show the edits to her, she'd argue with me, put stuff back into it, and then we'd reach a compromise. She loved making the book, and would laugh and tell her friends, isn't it strange, my daughter's a publisher but my book is being published by someone else. She was eighty-one when she wrote *The Gift of a Daughter* – it was about her experiences of working in the anti-dowry movement. She said writing it gave her a sense of freedom. Her only regret was that my father was no longer around to see the book. 'Poor man,' she said, 'he spent so much time being a bit embarrassed about his feminist wife! But this would've made him proud.'

We celebrated the book by doing what we often did together – we went out shopping. We often shared clothes, although of late she'd lost so much weight that I couldn't fit into anything of hers. She would often forget which clothes were mine and would have tailors take them in to fit her, leaving me fuming, and sometimes laughing.

One day in Zubaan I happened to read a small news item about a book in Hindi, written by a domestic worker, Baby Halder, about her life. Baby's life was like those of thousands of other Indian women: married at the age of twelve, a mother by thirteen, with a violent husband, poverty – until one day, now a mother of three, she decided to up and leave. She travelled, ticketless, to Delhi and, once there, managed to find a job with an employer who noticed her love of books. He encouraged her to read, and write, and Baby wrote her life. The book, called *A Life Less Ordinary*, became our biggest success and, for me, the most important thing was the rather piquant fact that it was a poor woman's story that did that.

A feminist publisher's life is really all about the books she publishes, and the women who write them. That's how it was for me: Baby's book was followed by a novel from a Tamil writer, Salma, a brave woman who battled patriarchy, conservatism and family pressure to make a name for herself as an erotic poet, a novelist and a politician. And then came Anjum Zamrud Habib, a political prisoner who'd been held on charges of terrorism in a Delhi prison for five years and was then let off, a woman who spoke movingly about being in prison, but refused to speak about her torture or any sexual violence that may have happened. 'The silence helps me cope,' she said. And she was followed by Revathi, a transgender person who was thrown out of her house by her family, forced to beg on the streets and become a sex worker, who faced ostracism, violence and hate speech, just because she wanted to be the transgender person she is today. And many, many others.

A feminist publisher based in New Delhi can also just sit in her office and access manuscripts written by well-educated, middle-class women and fool herself that she's doing the right thing. But, for me, it was the *Shareer ki Jaankari* experience – the book by the women of Rajasthan – that showed me that books weren't only about those who knew themselves as writers. Other women – the taxi driver who left a violent marriage to make a life, the Muslim women's group that set themselves up as a women's *jamaat*[2], the rape survivor who refused to be silenced – in other words, ordinary, everyday women, they too had a story to tell, a story of courage, of resilience, of the fierce desire to change their lives. And it was the feminist publisher's task to bring these otherwise marginalised voices to public attention.

---

2. A gathering or congregation

If that meant running a modest enterprise, earning a bit less, sometimes publishing fewer books, and always being careful about money, well, that was a choice I made. It wasn't always easy, and perhaps the most difficult part was to ensure that others who worked in this enterprise earned fair salaries – the balancing act was always tough, always challenging.

In some ways, by working with the street vendor, the domestic worker, the washerwoman, the typist, this is precisely what my mother was doing. And for us, one of the most exciting conversations became how we could create books about the lives of the women she encountered.

♦ ♦ ♦

In 2011 my mother died. She was a week short of her ninetieth birthday. Some six months before she went, she'd stopped going to her office, too weak now to climb those stairs. She was keen that I take over her work but by this time, my own had taken up most of my life and, although she understood this, she was also regretful that there would be one person less to help the many women who needed help.

The day she died, I held her in my arms as the life went out of her, and I like to think that she knew what was happening. Neither of us could have wished for a better way for her to go. Our feminist journeys had begun at the same time, but they'd taken quite different paths. As happens in life, by the time she was into her eighties, our roles were somewhat reversed, she the 'child', I the 'mother', both of us feminist, both of us working women, both of us Indian.

OVER MY SHOULDER

ANNIE ZAIDI

I had a rather sobering conversation with my grandmother the year I turned seventeen. I was lying beside her, my head resting on her arm, when she asked what course of study I intended to pursue. Before I could make any coherent reply, she asked me to consider the fact that there were only three professions suitable for girls: I.A.S. (Indian Administrative Service), doctor, teacher.

I was spending the summer with my grandparents after the school-leaving exam. It was a quiet house with just the three of us in it. Grandpa spent most of the day reading or writing. Grandma cooked, cleaned, sewed, mended, washed dishes, did the laundry. I spent most of the day reading novels but I was also trying to teach myself to type on Grandpa's old typewriter. I wasn't writing anything original, though; I just thought that typing made me a bit more employable.

As a seventeen-year-old middle-class girl in India, I felt remarkably unemployable. My grandmother was literate but never formally schooled and she may have been painfully aware of the importance of a good education. All the kids were sent to the best schools they could afford. She quietly hoped her children and her grandchildren would enter the most highly regarded professions. But for girls, the choices were as narrow as doctor, teacher, I.A.S. officer.

Timidly, I had ventured, 'There's also engineering.'

Grandma was not convinced. 'Engineering is fine for boys,' she said. 'They build bridges and dams. But engineers have to be in all kinds of places.'

I heard what she hadn't quite said. It was not so much that they have to be in all kinds of terrain but that engineers must deal with all kinds of men, and mainly with men. There would be few women colleagues, bosses or subordinates, which made the job unsuitable. What Grandma didn't quite say was that it might be unsafe.

Most girls in my class said they wanted to be doctors or teachers. A few said engineer, though they must have been aware that studying to be an engineer didn't mean you actually got to be one. We grew up in industrial townships where nearly all the residents were employed at a factory. There was not one female engineer in sight. The only women who held regular jobs worked at the township school, as my mother did, or at the medical dispensary.

The only other female workers in sight were tribal women who came in from the surrounding villages whenever needed – construction labourers, the occasional milkmaid, domestic workers (cleaners usually, the cooks were often male).

At seventeen, I knew of only the following jobs featuring women:
- ayah/nanny/governess
- sweeper/dishwasher
- receptionist
- typist/secretary
- phone operator
- salesgirl
- hairdresser/beautician

- teacher
- doctor
- nurse
- prime minister

'Prime minister' was a curious aside. I was six when a neighbour started teasing me, saying, 'The prime minister is what you'd like to be, isn't it?' I was dimly aware that this was a joke but it was a joke that held a glimmer of the possibilities our nation held for little girls. India did have a female prime minister, Indira Gandhi, who had been recently assassinated.

For all I knew, it was easier to be in parliament than to be a salesgirl. I never saw any salesgirls in local shops. Even in bigger cities like Lucknow, where we went visiting during the school breaks, most of the sales staff were male, even at stores selling women's underwear. Nor had I heard of women owning businesses, with the exception of Shahnaz Hussain, who started a line of beauty products and salons named after herself.

English novels had informed me that educated girls without an inheritance could become governesses. As for 'phone operator' and 'secretary', I must have got them from the movies. Few films showed women as industrialists, lawyers or cops, though a television series called *Udaan* was quite inspiring. The main character was a girl who joined the police force and we followed her trials – from the physically gruelling training process to the problem of wearing a sari just right, lest upper-class women decide that she belonged to the lower middle class – with avid interest. We had never seen any female cops in real life but a few girls had begun to talk about joining the police or the army.

For me, the end of high school was an uninspiring time. I was not interested in beauty products. Nor did I want to build bridges or join the army. I sat for medical and engineering entrance exams since most of my classmates were doing it, but was so uninterested that I drew patterns for dresses on the margins of the answer sheet. Somebody mentioned fashion design and I was toying with the idea. True, all the tailors I'd ever seen were men. But being a 'designer' was different, I told myself. Besides, Grandma sewed and so did all the widowed mothers of heroes in Bollywood films. There could be no doubt about the suitability of tailoring.

Clothes weren't my thing, though. Books were. For college, I moved from Science to Arts. My grandmother must have been disappointed but she assumed I'd end up teaching. Some people even held teaching to be the ideal career for girls. You could do it in any community and could move wherever your husband moved; you'd have time to cook since you wouldn't be expected to pull late nights at work; you'd have vacations at the same time as your kids; the kids might get discounted or free tuition. More than once I heard people say, 'At least teaching helps to pass the time.'

The assumption was that as a girl – and future wife – I'd be supported or subsidised by a husband and therefore didn't need a well-paid job. But my own mother was raising two kids alone, and many teachers at school were either single or subsidising their families. I also knew that teachers were barely keeping their heads above water (some private schools, even now, pay teachers as little as INR 5000 per month[1]). I had no overwhelming desire to be poor, nor did I fancy being stuck in a roomful of kids, day after day. So what was an 'Arts' girl to do?

In my final year of college, Mrs Mathew, one of the English Literature lecturers, pulled me aside and asked if I had a plan. I didn't. But I was starting to write, and was co-editing the college magazine. According to Mrs Mathew, journalism would be the best way for me to make a living.

---

1. Approximately US$75

I was pleasantly surprised at her interest in my ability to make a living. It was often assumed that the girls (particularly Arts girls) were not very invested in careers. One of the senior-most professors had said as much in one of her famous talk-downs: *Most girls just come to this college because it improves their chances at marriage.*

It made us squirm, as there was a grain of truth in it. We attended a well-regarded 'convent', exclusively for girls, and the matrimonial columns in newspapers did carry advertisements for prospective brides with 'Convented' listed among their many virtues. It was also true that some of my batchmates were resigned to arranged marriages. But many of us were also applying for a Master's degree in something or other. Some tried to crack the highly competitive C.A.T. (the entrance test for an M.B.A. degree at the highest ranked institutes) and once again, I found myself sitting for an exam only because my friends were.

I should have known better by then. A major clue was how I was conducting myself at this time. We had to travel to another city for the C.A.T. exam. It was a bigger city, with bigger, better bookstores. Instead of prepping, I spent nearly all my money on expensive goods like *The Collected Works of Saki* and didn't have enough money left for a bus ticket back to college. Mrs Mathew was right. I just didn't believe her yet.

Meanwhile, some of the girls in college were swirling in more glamorous currents of ambition. In the late 1990s, Miss Indias began winning Miss World and Miss Universe titles. They bagged modelling and acting jobs. They were on TV and in the newspaper. Their parents – many were middle-class professionals – looked proud. Girls began to want 'portfolio' photographs, even in smaller towns like Ajmer. One of the local photo studios was run by a man who had the rare distinction of being allowed into our strict convent to take pictures of cultural events. To him the girls went, armed with a change of clothes and diffident make-up.

The portfolio included one sari snap: a full-length picture showing a girl in her traditional avatar. She would often be holding the loose end of the sari on her left wrist, extended, to show off the rich fabric, just like the models in women's magazines. Then there was a close-up snap – a portrait where she smiled (but not too much). Finally, a 'Western' snap, for which a girl would put on a cobbled-together version of a business suit: black trousers or knee-length skirt with a blazer on top. Some just wore their school uniform blazer; some borrowed a black coat from their dads.

The photos, in soft focus that took away all blemishes of skin, served a triple purpose. First of all, we wanted to hold on to this version of us – young, hopeful, more attractive than we actually were. Secondly, the photos could serve as 'proposal snaps'. Parents didn't mind having a picture handy to send out to potential grooms. The third reason was professional. Some had secret modelling dreams and others wanted to be air hostesses. India had just permitted privately owned airlines to operate and there were advertisements in the newspaper asking for applications along with photos. The job was not only well paid, it was a symbol of great freedom. You got to travel without a chaperone. You could be out and about at any time of the day or night!

It was an exciting thought, but not necessarily for parents. A friend's father was working with an airline himself but he discouraged his daughter's air hostess dreams. I was thinking of applying although I had heard comments from family members about how air hostesses were just 'glorified waitresses'.

I still remember the sting of that phrase. Glorified waitress! It was inconceivable for an older generation of parents that a girl may actually want a job waiting tables. Nor did they think that travelling without family in tow was any kind of incentive. Anyhow, I was saved from having to argue about the suitability of air hostessing when I realised I wasn't tall enough to apply. I did want to do a bit of waitressing, though. I had read about girls in foreign countries waiting tables as they put themselves through college or struggled to become artists. But the fact was, I had never actually seen a waitress in any cafe I'd ever been to.

At twenty, my list of professions featuring Indian women was not much longer. The following items had been added:

- air hostess
- fashion designer
- film/theatre actor/director
- banker
- hotel manager
- journalist

I enrolled at a mass communication institute in Mumbai and worried about finding work. I often scanned the classifieds for Wanted ads. Several ads encouraged female graduates to apply for secretary or receptionist positions. A friend, studying for a Master's degree in English Literature, wrote to say that she worried about being unemployable.

I bravely responded, 'Well, we can both teach the primary section at school. And we speak English well, so we can be receptionists, at the very least.'

My friend was not consoled. If she showed no higher ambition, her family might ask her to sit at home until she got married. It would be hard to refuse an arranged marriage, especially if we couldn't support ourselves. At twenty-one, we couldn't even support our own correspondence. When my friend wrote, her handwriting would grow tinier and tinier as she squeezed as much into one blue inland envelope as was humanly possible. My letters were the same. Very rarely, on birthdays maybe, we'd call from the neighbourhood phone booth, one eye fixed on the red blinking electronic digits. Every sixty seconds, a beep scolded us: *Enough! Enough!*

While still studying towards a journalism diploma, I found work at a new web portal. Things started to look up. Grandpa being a writer meant there was more acceptance at home for journalism as a career. But I'm not sure my family had any inkling of what journalism actually entailed. The first time I was asked to take a night shift, my mother and older brother showed up at the office, ostensibly with my dinner. Mum was dressed formally in a crisp sari and had her stern face on. She asked if I was actually needed at the office through the night. The question was not addressed to me but to a male co-worker, the only other person on duty. My co-worker nervously shrugged and said he didn't know. My mother said, 'Well, then, she can go home, right?'

Home I went, and was never again assigned the night shift at that web portal.

A few months of editing and rewriting awful copy and I knew that it wasn't going to be enough. I wanted to write, and not just the feature stories that the website editors encouraged me to do. I wanted more, though I wasn't yet sure what the nature of 'more' would be. I figured there was 'more' wherever there was more newsy stuff happening. As soon as I had my diploma, I began to apply to newspapers.

Newspapers paid badly, worse than web portals, but I took a pay cut for a job at a city tabloid. This time around, I did my share of the shifts, same as the male reporters. An early morning shift meant getting up at 3.30 am, chewing toast with my eyes still half-shut at 4 am, standing at the platform to get into a train before 5 am. The graveyard shift ended well after midnight and I didn't get home until past 1 am.

Even at those hours, there were some women out and about. Fisherwomen with leaky baskets nodded off in the train on my pre-dawn commute. During the rush hour, we were crushed like sardines into the ladies compartment. Women stood waiting at bus stops. Women sold flowers and fruit and snacks on the streets. There were homeless women with kids, sleeping on the pavement at night. On the last train home, I'd travel in the ladies compartment along with bar dancers, still wearing the evening's glitter, teenage boys trying to sell make-up, hair clips and household appliances, and older women lugging bags full of snacks, like samosas and *vada-pao*. There was a lot of laughter around.

I felt bolder, surrounded by women with loud voices and bold eyes, all of them intent on making a living. But outside the train station my sense of safety dissipated. One night I was nearly ambushed by two men on a motorbike. I was heading home in an auto-rickshaw when they began to give chase, peering into the rickshaw and asking the driver to stop. I persuaded the driver to drive faster than the bikers and ultimately got home safe. But not before the auto-rickshaw driver had demanded a kiss from me. En route, he had begun talking, wanting to know what I did for a living, and refusing to believe that I was a journalist. According to him, I looked like I was a bar dancer.

I remember looking down at myself – at my loose, long, chequered *kurta* and *salwar*, no make-up, flat slippers. I used to try to dress down for work, afraid that taking pains with my appearance would be held against me somehow, that sources would take me less seriously and withhold information or, worse, that they would take too much of an interest in me. That night, the auto-rickshaw driver's insistence that I looked like a bar dancer was based on his assumption that a dancer has no right to reject any man's sexual advances. I shudder to think what would have happened to me if I was, in fact, a bar dancer.

I never filed a complaint about that driver, partly because I did not want to see his face again, and partly because I didn't want to go to the police station. I was afraid I'd have to listen to the cops discussing my appearance or question the necessity of my being out at night. I had done the court beat and visited police stations. There were very few female cops on duty. If the male cops misbehaved, I did not trust their female colleagues to stand up for me. In retrospect, I think what I was most afraid of was that fear and shame would settle deep into my bones, killing my desire to go out and do my job.

The last thing I wanted was to stop reporting and settle for something tame. Reportage was very hard work, especially for an afternoon paper. I didn't cover press conferences. I couldn't file stories that the 'morningers' were likely to break. I had to aim for six exclusives a week. But the quest for unusual stories was taking me to unusual places. I was tagging along with cops for a midnight raid on a brothel. I was putting myself in a wheelchair to document the city's accessibility barriers. I was calling up sleepy constables in at least a dozen police control rooms across the city, asking the same question over and over: *Do you have something?*

None of this was exhilarating. It was exhausting, frightening work and I was underpaid. But I kept at it, partly because I was figuring things out about the city, about human beings in general, and partly, I suspect, out of obstinacy. I wasn't going to be chased out of my job by random men who went about harassing girls. I wasn't looking to be tamed.

Harassment wasn't a new thing anyway. Girls across India confront the full spectrum – from groping and grabbing to suggestive comments being whispered in your ear to rape threats, stalking and unwanted attention from colleagues. I was experiencing it on the streets, in buses, in trains, in broad daylight, even in that safest of cities, Mumbai. But I rarely talked about it, never at home. My family had slowly got used to me being out at all hours. If I told them, they might panic and start pressuring me to quit, to move into a different line of work. Something that didn't require me to be out so much. Something that didn't require me to be out where all kinds of men were.

The commute was tough, the deadline pressure insane, harassment was a possibility that lay in wait at every corner. But my greatest worry was not finding a toilet when I needed one. Which was several times a day, every day. The city seemed to be lurching along anyhow, kidding itself that women didn't get out much and, if they did, it was never long enough for their bladders to fill up. Mumbai was rumoured to have public toilets, at least at train stations, but to my dismay and fury, I found that most toilets were either non-functional or locked up, especially at night. The official excuse was that women didn't use them anyway and that if toilets were open, they might be used for 'other' purposes.

Aside from a near-bursting bladder, I was mostly all right. I spent a few years working in Mumbai, then moved to Delhi. There were times I hailed a cab or auto- or cycle-rickshaw before sunrise, with the stray dogs still barking down the empty street, and it was all right. I travelled alone into villages and small towns where I didn't know a soul, and it was all right. Every other week, I was off on a train or bus, meeting new people who were – men as well as women – patient, generous and respectful for the most part.

However, I did look over my shoulder when I was out after sunset. I did cross the street to avoid a parked car with more than two men sitting inside it. I learned to gauge the safety quotient of a bar, restaurant, movie theatre, based on how many women were visible. Zero was not good. One was better than zero, but it still meant being in a state of high alert. Two was a relief. It meant I could stop exchanging nervous smiles with the only other woman present. Five was almost normal.

The more I travelled, the more I began to notice women's absence from public spaces. Over four years spent travelling to small towns and villages in central and north India, I met only one female reporter on the field. I met a couple of female I.A.S. officers, but no female peons in government offices. None of the budget hotels in small towns had a woman at the front desk. Forget drivers and mechanics, there weren't even any female cooks at highway eateries. Certainly no waitresses.

These absences were exhausting in a way that's hard to describe. They didn't register as gaping holes in my consciousness, nor was I afraid all the time. But whenever I ran into female activists or officials, relief flooded my bloodstream. It was like throwing off an invisible suit of armour. Perhaps they too felt the same way. A food security activist once told me that when she travelled alone at night, she would pretend to dial a number and have a long conversation – loud enough for the auto-rickshaw driver to hear – where she mentioned that she was related to a senior police officer. Just in case the driver had assault in mind. One of my bosses gifted me a can of pepper spray. Just in case. I had to deal with all sorts of men, after all, and mainly with men. My grandmother would have sighed and shaken her head. Indeed, she had told me so.

It wasn't as if there were no female workers. They laboured on construction sites, brick kilns, farms, stone quarries. They fetched water and chopped wood. They wove baskets and garments. But I rarely saw them in jobs with a pay slip and an office attached. The few who had regular jobs were often teachers or nurses. A smaller handful were doctors, I.A.S. officers and activists.

Even in the national capital, Delhi, women were not driving taxis or auto-rickshaws. There were no bus drivers or conductors, no female cops patrolling the streets at night. Nearly every vendor out there – subzi-wala, peanut-wala, gajak-wala, chaat-wala, ice-cream-wala, momo-wala, chik curtain-wala – was a man. The butcher, the baker, the tinker, the tailor, the soldier, and yes, even the underwear seller were still men.

I was very surprised one night when, looking for an auto-rickshaw at Delhi railway station, I discovered a female auto-rickshaw driver. During the ride, Sunita told me that she had to go to court to fight for her right to wear a vardi (government-approved and licensed auto-rickshaw drivers wear a uniform). The male drivers refused to let her work at first and they wouldn't allow her to join their union. She persevered and muscled her way in, but Sunita was the exception, not the norm. I have never seen a woman driving an auto-rickshaw since.

On one assignment, I had gone to meet a group of rescued child labourers in Delhi. Both boys and girls had been subjected to violence, even at so-called 'non-hazardous' jobs like domestic work. The rescued kids were being schooled and offered vocational training so they could find jobs later in life. The girls were being trained to work in beauty parlours or to use sewing machines. The boys were being trained to work as electricians or mechanics.

I remember pausing, notebook in hand, thinking: *That's how it's done.*

That's how they – perfectly well-meaning folk – perpetuate ideas about what girls can and can't do. That's how strengths and talents are kept in a box where women are not likely to deal with men. It's a different kind of *purdah*[2], a new sort of *zenana*.[3] I could have bet anyone anything that those rescued girls were being taught to sew only women and children's garments. They wouldn't learn to sew a man's suit. They wouldn't be taught how to measure a man. I suddenly understood the secret of the respectability of the widowed mothers of Bollywood films – they only seemed to sew frocks and blouses for women, and they always worked from home.

It is not as if nothing has changed since I was seventeen. In 2002, I stepped into a cafe in Mumbai and, for the first time in my life, saw a girl behind the counter. Over the next decade, there was a visible shift in our cities. New coffee shops and supermarkets sprang up where young women wore the same t-shirts and caps as their male co-workers. A few years ago, I spotted women working at a petrol pump in Mumbai. With security checks becoming mandatory, women are now hired as security guards at shopping malls, cinemas, airports, hotels, metro stations. There are more salesgirls and billing clerks too.

One of the significant changes at the turn of the millennium was the rise of business process outsourcing (B.P.O.) firms that took on

---

2. The Hindu or Muslim system of sex segregation, practised especially by keeping women in seclusion.
3. The part of a Hindu or Muslim house reserved for the women of the household.

jobs that foreign firms outsourced to cheaper labour markets. B.P.O.s employed tens of thousands of young men and women who worked through the night to cater to different time zones. This was a radical shift of the professional landscape for educated young women. The job didn't require a very high degree of skill and the money was good. Employees were dropped off home in buses or cabs. And yet this didn't guarantee their safety. In 2005, a woman called Prathibha Murthy, employed at a B.P.O. in Bangalore, was raped and killed by a taxi driver. In 2007, another B.P.O. employee was raped and killed in Pune.

There have been several reports since of women being attacked by drivers, security guards, deliverymen (pizza, cooking gas cylinders, mail). This is in addition to assault by partners, colleagues, family members, acquaintances and strangers. There have been brutal rapes not only at night but also in the day, not only outdoors but inside homes. On one occasion, a rape was reported to have taken place in a moving train, in plain view of passengers who were in the next compartment. In another case, the accused was a policeman.

Women keep trying to barge into professions that didn't look like options before. Along the way, our lives get twisted into painful, contorted shapes as we try to avoid rape and molestation. At the very least, to avoid the insinuation that 'she had it coming'. But the brutality of the gang rape of Jyoti Singh Pandey (commonly known as the Nirbhaya case) in 2012, shook us up in a different way. Our collective fear finally turned into public rage.

Jyoti was a young woman dreaming of a good job and a measure of independence. Our parents and grandparents have groomed us to become this kind of woman. People are sending daughters to schools and colleges in the hope that they will find work, find their feet, and will not be doomed to eternal dependence and poverty. The violence done to Jyoti was a violence done to all our hopes, and the grief and rage were so powerful that even the government seemed to be frightened by them.

The Nirbhaya case, as well as the 2013 gang rape of a reporter in Mumbai (known as the Shakti Mills case), was covered extensively by the media. Down the years, there have been some changes in response to women's safety concerns, particularly in services that are accessible to, and affordable for, middle- and upper-class women. Shetaxi, a fleet of taxis with female drivers, was set up to target solo female customers. Commercial services like Uber and Ola have started opening up to the idea of female drivers. There are reports of female bus conductors and metro train drivers. There is talk of hiring women to deliver flowers and food.

However, e-commerce entrepreneurs have expressed a chicken-and-egg difficulty in interviews. They would like to hire female couriers but who would guarantee the safety of their employees? Hiring a male chauffeur or security guard to trail the courier would inflate costs and make their business inefficient. Besides, the way the Indian government has reacted to sexual assault cases, they fear the business may be forced to shut down, as Uber was in 2014, after a female customer was raped by a driver.

Politicians are not helping women feel any safer. Some leaders have cited the eating of chow mein or meat as the cause of sexual violence. States like Haryana were already subject to pre-independence era laws that forbade women from working in establishments that serve alcohol. Mumbai has banned female dancers from bars, and also banned lingerie-clad mannequins. Governments, at both central and state levels, refuse to acknowledge the core problem: women do not feel safe in spaces where they are vastly outnumbered by men.

According to the 2011 census, women form 25 per cent of the working adult population in India, but the figures drop to about 15 per cent for urban areas. This means that for every one hundred people you see working in markets, factories, public service institutions, offices banks, only fifteen are likely to be women. The chances of them being outdoors and visible after 8 pm are negligible. Delhi, incidentally, has the lowest participation of women, at just 10.6 per cent. Delhi is also notorious for being unsafe for women. Coincidence? I think not.

Two decades after that sobering conversation with my grandmother, I am now forced to revisit the question of suitable jobs.

In neither Delhi nor Mumbai could I hope to hail a passing taxi and find that the driver is a woman. All the food and book stalls at railway stations are run by men. The street outside the apartment complex where I live in Mumbai is lively in the evenings, bustling with food stalls and neighbourhood stores. But no public toilets. Fruit and vegetables, sold by men. Medicines and milk, dumplings and dosas, sold by men.

There is a playschool, a dance class, some beauty parlours around. Women work there, of course. A doctor's clinic has a woman's name on it. One lone woman sits on the street with a sewing machine, altering clothes. But she's gone before evening falls.

There is one new development in town. In the ladies compartment of Mumbai's local trains, after about 9 pm, an armed railway police constable is deputed to travel. Sometimes, I am the first passenger to step into the compartment. I look at the cop and feel a mix of relief, sympathy and nervousness. I don't like guns. I would prefer a female cop. But then, who'd guard her?

Sometimes I wonder if I'd be a better writer if I ran into more female professionals. Would it make me bolder? Would I have deeper, more spontaneous conversations with strangers? Would I give out my phone number more easily? What stories would I tell if the auto-rickshaw driver, bus driver, mechanic, cobbler, plumber, packer and mover, deliverer of newspapers, fixer of gadgets, mason, gardener, carpenter and house painter were women? Would there be stories of pretend-talking on a mobile phone and pepper spray? And would I finally stop looking over my shoulder?

HOME GIRL:
A DAY IN THE LIFE
OF A SMALL-TOWN
SOCIAL WORKER

ANJUM HASAN

Manjula's daily work is to care for abused women and abandoned girls, and it is the attitude with which she does this that most attracted me to her. This young woman's tough pragmatism and wry affection for the strangers she meets and befriends every day made me curious about her background, which turned out to be very similar – in its traditional poverty and slow, tenacious journey out of it – to those of the women she works with. The oppression of women (as well as men) is a fact of life for Manjula. She is neither evangelical nor a harsh critic of her society but someone who has made the best of her limited opportunities and who uses the structures provided by the government to help the women around her. I had extended conversations with Manjula over the space of six months, observing her at work and at home, travelling with her and meeting her family. The following story is based on my many experiences, over these months, of seeing the world through her eyes. I've taken the liberty of using Manjula's name, with her permission. All other names have been changed.

Manjula wakes at dawn to a torrent on the roof, feeling the small body thrashing next to her. Four-year-old Rani has been running a temperature the last two days. Manjula gives the girl a drink of water, then pats her warm body back to sleep.

It's been a monsoon-soaked August and most of the thirty-odd girls at this government-run home have coughs and colds. They walk to and from school, their slippered feet sloshing in puddles and rain lashing at their bare legs. They've lined up twice in the past week for the visiting doctor. The youngest of the lot is the girl in bed, who's ravenous for affection. This scrawny thing and her solemn older sister were abandoned by their housemaid mother after their father died and she remarried. Their mother's brother took them in for a couple of years but he's getting married soon too, so he decided to drop them at the home. The mother hasn't been to visit since. The sisters look set to spend their childhood here. Still, in not having known life-altering catastrophe, they are better off than many of their companions, whose curriculum vitae feature mostly horror: father burnt mother to death in a fit of rage and went to jail, daughters sent here; parents alcoholics and beaters, daughter rescued and brought here; father married another woman, mother allowed daughter to be repeatedly raped for money, girl brought here by neighbours. The home, run out of the spacious premises of what was once a jail, shelters girls up to the age of sixteen. They go to school, play badminton and cricket in their free time, speak to a resident counsellor about their troubles, devise programs of dance and song for festivals, do yoga, and read picture books in English with a volunteer who visits a couple of times a week. After sixteen, they will be sent to the bigger town of Udupi to stay at a home for older girls, while they finish college.

When Manjula wakes a couple of hours later, the little girl is fast asleep, her skin cooler, the wrinkle between her eyebrows gone. Manjula bathes and dries her hair, her movements brisk and efficient, her mind always on the next thing. It will soon be time to go to the Women's Welfare Cell attached to the local hospital, recently set up to handle rape cases, where she spends her mornings. She is a social worker under the government's Department of Women and Child Development, which is responsible for both institutions. Manjula divides her time between the two. A girl came in last night, she and her family brought from a nearby town by a couple of policewomen. The doctor at the cell, a specialist in forensic medicine, has already examined her and taken samples, as has the gynaecologist, who would have given her emergency contraceptive pills.

'Done your maths problems, *kanno*?' Manjula asks ten-year-old Babita at breakfast. '*Namaste*, madam,' the roomful of girls yell at her through stuffed mouths. They are dressed for school, wolfing down their mounds of vegetable and semolina *uppittu* and lukewarm milk. Manjula devotes her afternoons and evenings to them, supervising homework, helping them tinker with the computers, watching TV together. Babita smiles ecstatically, even though the older girl knows maths is her great stumbling block. But in every other subject she is almost at the top of her class. Manjula has heard how someone called the child helpline about Babita and she was picked off the streets, begging. She had more lice than hair, sores all over her back, an attention span of a few seconds in class, after which she'd nod off, and no idea about using a bathroom to pee – she would just squat wherever. In four years Babita's become a new person, a quick-witted girl who loves to dance and authoritatively whacks the younger kids when they annoy her.

Manjula chats with the warden about Rani, who's still asleep in her room, then sticks her umbrella into her handbag and steps out. It's a ten-minute walk to the hospital. Rain-flecked cars cram the roads, driven by parents taking their children to private schools around town. Not for them the government school where the home's girls go, with its leaking roof and teachers armed with wooden rulers. Her phone rings, a cheap black Nokia that is welded to her palm; she tells her colleague Divya she's almost there.

At the hospital, a three-storey building of mildewed pink concrete, Manjula runs up the stairs to Room 26. A child who can't be older than fourteen sits poised and expressionless on one of the shoddy plastic chairs. Examining the posters on rape trauma syndrome and stress management are the two police officers and, huddled to one side, the girl's parents. One look at their weathered faces, sun-blackened complexions, rounded noses, the wrinkled hands and ancient eyes – all of which, she's well aware, belie their ages – and Manjula knows they're tribals, probably daily-wage labourers on one of the many coffee estates in the district. Divya, the counsellor who just called her, is writing in a file.

'I'm the social worker,' says Manjula to everyone in the room, and then, gently, to the girl, 'What's your name?'

The girl looks to her parents and the taller of the policewomen speaks. 'They came to us yesterday evening when she didn't get back from school. We found her and the boy on the estate. When does the lab open? We've been told she needs some tests done.'

'It'll open any minute,' says Manjula soothingly, then again asks the girl for her name.

Eventually, Manjula accompanies the still unspeaking victim, whose name, it turns out, is Maya, to the lab for blood tests that will determine her haemoglobin levels and HIV status. When she deposits Maya back in Room 26, Divya says she'd like half an hour alone with her, so the policewomen step out and Manjula takes Maya's parents down to the canteen for coffee.

She learns that their stick-thin daughter is sixteen and the boy in question perhaps eighteen or even twenty; they're not sure. They have three other children. Maya studies in class eight; she has known the boy for the last three years, was often on the phone to him. The police immediately looked in the coffee estate where the family works. The boy was picked up, denied the charge, was beaten, confessed. The parents filed a First Information Report at their local police station and the boy's in the lock-up. Manjula gives them her number; they are to phone her if they need legal help with the case. There's a government advocate attached to the cell and on call.

'Maybe the best thing is to get them married,' says Maya's mother.

'Useless, horrible boy,' blurts the father. He has the whole time been looking much more distressed than his wife.

'No!' says Manjula, raising her voice without meaning to. 'Don't you know that you could go to jail for marrying off a girl under eighteen and a boy younger than twenty-one? The same police who have arrested the boy will arrest you.'

It turns out that they didn't know. They go quiet then, nervously sipping their tiny tumblers of coffee, only breaking off to say that they have to get back to the estate soon; they can't both afford to lose a whole day's wages.

♦ ♦ ♦

Manjula joined the Women's Welfare Cell when it was set up in February 2015 in this small town in the southern Indian state of Karnataka. Each new encounter makes her reflect on previous ones. Seven months and twenty-eight cases down, she's starting to see patterns. Most cases that come to them only ostensibly involve rape. Love, instead, is the issue. Teenage couples across communities and religions elope and the girl's desperate parents file police reports accusing the boy of rape. When found (if not in the coffee fields, the couple is usually camping out at the home of a relative in the nearest town), the girls, sometimes as young as thirteen, are brought to the cell to be examined. If it's a case of underage sex, the boy is sent off to a detention home in Mysore or, if he's older than twenty-one, to the police to deal with.

Divya, tidying up a ledger of handwritten reports, recounts one of their earliest cases – the rich girl who fell in love with a house painter, obviously grossly unsuitable in her parents' view. She threatened to kill herself if she couldn't have him. The two ran away and when the police caught up with them, the girl refused to go back home. Her father and all the family's well-placed relatives – one a police officer, another a press reporter – did not let up, and even promised to consider the house painter.

'You think they would?' asks Divya.

Manjula nods emphatically. 'She's young. She'll feel differently in a few years.'

'She was afraid to go back home, said she'd be beaten,' says Divya.

'These girls,' says Manjula, calm and yet exasperated. 'They watch films, they watch TV and get the idea they can run away. They have no idea what will follow.'

Their talk turns to Maya and the harsh lives of the tribal workers on the estates. Manjula herself is tribal; she was raised for some years by an aunt and uncle who worked on the estates, and her brother-in-law is now a labourer too.

'What about older women?' asks Divya. 'We don't get any complaints from them.'

'It's not like they're never abused by their employers. But they don't open their mouths because their jobs are on the line. They just want to work and get their wages so they can eat,' says Manjula.

Manjula is a Yerava, one of several tribal communities based in this region, though her pale skin and slim frame don't necessarily give this away. She wears rectangular glasses on her small round face, long fingernails painted maroon, delicate anklets on her feet. In this season, she has a zippered sports jacket over her *salwar kurta*. She's twenty-eight.

Her parents' home – or rather her mother's, because her alcoholic father died when she was five months away from being born – is a three-hour bus ride and two-kilometre walk south of here. She comes from a tribal settlement of sixty-odd houses. Some of these homes are mere tepees – plastic tarp thrown over bamboo sticks. Her mother's house, built two years ago to replace a smaller one, is hardened, cow dung–slathered mud over a wooden frame, topped with a roof of terracotta tiles. Its three rooms and kitchen make it one of the largest homes in the village. Manjula allows herself to lapse into homesickness today; she's heading there on a monthly visit once work is through, and she hopes to make it before dark and the inevitable stampeding elephants.

Manjula's mother, Sidamma, dispatched her daughter early to study in schools and colleges further and further away from home, with the result that Manjula is now the most educated girl in her *haadi*, or settlement. She's also the only one who can chatter away in English, in addition to her Yerava tongue, and Kannada, the state language.

A little before one o'clock, Manjula walks back to the girls' home, looking forward to a hot lunch and a quick nap before she starts getting her things together for her trip home.

♦ ♦ ♦

Manjula takes a new, milk coffee–coloured, hand-knitted cardigan out of its plastic wrapping and holds it to her face for the texture. She went shopping yesterday and this is for her mother. Though she quietly accepts the money her daughter hands her every month, Sidamma never agrees to presents. Her standard reply, when Manjula asks, is: 'Get yourself something nice to eat instead.' But she relented yesterday. This was the best Manjula could find, and cost almost 500 rupees, a fortune relative to her monthly salary of 6000. Along with it, she's packing a tiny, frilly pink skirt for her cousin's toddler. She also bought a box of sweets, chocolate biscuits and some savoury *namkeen*. Her college-going nephew will head straight for her bag when he sees her. And relatives drop by all the time; Manjula enjoys offering them some town-bought titbit with their coffee.

By the time she's packed and changed, the girls are back from school, getting into their pyjamas. Not all of them have enough sets of day clothes so nightwear must do. There's *kadle* – horse gram – for afternoon tiffin today, along with bananas and coffee. They get free lunch at school but by this hour they're worn out and hungry. Manjula warns them to be well behaved as she says her goodbyes, then stops in the lobby on her way out. A woman is handing over a baby to two others while the staff of the home crowd around. This woman walked into a meeting of the child welfare committee yesterday, which comes together every week to discuss the case of each new girl needing rehabilitation. It turned out she wanted the home to take in her child – an eleven-day-old infant she doesn't want.

'What about your husband? Doesn't he want her either?' Manjula had asked.

'Definitely not. We get by on a small piece of land, that's all. We already have two girls. We can't raise a third.'

What about your parents-in-law, Manjula wanted to add, but didn't, for she was sure they were highly encouraging of the plan.

The woman said the nurses at the maternity ward had tipped her off about the home and the committee's weekly meetings. Her husband was with her till the baby arrived, then went back to the village, leaving behind instructions to get rid of it. The committee folks had called up a rehab home for abandoned babies in a nearby town. It is their representatives the baby is going over to now – two serious women in bright nylon saris. The cooks and cleaners on the staff coo over the child as she is bundled into a blanket and Manjula is suddenly crying. She held this baby yesterday, all wrinkled and new, and wondered what it might feel like to discard someone so utterly blameless. She opens the door to leave, and looks back once more at the mother. Her face says nothing.

In the town centre, Manjula finds a run-down private bus, blasting a jubilant film song, going halfway to her destination. The town is quickly left behind, replaced by silver oak–dotted coffee estates and forests of acacia and teak. Hidden away behind them is the world she came out of – small holdings on which poor peasants like her mother toil, growing paddy once a year and then leaving the land fallow the remaining months because there is no irrigation other than the monsoons. It is transplanting time right now, the tender green shoots of rice evenly sown into the mud of the fields, which will be their home till the winter. She is still thinking of that scrap of a baby when her phone rings. It's the superintendent of the girls' home calling about fifteen-year-old Shahana, whose case is the most nerve-racking rigmarole Manjula and her colleagues have ever been involved in.

A rich local businessman called Adnan had apparently, over the past year, been running an elaborate hoax to blackmail tourists. Young men from the adjoining state of Kerala, interested in coming over to find brides, would be invited by a middleman to stay at one of the small guesthouses in town that Adnan owned. But instead of prospective brides, an older woman and a young girl, both in a state of undress, would turn up and attempt to seduce the men. Before they had made much progress, police would arrive on the scene armed with cameras, and confront the Keralites. They were to pay up for having illicit sex else their pictures would be in the following day's papers. Only this wasn't the police at all but Adnan and his friends incognito. They were said to be raking in hundreds of thousands of rupees.

One of the men from Kerala had seen through the lies and complained to the police. Along with Adnan, Shahana and her mother were taken in. It turned out that Adnan had promised to build the family a luxury home if they went along with his plan. Manjula didn't know if the house existed but she did learn that the girl had told the police the following: Adnan had raped her, several times, and threatened to fling acid on her face if she let on that it was him; Shahana's younger sister was an unpaid housemaid for one of Adnan's married daughters; Shahana's mother had received money for keeping quiet; and her father seemed to be mentally disturbed.

Shahana is in the girls' home for the time being. And now, the superintendent tells Manjula on the phone, she is threatening to kill herself unless she's released; she seems certain that Adnan is planning revenge and worried about her parents or sister being murdered because of her revelations to the police. Manjula groans and the two women can't help but marvel at the mess. Then they worry about how all this will end for the traumatised girl.

As soon as she rings off, there's another call. It's her best friend Bhim, checking in, as he does a few times every afternoon. She tells him about her day and he says he'll wait for her at the bus stop and see her into the next bus. He happens to live in a village on this route. She's brought a couple of Kannada magazines for him, her young farmer friend who loves her and whom she thinks she loves back. But it's not romantic. They don't allow their thoughts to run in that direction; at least Manjula doesn't. She sometimes feels she's fine as she is – carefree and single, unlike the other girls in her community, who all marry early. She wants to find a better-paying job and is willing to move town, even leave the state; she enjoys being surrounded by people, working with and for them. Marriage will tie her down, she's certain, unless she meets someone who is not insecure about her leaving the house. Someone like Bhim, that is, who cares, calls her every single day, tries to help whenever she's in any kind of trouble or need. He's a friend of the family too, particularly of her nephew, and he's visited Manjula's village. They've all taken to him. The problem is that he's a high-caste boy from a well-to-do family who's given up his studies to manage the family lands, and she a tribal girl from a dirt-poor background who has risen in life but still just about gets by. There's little they don't share with each other, and yet they're tragically incompatible – there'll be trouble for sure from his family if they consider marriage. Her relatives might have things to say too. So they've both decided to put the idea out of their minds. He's told her, jokingly perhaps, but with honest intent, that he's on the lookout for a groom for her.

As he comes up to her, grinning, an hour later, dressed in stylish jeans and a shiny t-shirt she hasn't seen before, holding out a strip of the tablets she had asked for to ease the headache she feels coming on from the rattling bus, Manjula thinks again about how young he is. She's two years older and is sometimes convinced he's a child. She gives him the magazines, and he asks why she'd been crying. She hadn't told him about the baby being sent away; he guessed from her voice on the phone. They chat till the next bus takes off; she waves from the dirt-clouded window.

Soon enough, Manjula passes the landmarks that signal she is nearing home. The bus speeds past the unpaved lane leading to the village she was sent to at the age of five, to live with a maternal aunt and her family so she could be near the *Anganwadi* playschool[1] and then the free government school. Sidamma paid for her daughter's requirements with the meagre money she made from her fields and from raising pigs to sell for meat. Ten minutes later the bus is at her former high school; its large playground and immaculately painted buildings were a wonderful contrast to the dismal structures she'd known as school till then. She was an average but always interested student at school and then through junior college in another nearby town. Back home after this, she was roped in by a local N.G.O. to tutor village girls who'd stopped going to school. The dropout rate was high among tribals, and the N.G.O. staff felt that achievers such

---

1. *Anganwadi*s are government-sponsored childcare centres.

as Manjula could inspire the girls to go back. She and a friend set up classes at the offices of the N.G.O. for a few months. Noticing the girls' motivation, the friendly head of the organisation offered to fund their further education, advising them on suitable courses of study and helping with admissions. Both girls then went off to the port city of Mangalore, the furthest from home they had been till then. Manjula joined an undergraduate course in social work.

Mangalore was a make-or-break experience for the twenty-year-old. English as a medium of instruction baffled her; the food at the hostel was never enough; she got malaria thrice; she was failing exams; and for each of these crises she had no one to turn to but friends grappling with similar problems. But by the time she enrolled for a Master's in social work the experience had toughened her. She passed with distinction.

It was not at college that she really learned to speak English, though. That happened when she interned one summer at another N.G.O., run by Tamil Christian brothers, based in the state capital, Bangalore. Many of the country's tribals lived off the land, either on forest produce or cultivation, and had done so traditionally, but they did not have legal rights, nor were they familiar with this new-fangled concept of ownership, which made them highly vulnerable to exploitation. To remedy this, the Indian Parliament passed the *Forest Rights Act* 2006. The N.G.O. put their weight behind raising aware-ness about the Act and helping tribal families cut a swathe through the bureaucracy to get title deeds to their land. Manjula got absorbed in the cause as well, and among the people she met in Bangalore was a visiting resource person who'd speak to her only in English. She was soon answering in the language. Later, after finishing her Master's, she returned to work at the N.G.O. for a couple of years at what became her first job.

Manjula gets off the bus, and flags down a rickshaw for the four-kilometre ride to the turn-off for her village. The day is ending by the time she pays the driver, and the way home is a kilometre and a half of dirt path through paddy fields. Months of rain have rendered it a chocolatey mud slick but Manjula, one hand lifting her *salwar* to keep the ends dry, the other clutching her bags of gifts, makes her way with élan. She stops briefly to consider the enormous, fresh footprints of a wild elephant in the mushy grass. Her village and the surrounding ones happen to be within the confines of a government-designated national park. Across one field she can see a tree house that village men have built to stay nights and watch for hostile animals, sounding an alarm if they spot any. She knows people who have been mauled by elephants; her mother once had one staring her down in her backyard. Recently, workers from the forest department dug a deep trench behind the house to prevent future encounters.

Just as the final dregs of watery light in the wide open sky are extinguished, Manjula walks through a brood of chickens and one shrieking turkey to a mud hut with a sloping roof, where two women are waiting on the verandah. She is home.

◆ ◆ ◆

The nights are extraordinarily silent and black here, punctuated only by the distant explosions of firecrackers meant to scare off elephants and, nearer, the sudden, frightened bleating of the goats her mother rears. As for light, the forest department is opposed to putting in electricity lines out of consideration for the wildlife. A few years ago, a government scheme allowed for the installation of solar-charged lampposts in some houses. Manjula's family has one in the backyard now, lighting up their small patch of coffee bushes, the cane ramp on which the chickens have gone to sleep, the guava, passion fruit and coconut trees and the exterior of her sister's house, which is next door. Inside, they move around with the help of small kerosene oil tapers. Manjula is relaxed after a bath; the hot water is always simmering on the wood fire in their little bathroom. There is no toilet, though; they head to the fields for that.

After a dinner of rice and *sambar* – pulses, soy flakes and potatoes thick in a spicy stew – eaten sitting cross-legged on the bare floor, Manjula, her mother Sidamma, her older sister, whom she calls Akka, and her nephew Tilaka, are sitting on the verandah trying to catch, on a patchy FM signal coming through Tilaka's mobile phone, the sermon of a guru Sidamma visited in town that afternoon, being broadcast now.

'What did he talk about?' Manjula asks her mother.

'If you're thinking the wrong thoughts,' Sidamma answers, 'he'll set them right.'

She listens intently to the crackle from the mobile phone. She is a dignified woman of fifty-six, with a grave, lined, beautiful face, who has studied till class five and can read and write, has spent most of her adult life working the land and providing for her children, and who does not brood despite her various tragedies. Husband dead when she was not yet thirty; five of her seven children dead of various illnesses, mostly unidentified.

Manjula goes in and brings out the new cardigan to show off again, and her family looks at it in the near-dark with wordless approbation. Sidamma says she'd like to go listen to the guru again, he's a good one. The paddy transplanting is done, so she's a little freer, but getting into town and back before nightfall is always hard.

'There's no road, that's the problem,' she says, in the same level voice in which she has expressed this woe so many times before.

'A road will make you lazy,' Manjula teases her mother. 'Just as the provisions you're getting from the I.T.D.P. will.'

Manjula worries about laziness just as much as she knows that they need both a road and, for six lean monsoon months each year, the limited amounts of free rice, sugar, cooking oil, eggs, soy flakes and so on that tribal families get, thanks to recent government largesse in the form of the Integrated Tribal Development Programme. She is glad about the lamppost, however, and especially grateful for the battery box at its base. They charge their phones here, as do their neighbours. Earlier they'd have to walk through fields and mud to the main road where a little grocery store did it for them at ten rupees a shot.

She passes around the box of sweets, while Tilaka dispenses with the packet of biscuits. He is studying for a B.A. in business administration and hopes to do an M.B.A. after that; Manjula asks him how his English is progressing and he says it's awful, too shy to try it on his fluent aunt.

They turn in early, as everyone in the village does. Manjula shares her mother's bed and Sidamma is snoring richly in seconds while she herself does not take long to arrive at the border of sleep. If there are things that cut into her as her mind roves over the day – the raped child's clouded future, the rejected baby growing up unloved – there is also much to cherish: the tender shoots of bamboo her sister has gathered from the forest, which she will carry back with her to cook in a curry; the delicious raw guavas she'll bite into tomorrow; her mother's imperious turkey, which will follow her everywhere as she helps with tasks around the house; and most of all just this – a roof over her head, a warm blanket, the life she and her family have built, which is very precious and very hard-won.

BEYOND MEMORIES

SALMA

Translated from Tamil by N. Kalyan Raman

Unfettered
The monkey,
sitting placidly
on the tiled overhang
with her sagging, distended
belly and scratching
her head, isn't at all
nervous about having
to find her own food,

about the safety
of the burden in her womb,

or even about
whose child it might be.

1. My father

My father's first wife had three girl children. Every time she gave birth to a girl, my father would rage at her for increasing his burden, for not giving him a male heir.

They were illiterate people from a small village who did not understand the scientific truth that it was the X or Y chromosome in the father's sperm that determined the sex of a child. That simple village girl was now carrying her fourth pregnancy with a sense of dread.

During the pregnancy, her husband frequently threatened to divorce her by *talaq*[1] if this one also turned out to be a girl. When she went into labour, she was gripped by anxiety. On her journey to the hospital, she moaned to the female relative who was accompanying her, 'This one has to be a boy.' Minutes later, she delivered the child – right there, inside the car on the way to the hospital.

She eagerly asked the relative about the sex of the baby. This one, too, was a girl. Still dazed by the pain of childbirth, the poor woman fainted, and she expired soon after. A few minutes after the mother's death, the fourth girl child, too, breathed her last.

My father never experienced a moment's guilt that his threats had ended his wife's life. He got married again – to my mother this time.

When my mother became pregnant for the first time, she too faced the same pressure. Throughout her pregnancy, he told her this one had to be a boy, or else she would be packed off to her parents' house.

I was the child she delivered: a girl. My father refused to visit his wife and her newborn child, and made the following demand: the wife must come back alone. The girl child was not wanted.

My mother took me to her mother's village and, after leaving me in her parents' care, returned to her husband's village.

---

1. A form of divorce under Islamic law in which the husband repudiates the marriage by saying '*talaq*' three times.

2. Preparing for marriage

While I was away, my mother delivered a son, my younger brother. My father was so pleased at finally having a male heir that he agreed to have me back at his house. So, when I was five years old, I was snatched from the narrow, dusty streets of that tiny village and taken by my uncles to my father's village in order to start school.

I would be going to school until ninth standard. This was the maximum educational level of most Muslim girls in our village, for it was during ninth standard, at the age of thirteen, that girls got their first period.

At that point, a girl's life changed instantly. She had to adopt an absurd way of life, in which she never saw the face of any man or learned about events in the outside world. She would be confined to her house, huddling inside the inner rooms to avoid even the smallest ray of light from outside, preserving her beauty for a face-less stranger whom she would marry someday. During this time, she was taught all of the skills necessary for married life and for looking after a family, such as how to cook and clean. Depending on the girl's family background and economic status, she may have to wait only a couple of years before being married off; others waited for many years.

With great trepidation in my heart, I watched my sisters and other girls in my village go through this ritual, wondering how they were able to accept married life without protest. And I wondered when my turn was going to arrive, realising at the same time that I couldn't reject the system myself.

3. The library and the cinema

A few weeks before I turned twelve, a small library opened on the way to my school. I was thrilled; I saw it as the greatest blessing I had received in my life thus far. Situated halfway between my home and the school, the library became a refuge in the hours after school. I spent all of my leisure hours there, indulging my passion for reading.

One Saturday morning, during the school holidays after our half-yearly exams in the ninth standard, I was sitting in the library with a few other girls, immersed in books. Music from the cinema, just ten feet away from the library, signalled that the matinee film was about to begin. We saw the crowd swarming outside the theatre and all of a sudden, we were struck by a foolhardy impulse. Could we go to the cinema without seeking permission from our mothers? Even if we asked, would permission be granted? We decided to do it, without telling our mothers or anyone at home.

Once the movie started, the doors closed and our group of four was stranded in a theatre full of men, with no other female members in the audience. We sat through the entire film with our heads in our laps, our eyes closed, and our bodies shrivelling from shame. When I timidly returned home that evening, I was ordered to stop going to school, from the next day. In fact, from then on, I wasn't allowed to leave the house at all. That day, I learned that a girl who watched a forbidden film brought ignominy upon her whole family. It was a rule reserved solely for women. No such restrictions were placed on my brother, who had watched the same film with us.

4. A poet is born

It was during that phase of my life, when I was engulfed by solitude, that I began to write poems to transcribe my feelings.

My poems were full of questions and critiques about how the lone difference of gender was used to strangle women. Rather than expressing a young woman's typical feelings of joy and celebration, my poems spoke of grief and loneliness. I started writing them on post-cards and, with the help of a male cousin, sending them to publishers whose addresses I found in the magazines I had read. Eventually *Little Magazine* published my poem *En Swasam* (Breathing).

When the postman delivered the magazine to my home, it created a furore within my family and my village.

My work was condemned for two reasons. First, a Muslim woman who had to keep her identity hidden and lead a cloistered life inside her home was expressing herself through poetry. Second, the poems were critical of our narrow, closed society.

Instead of feeling anger or sadness about the savage comments people made about me, I felt a profound joy from knowing that my poems could shake up my society, at least to a small extent.

Breathing
Everything happens so quickly
before I can feel it.
I keep trying to feel something
before it's too late.
It all happens in my name
without me being there.
Flowers, people,
the world is so much bigger than me.
Should I carry on breathing
If I'm not really here?
(Translated from Tamil by Hari Rajaledchumy)

5. Betrothal

During this time, I was betrothed to a boy from my village. My future in-laws stood before me and demanded that I promise to never write again. It was only then that I realised that just as a woman was denied the outside world, she was also denied the activities that could give her freedom, recognition and an identity.

I suggested that we call off the wedding.

The anger and scorn of my in-laws made me realise that they were not used to a girl talking back to them.

My opposition to the marriage plunged my parents into profound anguish and sorrow, but I didn't want other people to interfere with my journey towards making a place for myself in the world. I believed that the survival of my individuality and identity, at least as a speck in this vast world, was far more important than anything else – and it is this belief alone that brought me to where I am today.

The following year, I was made to go ahead with the wedding. After hiding within the lime-coated walls of my parents' home for several years, I moved to my husband's family house on a neighbouring street and was enclosed by brand new walls, freshly coated with paint.

A marital relationship is more than just migration to a new home; it is a site where the man and his family can wield maximum authority over a woman. It was then that I began to feel and experience the full force of that authority, which far exceeded what had been my understanding until then.

A daughter-in-law's sole duty was to earn a good name and social approval for her husband and his family. If she had any desires, hobbies or ideas of her own, this was tantamount to insulting the family.

Writing poems and reading books were considered serious crimes. My husband warned me to stop reading. He threatened that if he happened to see any books lying around the house he would burn them, and if he saw me writing he would break my fingers.

I also had to give up my *identity* as a poet, which I had fought so hard to establish between the ages of thirteen and twenty-one. The expectations of my in-laws threw me off balance. I did not understand why my reading and writing should upset them when everyone in the house was doing whatever he or she wanted to do. Everyone considered the activities they pursued as right or important for them. In the same way, my activities were my own; how could they have an impact on other people? I was not troubled by anyone else's desires; why were my activities alone deemed dangerous to them? Bewildered, I sought to understand the reason behind such a notion and came to the following conclusion: it had to do with the place of a woman. In a world full of women who lacked a place in society but were unaware of this deprivation, no one was ready to accept me as a woman who was aware of her existence as a distinct individual. I experienced this truth through the strictures imposed on me by my husband and his family.

I recall one incident distinctly. It was around six in the evening and, as my husband didn't normally return from work until after eight, I was sitting alone in my room, reading a book on Gramsci.[2] It was a thick volume, which had been translated only recently by a friend of mine.

There was a knock on the door. I got up to answer it, wondering who it could be. My husband stood there.

'What are you doing at this hour, behind locked doors?' he asked, angrily.

'Nothing really. I was resting,' I said, and went back to sit on the bed. That fat book lay open on it.

With mounting fear and anxiety, I realised there was no time to hide the book. He walked over to the bed and picked up the book. His face turned red. 'So you lock yourself up and keep reading and writing, don't you?' he bellowed. The anger in his voice made me tremble. Don't let your fear show, I thought; that would be humiliating.

He started searching around the bed, then he lifted the mattress to check whether I had hidden any of my writings there. Many times previously, he had found my poems and torn them up.

'Why shouldn't I read? I read to pass the time. What's your problem?' I wanted to scream it, but I was so scared that the words caught in my throat. Those feeble-sounding words of resistance fuelled his anger.

---

2. An Italian Marxist theoretician and politician active in the early twentieth century

'Don't talk back to me. How dare you ask me why your reading should bother me? These books have made you so arrogant.'

He flung the book into a corner of the room.

'Let this be the last time. If I see you reading any kind of book or writing anything, I'll turn really nasty. You won't have fingers to write with anymore. Remember that!' he shouted. He picked up the paper bag filled with eggs that I had on my table, and threw it on the ground before he walked away.

The yolks of the broken eggs splattered all over the floor and across the walls. I stood there, numb with shock, humiliated and weighed down by the silence.

6. Writing in secret

Sometimes, in the middle of the night after my husband had gone to sleep, I would smuggle a few blank sheets of paper and a pen into the bathroom to write my poems in the dim light that trickled in. I would write down those lines of poetry urgently, anxious that I might forget those feelings and metaphors by the morning, and exhale deeply. I would hide the poems in a cupboard in the bathroom, then retrieve them the next day when my husband was not at home, and hide them between the pages of my diary.

I sent the poems that I wrote clandestinely, as if writing them was a crime, for publication. Once they were published, the problem became more serious. Some men don't flinch from using violence against women who resist their authority and disobey their commands. For an Indian man, it is not that difficult a task.

Almost daily, my husband would pick a fight with me. He would use cruel words to tell me not to write; if I stayed silent or talked back to him, he would bang his head against the wall. Time passed in a series of sleepless nights and silent days. While this torture adversely affected my mental state, my resolve to never give up my individuality or identity for such triviality grew stronger.

I decided to hide my real identity behind a pen-name – Salma – and send my poems for publication anyway. It was only when I changed my name to the pseudonym that I reached a state of total freedom, and could finally experience the creative freedom of an artist.

Living in my husband's house, it was impossible for me to send the poems to various magazines by post. I couldn't get out of the house and go to the post office to mail them. Nor could I ask others for help. Similarly, no magazines could be received at my address. If they arrived, they would have created problems for me. It was under these circumstances that I would send the poems hidden in a cloth bundle with my mother. My mother would get someone's help to post them. She would bring the mail I received from magazines in a cloth bag. I would read them without anyone's knowledge, and stash them away between the stacks of dresses in my clothes cupboard. This went on like a hide-and-seek game for several years.

After a certain period, a publisher brought out a book of my poems. Unbeknownst to my family, the collection helped me to achieve wide recognition in society as a poet.

8. Betrayal

I cannot so easily forget those countless gruesome nights when my husband threatened to hurt me, or announced that he was going to kill himself, if I didn't promise to stop writing poems. I often wondered if those long, sleepless nights, filled with my husband's pleas and menacing threats, would ever come to an end. My futile yearnings spread over me like a grim fog.

One night, after I had gone to sleep, I heard someone trying to wake me by pummelling my pillow. I awoke with a start.

'Why are you sleeping? Get up!' It was my husband.

Frightened by his voice, I sat up hurriedly and said, 'What is it?'

'So, a monkey cannot identify its husband; and its young one doesn't know its father, is it?' he lashed out, referring to my poem 'Unfettered'. 'If you wanted to live like that, why did you get married?'

Not knowing what to say, I sat trembling on the edge of the bed, looking nervously at the faces of my children, afraid that their sleep might be disturbed by the light.

'Why don't you listen when I tell you so many times not to write poetry? How dare you defy me?' he hissed into my ear. 'Say it now, that you won't write anymore,' he said, as he flung open the door of his cupboard and picked up a small bottle from a shelf. 'Look, this is acid. I bought it just to throw it in your face. Tell me you will never write poems.' Although in the semi-darkness I couldn't see the small bottle or its contents clearly, fear wrapped its grip around my insides.

'Promise me now that you won't write another word. This poem shows your true character – that you are a whore. If they had sent you to college and let you loose in the outside world, you would've slept with a thousand men. You've written as much in this poem.'

Disgusted at hearing those words, I sat still, without any response. What could I say?

After a brief period of silence, I heard the sound of his banging his head repeatedly on the wall. I watched him in disbelief. I didn't know what to do.

I momentarily considered telling him that I wouldn't write anymore, but my anger at the vile abuse he had just flung stopped me from doing that.

After a few more minutes of beating his head against the wall, he stopped and picked up a bottle of kerosene that he had brought into the bedroom earlier. 'Look here, I am going to drink this and die. You can live in peace,' he said and started drinking the kerosene.

Wailing, I ran to him and tried to snatch the bottle away. When the struggle between us came to an end, I made a solemn promise that I would no longer write or read. I stayed awake the rest of the night, weeping and hugging my children, thinking about what I had just witnessed. The arrogance of being a man had fused with an inferiority complex, and this torment had affected my husband's psyche. And within me there was searing uncertainty about how I was going to get through what remained of this life.

Every minute was like living in hell. Giving birth to my children forever closed the possibility of choosing to evict myself from this life. It would be no exaggeration to say that societal and familial pressures pushed me to seriously consider the idea of eviction.

When a woman is unable to choose whether she needs an education, or whom she should marry or at what age she should marry, or when she should have children and how many children she should have, how can she find happiness?

It was during this time that I finished writing my novel. For three years I had been writing in notebooks which I had kept buried among my saris. Anxious that the key to that cupboard should not fall into my husband's hands when I was asleep, I would hide it in a different place every night and retrieve it in the morning. One day, when I returned from a visit to the hospital because my child had fever, I found that the entire manuscript had disappeared from the cupboard. It was three years' work. I wept and pleaded with my husband to return the notebooks.

'I have burned them,' he replied.

9. Freedom

I will never forget how I cried that day. I lived like a walking corpse for the next few weeks.

The emotions I felt when I happened upon the notebooks in my husband's cupboard cannot be described in words. Eventually, I recovered the manuscript without his knowledge. My novel, *Irandam Jamankalin Kathai (The Hour Past Midnight)*, was published in 2009.

Salma would never be voiceless.

THE VILLAGE
WITHOUT MEN

ANITA AGNIHOTRI

Translated from Bengali by Arunava Sinha

As a writer and development worker, I have travelled extensively, exploring the faraway and uncertain terrains of India, a large, complex and diverse entity. The Sundarbans is a fragile, biodiverse zone in Eastern India, where human existence has been made immensely difficult by the fact that forests are protected in the south. The crisscrossing of turbulent rivers surrounding the islands has always fascinated me as it challenges the reality of human development. Around four million people live in this region. In the last decade, I have had the chance to explore the Sundarbans several times. Each time I come back with a feeling of deep anguish and determination to initiate change after meeting women (single and in groups) in desolate villages where men have mostly migrated for work.

Cyclone Aila hit the Sundarbans in 2009, causing severe damage to the embankments and land, destroying the already thin support system that the poor had. The day I spent in the village Mohanpur, months after Aila, has remained vivid in my memory.

It was on this day that I met Taramoni, a single woman in a household, who to me represented all the courage and fragility of a woman who has been left with the task of running and managing a household alone while waiting for better days.

The narrative that follows is the story of Taramoni in a village of no men. But it is also a story of each and every woman of the Sundarbans.

◆ ◆ ◆

Cyclone Aila struck in summer.

It was dawn. Satyen, Taramoni's husband, had gone to the field behind the house to clear his bowels. He came rushing back: 'The water's broken through the big embankment! We have to leave at once!'

Within moments, the salt water had entered the village.

It was already flooding into the house.

Somehow Taramoni and Satyen managed to wake up the two sleeping boys, make a bundle with whatever dry clothes were within reach, collect the money tucked above the bamboo beams beneath the roof and leave, taking shelter in the raised verandah of the middle school.

They saw numerous other families like theirs from the village rushing in, one by one, with a few meagre possessions.

The speed of the wind rose as the day advanced. The raging storm was uprooting trees and dislodging tin roofs from houses. They let Bhanumoti the cow loose so that she could escape the flood, but what if she was killed by a flying tin roof or a falling tree?

How could the strong and sturdy embankments, built during the era of the zamindars[1], actually break? That morning when Aila came, bringing with it such chaos, there was little time to ponder this.

---

1. Landowners who leased their land to tenant farmers

◆ ◆ ◆

Taramoni had seen it rain all night, and witnessed the upheaval of the tides on countless occasions. Storms, hurricanes and tornados were a regular feature in the Sundarbans. There had been a cyclone the year before Tara's wedding. This time, however, the water rose when the tide flowed in, but refused to subside when the tide ebbed. And yet how they suffered from a lack of water! There was no water to drink, to bathe, to clean themselves after going to the toilet. Neither for humans nor for animals. People were dying, gasping for water. The stagnant water in the rivers was giving off a stench, as though something organic were rotting in it. Flies swarmed everywhere – on the floor, on beds, on utensils. People were crowded together on the verandah and in the hall. Wailing babies, old men beating their breasts.

◆ ◆ ◆

Weeks and months passed, but the wounds still did not heal. The memory of that dawn sent shivers down Taramoni's spine, every single day.

But at least they had survived.

◆ ◆ ◆

Six months on, Taramoni found herself gazing emptily at the drumstick tree near the front verandah. Bereft of leaves and fruit, the tree looked like an emaciated spirit, dying slowly. A flock of chirping grey sparrows was tumbling in play under the tree. Taramoni could hear them faintly, like murmurs floating in from the distance. The afternoon was strangely calm: the winter sky a deep blue, without clouds. A dove was calling from the distance amid the silence in the bamboo grove.

It did not ring gladly in Taramoni's heart. The river Gomar was in high tide at midday. The water made splashing sounds in the wind.

She was grateful that they at least had drinking water now; all the hand-pumps were back in operation. Still, Taramoni walked half a kilometre every day to fetch water for drinking and for cooking, storing it in buckets.

Finding drinking water wasn't Taramoni's only problem. She tethered the cow to the drumstick tree and let it graze – but there was no grass. She had to collect leaves and straw from the edge of the forest and store them. There had been no rice this year, and no hay either. The once-bounteous cow's ribs and bones were visible now, and her tears had dried beneath her eyes. She had a strong appetite. But because Bhanumati the cow understood Taramoni's sorrows, she did not low very often these days, only staring straight ahead with her large eyes, the lids always open, and licking Tara's hands.

The hours were ticking past, the hours of a winter day.

It was time to let the cow loose and tether her in the shade. But where was the shade? The trees had been submerged in waist-high water. The roots had rotted away underwater. Salt water had gathered in the rice fields. Water was everywhere, and there was no question of re-entering their old home, but still Taramoni's heart was yearning on the verandah of the schoolhouse.

After Aila had struck, Taramoni waded back from the safe shelter of the school for a glimpse of her beloved home, bursting into tears at the sight of the devastation. The tin roof had been blown off by the wind, landing in a distant field. The swaying walls had collapsed over one another, although the walls of the kitchen at the back had miraculously survived. During Diwali, Taramoni had added a layer of red clay to the front wall and drawn on it with her own hands. As though the wall were a gigantic screen and Taramoni, a rapt artist. She had drawn such beautiful hibiscus flowers, scarlet with green leaves – not like actual hibiscus, but so what? Satyen had made fun of her art, and Taramoni's indignation and embarrassment had reddened her cheeks. The home that they had made bit by bit, with so much love, like the painted wall, with so much blood and sweat over twenty years, had been demolished in just a few seconds.

Her favourite wicker basket, the dolls displayed in the wooden cupboard, the silk clothes for herself and her family, bought with patiently accumulated savings, were all underwater, rotting away. Water snakes were moving about in the room, scorpions too, the bed-clothes covered with swarming black flies.

They had not been able to get their possessions – who was going to risk his or her life to retrieve them? It was Taramoni who had asked her husband and sons not to try.

Satyen had not grieved openly as she had. Men had appearances to maintain – they would not weep, even if they wanted to, in the presence of others. But Taramoni knew of the tempest in her husband's heart. He was a singer. His harmonium and cymbals had all been damaged by the water.

◆ ◆ ◆

Even now, six months on, a cold current of fear gripped the people of Mohanpur when the round full moon rose in the sky and a liquid silver melded into the water of the Gomar. During high tide there was always the anxiety that the fast-flowing water could attack through cracks in the embankment. The damage to the Mohanpur embankment had not yet been repaired.

◆ ◆ ◆

Taramoni's new home was built with bamboo poles, bamboo screen walls, and a sheet of black polythene tied to them with ropes. Fortunately the kitchen wall of the former house had survived, or else they would have had to cook in the open.

'This is our new home. Do you like it?'Taramoni asked me, on that day of my visit to Mohanpur. She had dark circles under her eyes. Her tears were overflowing on her cheeks.

The new house, comprising a single room, was twelve feet long and twelve feet wide. They couldn't make a larger house. The government had given them ten thousand rupees after Aila to rebuild their home. It was impossible to build a house with that kind of money. Many of the people in the village had spent it on food. Taramoni had kept the money safe, without letting anyone use it to buy anything else.

'If you did build a house, why couldn't you have made it a little sturdier, Taramoni?' I asked her gently.

'What kind of sturdy house are you talking about? The paddy harvest was ruined completely – the rice fields were under salt water for a month. The plants just stood there and died. It's Durga Pujo time, and we have neither rice nor hay at home. What am I supposed to make the roof with? We cannot wedge in wooden planks – this is the Sundarbans. The police will despatch us to Alipur Jail if we so much as touch the trees. So all we were left with was bamboo, and these polythene sheets the government gave us.'

♦ ♦ ♦

It wasn't just the makeshift house and the daily task of transporting water that Taramoni had to worry about. No plants were growing in Mohanpur. The plants and trees around most people's houses had been killed by the salt water. Winter crops had been sown on more than half the land, but the crops, too, had been spoilt by the salt water standing in the fields after breaking through the embankment. The rural economy had collapsed in the absence of a harvest. There was no hay, no work on winnowing. The self-reliant team of women who used to trade in rice had no work either. Most worryingly, farmers had no seeds to plant for the next season.

Wives and daughters like Taramoni were carrying the burden of the entire family. Now they had to buy all their vegetables, which posed a new crisis. Earlier, small farmers used to get rice for their families every year while their kitchen gardens yielded vegetables like drumsticks, eggplant, gourd, pumpkins and tomatoes. They spent money only on oil, salt, sugar and clothes. But now they had to buy everything they ate, which meant they needed cash.

♦ ♦ ♦

The village of Mohanpur had been emptied of its men. Only the women and old people incapable of physical work had stayed behind.

Even Taramoni's husband, a talented musician, had been forced to leave in search of a living. There was simply no work to be had in the village, not even as a labourer. And Satyen Sardar's harmonium and musical instruments had fallen silent, ruined by the water and the mud.

Labour contractors had come scouring all of the Sundarbans. There were two or three of them for each village, finding work elsewhere for the residents. And so the people from the Sundarbans went to work at brick kilns and cotton mills in other states, sometimes at cold storages in other districts of West Bengal. Those who went to work as masons got work in Chennai, Hyderabad or Bangalore at 300 rupees a day or more. The company also made living arrangements for them on the site. The village people sent their earnings home every month.

But this life was associated with unknown dangers. Sometimes the men returned to the village seriously ill or injured, without money. This being an unorganised sector, the contractors did not look after the workers' interests: for example, the owners of the brick kilns seldom paid properly, and fate often held physical torture for workers; there was frequent news of brick-kiln workers, who had left their homes and families behind, being rescued by the police or by voluntary organisations. They had to return home without insurance or compensation.

◆ ◆ ◆

Taramoni had two sons. One was twenty and the other eighteen. They too had left the village after Aila.

I asked her where her sons had gone.

'I don't know,' she said. 'The contractor who gave them work had said he would let us know, but he hasn't been to the village since then. I don't know their address either. Nor did they say when they would return.'

'Have they sent any money through money orders?'

'No.' Taramoni shook her head. 'They are young, they haven't learned any trade. They will ruin their health if they're working at a brick kiln. And if ...' Taramoni fell silent. I knew the apprehension that had cast a shadow over her – the fear that her boys would come back with diseases or disabilities. As their mother she couldn't express her inner fears.

◆ ◆ ◆

Traditionally, when the farming season ended, the men had taken their boats into the jungle to fetch honey and wood fragments, and to catch fish and crabs. The water was infested with crocodiles and snakes.

The women did not go into the forest alone in boats. But by way of work now, they had just one option: trapping shrimp prawns in the river below the embankment with homespun towels. It wasn't just shrimp that got trapped but also other small fry. They caught the fish while wrapped in drenched clothes on winter evenings, averting crocodile attacks. The owners of hatcheries bought the shrimp. Some people sold the rest of the catch, while others cooked it with a little oil. But catching the small fish meant destroying biodiversity, and the number of fish wasn't increasing. The women said they were helpless. They only caught the fish because they had no other choice.

◆ ◆ ◆

No woman who had to guard her house in a village of no men could sleep well, and the deep dark circles under Taramoni's eyes indicated that she had not slept peacefully for many nights.

'Didi, do you have sleeping pills? Will you give me some?' Taramoni held out her hand to me.

Tigers were partly to blame for her insomnia. Royal Bengal Tigers. There were dense forests to the south of Gosaba Block. The distance between the two banks of the Gomar was not far at Mohanpur. Wire fences had been erected along the riverbank, but there were gaps in it for people to pass. This was the route tigers took into the river. And then they swam up to the villages. They took away calves or goats or anything they could find. Ancient occupants of the forests that they were, the tigers' sanctuary had been destroyed by human habitation. Their sources of food had been reduced. The tigers had not forgiven humans.

'I can't sleep nights,' Taramoni said. 'I live in this large desolate room protected by bamboo. I stay awake worrying, what if a tiger attacks me? I keep jute stalks and matches close by. Only when the breeze at dawn makes me drowsy do I go to sleep.'

◆ ◆ ◆

The day was declining. The colour of the sunlight had changed. Daytime yellow had acquired a hue of saffron. The water of the Gomar splashed louder in the restless afternoon wind.

Pointing to the south-east, Taramoni said, 'Midnapore district lies that way. That's where my parents lived, in Rangini village in Ghatal. I got married at fifteen and came to Mohanpur. I came to Satyen's house. My father was swept away with joy by my husband's singing. My husband never owned much land or anything, but we were happy. Both our sons were born in that house you saw destroyed by the flood. That was where they crawled, played, grew up. On full-moon nights my husband would take his harmonium down to the river and sing, with someone playing the drums. I played the cymbals. We were happy ...'

My motorboat left Mohanpur for Rangabelia before the darkness turned dense. Taramoni stood on the bank. Her figure grew smaller and dimmer, while the line of the bank vanished. A torrent of water at the confluence of the Gomar and the Vidya made the boat sway on the waves of the high tide.

Taramoni Sardar had told me, 'Write about me, didi. Publish it. People will read.' Here, I have written Taramoni's story. Along with the stories of hundreds of solitary women like her who stayed awake nights.

I still regret that I couldn't give her sleeping pills.

TICK TOCK

TISHANI DOSHI

In 2022, India will be the most populous country in the world. It would not be an exaggeration to say that we are a fecund people. And that at least part of our fecundity is thanks to our mothers.

As a nation, we are extreme in our obsession with the Mother. Mothers are goddesses – deified (if they're lucky), vilified (if they're not). May you be the mother of a hundred sons (and 91.4 daughters), and so forth.

Mother's milk, mother tongue, Mother India, motherfucker. No other country will offer you such dazzling and diverse epithets as we have for mother. Entire philosophies rest on the idea of a divine female principle: Shakambari – Bearer of Greens, Shakti – The Powerful, Sita – Paragon of Woman. Even the holy cow is a personification of motherhood: Kamadhenu – divine bovine goddess!

We have Great Mothers in the shape of wide-hipped Harappan terracottas. Warrior Mothers like the goddess Kali, who offers her breasts to her husband Shiva, so her milk can negate the poisons of the world.

And should you imagine that our mothering is restricted to the mere heavens and mythology, fear not! We have mothers of the earthly realm too. Mothers-in-law, mummy-jis and MILFs. Single mothers, working mothers, surrogate mothers, unwed mothers, burning mothers.

And then we have the most powerful mothers of all. The mothers who are childless. Divine Mothers like the 'Hugging Amma', who dispenses her benediction by enfolding you. Political Mothers like the chief minister of my state, Ms Jayalalithaa, former film star, now mother, or 'Amma', to her entire electorate. These women are chaste, desexualised, scrubbed free of even the most molecular immoral thought. They are powerful precisely because they have relinquished their reproductive rights in order to be mother to millions.

But what of a woman who doesn't lean towards a career in the divine or political? Can she opt for a life without babies? The 32 million Indian women who have no access to modern contraception must keep banging them out, or hope to be part of the 4.6 million who are sterilised each year. And the 'modern' Indian woman – she who has the world at her manicured fingertips? The answer is yes and no. There will be resounding cries of 'Get thee to a fertility clinic!' should she decide to remain childless. But if she approaches her resolve with humour and the hide of a buffalo, she may proceed with caution.

◆ ◆ ◆

Many years ago, in the genial hubbub of a hotel lobby, I had an epiphany about children. There was a family checking in at reception ahead of me, an ordinary kind of family: Mama, Papa and two ungainly, surly teenagers. I remember watching them – the vast space between Mama and Papa, the complete boredom and disdain their bodies held towards one another. And I remember thinking, 'That's funny! At some point, long ago, these two people must have had sex at least twice in order to produce those two skulking creatures.'

Once this idea took root in me I found myself leering at families unabashedly. Families at the beach, families at dinner, families on aeroplanes (the worst). It intrigued me to see how genetic codes survived the generations. And if there happened to be grannies and grandpas on hand, greater joy still to see who inherited the crinkly hair, the propensity for freckles, the large, lumbering bottoms. Always there was the inescapable fact of it: children are a by-product of sex.

Of course, I've known this since I was twelve. One of my friends at school, whose mother was a doctor, had shown us a book which explained what happened when a boy's thing went into a girl's thing. We sat on the school wall – a line of us girls in blue uniforms, peering at lacklustre diagrams of appendages and labia majora, which sadly didn't stir the requisite shivering in the loins we'd hoped for. Sex was as distant as the moon, and as incomprehensible as the gonadotropins coursing through our bodies. But we were children, and believed as all children do, that the universe existed for our benefit. Our narcissistic egos would never allow us to see ourselves as by-products. If anything, it was our parents who were utterly by the by – present in relation only to our own exalted beings.

Long after you've come of age, though, and begun actually engaging in sex, you start to forget about this interwoven destiny between sex and babies. At least, those of us with access to birth control do. We confidently go about our mammalian task of coitus without worrying about side effects. But gawking at families in their natural habitat remains a vital hobby for me because it reinforces a primeval link. It also highlights a condition I have so long angsted over: should I or shouldn't I have children?

I should say here that I like kids. There are women who've always known they wouldn't have children, but I'm not one of them. I grew up in a happy family (sorry, Tolstoy) and, despite the difficulties of growing up with a brother with disabilities, the family was reinforced as the exemplary model for living. In fact, until my mid-twenties, children seemed inevitable – a distant and somewhat terrifying prospect, reserved for a phase in my life which always seemed to be moving further and further away.

In my mid-twenties, though, I met someone who would challenge those ideas and offer me a periscopic view of an alternative lifestyle. Her name was Chandralekha. She was a choreographer who transformed me into a dancer, and she lived in a house by the sea, ten minutes from my parents' home in the conservative coastal city of Madras, now Chennai.

Chandralekha was a rebel. Born in 1928, she had declared precociously at the age of fourteen that marriage was a form of slavery for men and women. When I met her, half a century separated us. She was a beauty, with astonishing silver-white hair and piercing dark eyes, and she delighted in calling children 'little terrorists', with their demands of 'goo-goo ga-ga'.

Deeply involved with India's earliest feminist movement, she routinely worked with women in workshops, trying to get them to use their bodies differently from the usual washing, scrubbing, cooking, sweeping. For Chandra, the body was a repository of energies, and the spine a metaphor for freedom.

In her choreographies she relentlessly explored the idea of femininity in the bodies of women and men. This reclamation of the female principle was integral to all her work, because she saw *Shakti* as the source of all creation. 'When I say creation I don't mean procreation,' she once quipped. 'I mean *all* of creation.' She was recalling those other kinds of mothers, who stood with their spines erect, who spread their terracotta thighs and gave birth to all the vegetation of the world.

To have met Chandra at that particular juncture of my life was, in a way, to begin again. Not just with my body, which was changing and transforming through dance, but in my ideas. We don't necessarily have to inherit the life offered to us by society. It seems an obvious point, but to arrive at this emancipation requires instinct, or, at the very least, epiphany. And I had it through Chandra. I saw what it meant to choose the life of an artist. And more: what it meant to be an artist and a woman in India.

I did not, however, share the militant views of my mentor when it came to children. I always believed I had the right to change my mind if ever the mythical 'tick tock' should return from walkabout. I made a pact with myself: if ever I met a man who made me think, 'Ooh, I've just got to have me some of your babies', then I would reconsider.

◆ ◆ ◆

People say they *just know* when they want to have kids. They walk past Baby Gap and their hearts turn to mashed bananas. They call it baby fever. Scientists have recently confirmed that these urges are not grounded in a primordial clock ticking inside our wombs, but are in fact a result of social conditioning. Evolution does not give us the desire to procreate, merely the desire for sex, and the physical means to bear children. Until recently, though, if you were going to spend any amount of time rolling around in the hay, babies were inevitable. My generation is part of a fledgling generation of women who can opt out of species continuity if we want. Culturally, though, the pressure to procreate remains a powerful force. Particularly if you live in India, as I do, where no matter how liberal the society you keep, the possibility of having to answer for your childlessness is high.

You could be at the gym, and someone you barely know will engage you at the water filter and ask, 'Any good news?' (A colloquial way of saying, is there a bun in the oven?) You could be sitting with family, when a gaggle of aunts gang up on you and try to convince you that being a writer doesn't mean you can't be a mother. You could even think you're in safe territory with friends, and one of them will say,

'You're *really* not going to have children?' Because while sex in India is like tuberculosis – behind every curtain and down every alleyway, ubiquitous but invisible – motherhood, by contrast, is a never-ending road show. And even though India ranks 140th in the global motherhood index, which means there are only thirty-nine countries where it's worse to be a mother, any rejection of motherhood requires some major upholding.

◆ ◆ ◆

Picture this: I'm at a friend's wedding in Bangalore. The scene is lavish: *Monsoon Wedding* to the power of twenty. Marigolds, roses and jasmine bedeck every conceivable surface. I feel I'm knocking about inside of a perfume bottle. Women in bright saris totter on heels. Men in turbans slap one another on the back. The bride and groom sit around a fire. Indian drums and pipes waft up from the stereo, food in giant vats is being carted out, colourful glasses of non-alcoholic beverages sail by on trays (the champagne is for after the religious ceremony). In the midst of all this celebration, I find myself cornered, somewhere between the *rasgullas* and the black forest cake, by a former classmate – a man who decides this is a good time to get into a discussion about parenthood. He tells me it's the best thing that ever happened to him. That it took him out of himself like nothing else, that it diminished his ego, expanded his capacity for love. And when I merely nod noncommittally, he signals the end of the discussion by saying, 'You know, you should really think about it. It would do you good.' As if having a child is like taking up transcendental meditation or trying an Ayurvedic diet.

One of the drawbacks of choosing not to have kids is that people who have gone into the Mini-Me-making venture feel they can casually quiz those of us who haven't about our decision not to breed. Worse, in the fashion of many religious born-agains who have 'seen the light', they feel they must convince us of the error of our ways. And this is not an activity that's restricted to India. I can't tell you the number of times I've been cornered at a party by a stranger who launches in with a personal question about the state of my ovaries, and when I patiently outline my reasons – that I can't afford kids, that I love the coupledom I have with my husband, that growing up with a brother with Down's Syndrome I know that children are a responsibility for life, and that I'm actually happy with the life I have right now, thank you very much – they cast their big saucer eyes at me and say, 'Oh, that's so sad!' Then, I start flailing like a drowning woman, talking of the body, and how I'm a dancer, and that if my body were screaming 'give me a baby', I would definitely hear it screaming, and I would give it a baby, consequences be damned. But it's too late for all that. They've judged me, and I have certainly judged them.

It's not always this way, of course. Some people are kind. They want to tell you about the entire range of human emotions you're missing out on, which you cannot possibly know about until you've squeezed a thirty-five-centimetre head through your vaginal introitus. They'll tell you that until you've held a being of your own living blood in your arms and looked into its eyes, you haven't really understood the power of love. And this is somehow more offensive to me, because if love were really going to be judged as if it were a hierarchy, then surely a more powerful kind of love is that which is inexplicable, which has no familial DNA running through its cells? You'd think that a person who ethically chooses not to overpopulate an already overpopulated planet would be congratulated for her choice. That Indians, with our 1.2 billion and still going strong, would have greater appreciation for this gesture of stepping out of the genealogical race. But no.

Why is it that people who don't have children are by and large respectful of the decisions of people who have them, but rarely vice versa? I would never (although I've often dreamed it) go up to a family on a day when they're at their spectacular unbest and say, 'Excuse me, but do you ever regret having children?'

And yet, people who proselytise about parenthood are free to pronounce, 'Oh, you'll change your mind eventually', or 'You'll regret it'. But before I can holler 'Glorify it as much as you want, but your little bundle of joy has arrived on this planet only by way of a (choose your adjective) sweaty/prolonged/painful/blissful/hesitating/steadfast/forgettable fuck,' they've already rushed back to their harried lives.

◆ ◆ ◆

Lying at the leafy nub of this debate is, of course, the idea of womanhood. To be a man who decides not to have children barely registers on the seismograph. To be a woman who says 'Actually, babies aren't for me' is to unleash a minor tsunami. It isn't just a personal rejection of what's considered a woman's unique quality – her ability to bear children – but a challenge to the entire society.

From my late twenties to my mid-thirties, every birthday that passed was signalled by my mother saying, 'When I was your age, I had babies/toddlers/school-going children.' She didn't press too much, but there was always this gentle urging. *What will you do when you get older? Won't you regret it? Won't you be lonely without a family?* At some stage these exhortations ceased. There seemed to be a realisation on her part that I had chosen a radically different life from hers, and that this was okay. But more importantly, that my life-choices were in no way a backlash against her choices. That by choosing childlessness I was not undermining her entire adult life, which was, first and foremost, to be a mother.

There will always be moments when I think, *What if?* What if my mother was right? What if that condescending classmate had a point when he said having a child would do me good?

♦ ♦ ♦

During an interview in Germany once, Chandralekha was asked whether she ever regretted not having children. And Chandra, in the way that only a dancer can, cupped her breasts and said that she was proud of her 'undrunk breasts'. In Sanskrit, there is a term for it – *apina vakshoruham*.

Chandra did not have an easy time of it. Her rebelliousness had ostracised her several times over. In some respect, she must have thrived on it. 'I exist in spite of you,' is what she liked to say, of institutions, of the government, of anyone who tried to box her in. Ironically, towards the end of her life she became something of a national treasure. Officials (the kind she despised for their fickle sycophancy) dived at her feet for blessings, newspapers extolled her work as groundbreaking. And because I only knew her in the last five years of her life; because I saw her struggle with the decay of her body, which for a dancer is no easy thing; because I was there the morning we carried her body out from her house of swings, I saw how surrounded by love she had always been. That while she must have suffered and sacrificed, as we all do, this was a woman who had lived the life she constructed for herself, who had made of her friends a family. And it was what I set out to do myself. Not with quite her brand of ferocity, but with the knowledge, at least, that it was possible.

♦ ♦ ♦

'Mothers ... If only we could be born without them.'
– *All Decent Animals*, Oonya Kempadoo

Let's get back to that ungainly stegosaurus in the room: sex.

It used to be that to make a child, sex was involved. Sex for homo sapiens is a legitimate biological urge, yet we're so hung up about sex that in cultures across the world there have been concerted efforts to separate the act of sex from the act of birthing. Ergo, baby lore such as: We found your sister under the cabbage patch! Or, the stork brought her! Or some other cock-and-bull story along the lines of birds and bees in order to make the whole enterprise respectable. Now, of course, Assisted Reproductive Technology has changed everything, and made it so a man in a dark room with a cup and a woman renting her womb in a surrogacy clinic can produce a baby without even holding hands. Parents can truthfully say 'The petri dish brought her!'

Surrogacy in India is a multi-billion dollar industry, but it has been likened to a Wild West situation, given there is very little legislation in place to protect the surrogate mothers. These surrogates are often from indigent backgrounds. They aren't allowed to have natural births. They cannot touch or see the child once it's born. They must often stay in the clinic for the entire duration of the pregnancy to ensure nutrition levels are met. They are not paid if they miscarry. If the surrogate happens to die due to complications connected with childbirth, her family won't be compensated properly. Besides all these possible pitfalls the surrogate must also bear a degree of social stigma because the act of carrying another man's child in some communities is bizarrely equated with prostitution. For all their efforts, these women are paid US$5000. But make no mistake about it: India loves her mothers.

♦ ♦ ♦

Nostalgia for a road not taken is inevitable with most hard-wrought choices. But when you live in India, where the pressures and expectations of motherhood perpetually press down on you from all sides, the what-ifs can be particularly poignant. After all, what can we say of the future of a childless woman among these myriad kingdoms of families? Will she really lose her sense of beauty and strength once she is past child-bearing age? How will this affect her identity? Will she really be alone? These are the questions I hope to find answers to, or at least illuminations of, in my lifetime.

◆ ◆ ◆

It was shocking, in a way, for me to encounter Chandralekha in the city of my birth. To sit on the parapet of the beach outside her home and talk of this and that while watching the rising moon. 'Always walk alone,' she told me. 'A woman is nothing without a sense of politics and sexuality,' she told me.

But remembering her this way makes her sound so much more serious than she could be. For she was childlike as well, took delight in staying awake to watch the petals of a lotus open and close, or to catch a mongoose skittering across the garden. Her house was a house of swings and all kinds of people would pass through it – doctors, painters, mango farmers, poets. They eschewed gossip and the usual dinner-table banter, spoke instead of real things. Of politics and desire and resistance. I had travelled all the seven continents of the world and never met a woman like her. I suspect I never will again.

◆ ◆ ◆

When I was thirty-five I met a man who gave me reason to pause. I knew I would marry him within months of meeting him, and in the most abstract fashion I began to fantasise about the kind of children we might have. There was just one thing, though: he already had a child. A sweet, seven-year-old boy I'll call Tom. Every time I saw Tom, I used to think just one thing. You guessed it! Two people had sex to make this boy, and one of them was my soon-to-be husband.

At thirty-five you don't expect your relationships to arrive in a quiet fashion or to be unsullied. But the presence of this child, even though he lived for the most part with his mother, tore me up.

It wasn't so much retroactive jealousy, but the foreverness of the situation pressed down on me like an entire galaxy. From here on out, till Tom came of age – summers, Christmases, New Years, birthdays – all plans hinged on the vagaries of a woman I had nothing to do with.

And there was the question of Tom's face – his mother's startling wide-set eyes, her chin, her pursed lips. His father's eyebrows and high forehead. A crucible of genes collected in his face, which served as a reminder of all the sex that had gone into making him, all the ideals and dreams and whispered words that might have accompanied that act of sex.

I was a mess. For the first few years, when Tom visited us, I frequently found myself bawling on the floor of the bathroom. Real, drawn-out howling, the kind I hadn't engaged in since I was a teen-ager. It was unbearable for me to watch my husband morph from my lover to someone's father. He was so good at fathering: intelligent, funny, tender, wise. But it was as if he could be just the one thing: lover or father. And because he suffered the guilt that most separated fathers feel (rightly so), the time that he and Tom spent together was always a kind of grasping, cloistered, intense twoness, which left little room for me.

I began to think that my emotional state was merely my body's way of saying 'Hey, I want one too.' Girlfriends would visit with their kids, which always heightened the baby dilemma. We'd begin chatting, but before anyone could really hit their stride, sentences were forci-bly abandoned, words and ideas kneeled in submission to the little person, close at hand, who always had something to say that was far more important. Goo-goo, ga-ga. I shared the love, read storybooks, treasured the crayon masterpieces. And as soon as they left, when the house was a quiet cathedral again, I'd breathe easy and think, 'No, I don't want a baby.'

◆ ◆ ◆

What I wanted was a life of freedom, of travel and writing and friendships. But I now loved someone who had a child, so, by default, I was going to have to make space for that child in my life. It's taken five years and, while the writhing incidents on the bathroom tiles have come to a halt, there are still twinges. Particularly when I see how their bodies tuck into each other, the limbs, the resting head on shoulder. I know I will never have *that* kind of physicality, that kind of unquestionable belonging. And I know that part of the bitter-sweetness of it is that I can't forge ahead with my freedom in entirety, that I must always be reminded of my decision *not to*, because from time to time, I must watch father and son stride off into the sunset, while I teeter awkwardly in their wake. And I'm okay with that. Sort of.

I've learned to excuse myself from the drudgery duties of parenting, like trips to Disneyland and school performances, to engage instead with the marvel of how a human being grows and changes and finds his place in the world. It turns out I'm able to share a stake in this child. To see him as his own entity – separate from his genes and the history of intimacy that made him. And perhaps, one day, even to love him.

SCENES FROM A MARRIAGE

ANONYMOUS

Always heed the warning.
Love will let you down.

◆ ◆ ◆

I never knew rape until it happened to me. It was a concept – of savagery, of violence, of violation, of disrespect of a woman's body. I had read my share of Kate Millett and Susan Brownmiller but nothing prepared me for how to handle it. Within a marriage, fighting back comes with its consequences. The man who rapes me is not a stranger who runs away. He is not the silhouette in the car park, he is not the masked assaulter, he is not the acquaintance who has spiked my drink. He is someone who wakes up next to me. He is the husband for whom I have to make the morning coffee. He is the husband who can shrug it away and ask me to stop imagining things. He can blame his actions on unrestrained desire the next day.

There are no screams that are loud enough to make a husband stop. There are no screams that cannot be silenced by the shock of a tight slap. There is no rigidity that can guarantee a shield against penetration. He covers himself with enough lubricant to slide past all my resistance. My legs go limp. I come apart.

◆ ◆ ◆

The rape that happens to a grown woman is different from the rape of a child. When I was little, I did not know what was going on, or its magnitude. I did not know that I was the same as the grown man forcing himself on me – I was small, I was powerless, I was sad; everybody thought I told lies all the time.

A million things happen in a child's mind; a million things happen to a child's body. But, to an eight-year-old, something has *happened* only if there are adult witnesses, only if others agree that it actually *happened*. A man sticking his fingers into me, a man pushing his penis between my thighs, is as real as my grandmother giving a bigger portion of the cake to my younger cousin. No one else sees the partiality, so it does not exist. No one else sees the creepy fingers, no one else notices the sticky white thing he leaves on me, so it does not exist. Everything else is make-believe. Child, don't make up these stories, they say.

The child grows up to be a storyteller. Sadly, that eight-year-old girl also becomes a woman who can confirm the world for herself. She does not need adult witnesses. She feels its footsteps as it makes its way towards her, she recognises a rape even before it looks her in the face.

◆ ◆ ◆

'Will you walk out of this marriage?'

It's a question I never answer one way or another. I answer my husband with other questions, or with a declaration of everlasting love.

There's no honest answer. Only answers that make my life safer, the nights less painful.

The brave die every day because they do not get broken.

♦ ♦ ♦

'Will you walk out of this marriage?'

This time he does not even wait for an answer. He provides it.

'Nobody is going to save you. The men who are out there, waiting for you to walk out, are waiting for their turn to ride you. The women cheering you to leave me have two intentions – they want to see you ruined, lonely, miserable. Or they want a drama absent from their own lives. If you're banking on these men or women to fix up your life, you are making a mistake.

'Your fellow feminists, middle-class petit-bourgeois women, have found the "freedom" they need by getting rid of their men and are free to fuck around. When they get you, it means more holes at their orgies. They'll invite three more men. If that's the freedom you're looking for, leave me now.

'Go, make yourself useful.'

♦ ♦ ♦

I try to marry the world that I witness with the linguistic theory that I have learned.

Man made language. I have read that bit.

Man made language to (also) rape women with his words. This, I learn. This, I experience. This, I hear from my husband's mouth. When he begins to shout, I shrink from shame.

Here, the inversion of Luce Irigaray. Not: *Ta langue, dans ma bouche, m'a-t-elle obligée à parler?* Was it your tongue in my mouth that forced me into speech?

No, Lucy. Not speech, but silence.

This is never a question to be answered, not something to be taken up for consideration. Within my marriage, I have the stock-sure method of knowing: it was your tongue in your mouth that forced me into silence. It was your tongue in your mouth that forced me into submission. And then, it was your tongue in my mouth that forced me.

◆ ◆ ◆

Sex, actually rape, becomes his weapon to tame me. Your cunt will come apart, he tells me. Your cunt will turn so wasted, so useless, you will never be able to offer yourself to any man. It'll be the loosest bag, a literal begging bowl. *Koodhi kizhinja, paati surukku pai pola iruppadi.*

I imagine it falling out of me like spare change. Not with jingling noises, but in a squishy, silent way, of something habituated to water. Carrying the purple of dying roses.

When he takes me, I dream of how I'm going to lose it.

Perhaps it'll come away in slabs of blood and pink flesh. It may not go alone, bringing my uterus and woman parts out with it. On a toilet seat some day, I will notice that I'm passing my pleasure. A slow death by disintegration.

The fear makes me withdraw into myself. The terror seizes me like a spirit the minute I spread my legs.

◆ ◆ ◆

'Why are you so fascinated by other men?'

It's the only question that I summon the courage to ask.

'Don't dream of it,' he tells me. 'Don't dream of a day where you will carry your cunt into another man's bed. When I'm through, what you have will be torn, tattered. After a child, it will not even be recognisable.'

That is the aim of his rapes, all this rough sex. Not just a disciplining, but a disabling. He believes that after him, I will have nothing left in me to love, to make love, to give pleasure.

This is a man breaking his own wife. This is a man burning down his own house.

I need to run away, I need to run away, I need to run away.

♦ ♦ ♦

All that I need, I carry with me. My bag holds it all.

Passport. ATM card. Laptop. My phone, which he never let me use.

All of this is mine.

This is all I could think of taking. This is all I had the time to take.

The moon is on my back. The auto races into the night. I shed this miserable city like a second skin. I have got away, at last.

LOVE IN THE TIME OF THE INTERNET

IRA TRIVEDI

When I moved back to India in the ninth grade, a boy asked me to be his friend. Even before this I'd had a feeling that it may not be a normal sort of friendship. He had crank-called me for two weeks, had written me anonymous notes and then one day, when I stood lost in the hallways of my new school, he came up and introduced himself.

'My name is Kunal. I am Jawahar House prefect. Will you be my friend?'

I thought this introduction a bit odd, but he was cute, he was in the twelfth grade, and being the new girl in school was awfully lonely. Our friendship was short-lived: I soon realised that this friendship wasn't ordinary; it was a 'special' friendship where he would write me love letters, ask me to meet him in empty classrooms and place toffees in my desk. Once he even tried to hold my hand.

Over the next few years at high school, in the town of Indore in the central Indian state of Madhya Pradesh, I realised that a 'proposal for friendship' was a mime for dating – boys officially 'befriended' girls by presenting them with a card and a rose, nervously clearing their throats. Over the years to come I got many proposals of friendship, and I made (somewhat) wiser decisions.

All this seemed a dreamscape, an antiquated world, when I moved away to the U.S. for college, where mating and dating were uttered in the same breath. For me, a girl who had only ever been 'friends' with boys, this was utterly frightening. Nervous about the prospect of what 'American' dating entailed, I stuck to hanging out with girlfriends and only eventually found a boyfriend – a nice boy from India who, while he didn't 'propose' friendship, took me out for many lovely meals and seemed to be a suitable prospect for a long-term relationship leading to marriage. I dived right in.

But alas, my college sweetheart did not become my husband and I moved to New York after I graduated. Here speed dating was all the rage. I did not realise how much my high school days had affected my perceptions of dating.

'Did he pay?' my roommates would ask after I returned from a night out on the town with a new gentleman friend.

'Yes,' I said, embarrassed. 'I offered though,' I hastily added.

'What did you guys do?' they curiously asked.

'A play and dinner,' I said.

'That's a date!'

'No,' I argued, 'but we are just friends!'

'In America,' they joked, 'that would be considered a pretty hot date.'

While I was going out for what were obvious dates, I was in denial for no good reason at all. In my mind, 'dating' was what you did when you really liked someone, when you wanted to have a serious relationship, which would eventually lead to marriage.

◆ ◆ ◆

Fast-forward six years, and I have moved to New Delhi, single and ready to mingle and hopefully, for my parents' sake more than mine, settle my personal life.

Here all my friends bitterly complain: we want to date, we want to meet new people, but there is no scope. New Delhi isn't like New York, where you see a hot guy at a bar, walk up and say hello. Here everything seems to happen with hooded eyes, with tense smiles across crowded rooms, or running around trees like in Bollywood movies of yore. The only real way to meet people is through friends, or friends of friends – and, eventually realising how limited this is, most young people grudgingly allow their parents to get involved, though that has its obvious pitfalls: involving parents means getting serious, which in this case means marriage.

My friends aren't the only ones who are frustrated. As I wrote my book *India in Love*, interviewing hundreds of young people across the country, I realised that the frustration seemed to be on a national scale. Educated young men and women, who grew up watching *Friends* and new-age Bollywood films where dating was in vogue, seemed desperate to have romantic relationships outside of parental pressures and marriage, but since there was really no concept of dating, or no way for them to meet people other than those in their immediate ambit, they came up with creative solutions, as young lovers always seem to do.

Many young Indians began using the numerous matrimonial websites to 'date', with little or no intention to marry. This created problems for the websites as parents complained of the 'seriousness' of the candidates their sons and daughters had met online. Several of the larger websites created an 'offline' marriage bureau, hoping to build customer trust.

But even brick-and-mortar marriage bureaus and flesh-and-blood marriage brokers were becoming frustrated as young people chose to date instead of getting married.

'Ira-ji! These people never make up their minds! They keep on meeting and meeting and meeting. What is all this? Why don't they just say yes?' asked the marriage broker I was spending time with, in the line of my research. He refused to say the word 'date', which was a bad word, just as 'girlfriend' and 'boyfriend' had been back in high school, where we cloaked the words with 'friend' and 'friendship'.

According to another, more savvy, marriage broker, who matched people on chemistry and compatibility instead of the older tropes of caste and class, 'These people, they come to me for marriage but they have no intention of marrying. They meet, they sleep with each other, holiday with each other, and then they move on saying that they aren't compatible.'

◆ ◆ ◆

Enter 2016.

Across India, young people, straight and gay, are downloading and swiping right. Unlike in the West, the concept of 'dating' has never really existed in India, but now the Western concept of dating has captured the imaginations of India's young, quite literally at cyber speed. While dating is largely an urban, middle-class phenomenon, in cities big and small India's young are choosing their own partners across caste and community lines.

At the offices of Truly Madly, a dating app, young Indians lounge around in hoodies and skinny jeans, working on their MacBooks and sipping on lattes. Inside the sleekly designed Facebook-style offices, with beanbags and exposed brick walls, one could be any-where – San Francisco or Stockholm – but outside we see a hip, up-and-coming India.

I have joined the board of this company started by three men, all successful entrepreneurs.

Sachin Bhatia, previously the co-founder of makemytrip.com, one of India's first and most successful travel websites, founded the website when he saw the widening gap in the market and because he was seeing Indian women taking matrimonial decisions into their own hands.

'I saw my neighbour's daughter, a highly qualified doctor, get matched to someone with fake credentials on one of the matrimonial sites. I was hearing of more and more such cases where online profiles were fake or there was little or no compatibility between the man and the woman, yet matches were being forced down people's throats. I realised that the solution was to give girls options early on. An Indian girl should have the option to suss out a bunch of guys before she decides who is right for her, just like she has the option of going into a store and trying out a few pairs of jeans and deciding which one is the right one for her.'

But starting a dating app in India is no easy task, especially when 'dating' remains taboo. So much so that many of the young men and women who work at Truly Madly have not been able to tell their families the true nature of their jobs.

'If I tell my mum I work at a dating app, she'll freak out,' says a twenty-something employee – a recent graduate of one of India's top engineering colleges.

'What do you tell her, then?' I ask.

'I just say that I am working with a start-up,' she says with a grin.

Another employee says that she tells her parents that she works at a matrimony website.

A third says that he told his parents, but they aren't too happy about it, preferring he get a government job instead.

But these young people are excited and passionate about what they do – the company has raised millions of dollars from venture capitalists, they have over a million users across the country, and they are now the biggest player in the Indian online dating space.

Most exciting are the stories of users that are constantly pouring in.

Take the story of Shilpa, a young woman who worked at IBM. Her parents found her a match on the matrimonial website shaadi.com, and she got engaged. But her fiancé's family wanted a dowry, and they would not relent. Eventually Shilpa put her foot down and decided to call the wedding off. Jaded, she downloaded the app while having a drink with her friends at a bar, and within minutes she swiped right and met the man she would marry six months later.

Another is the story of a Muslim couple, Salem and Alia, who met on the app but are from different communities. He is Shia, and she is Sunni. Initially their parents were dead-set against this inter-caste marriage but, after a year, the young couple finally persuaded their parents, and were wedded a few months later.

Then there is Mira, a PR consultant who found her boyfriend on the app. It turned out that he worked in the same office building as her, just three floors above, but they had never met till they both downloaded the app.

I am not the only one who has harboured warped notions of dating, and one of the first things Truly Madly does is run a campaign to educate people on dating.

#Itsadateif goes viral and, within hours of launching the Twitter campaign, it is trending not just in India, but also in the U.S.

Responses pour in.

Some innocent:

#Itsadateif you both dance like no one's watching, even with your two left feet.

Others not so much:

#Itsadateif she wears a thong, someone writes.

Then, a few days later, Truly Madly launches #Itsnotadateif and this too goes viral.

If she keeps on checking out her Twitter, you're clearly not the top trending topic on her mind! Sorry, bro. #EpicFail

#Itsnotadateif she brings all her friends along.

Offline, Truly Madly hosts block parties in Delhi, Mumbai, Hyderabad, Pune and Chennai: young men and women pour in, shimmying to electronic dance music, drinking beer and looking for people to date.

Perhaps the most well received approach is a TV ad called 'Boy Browsing', which involves young girls choosing boys. Now, while this may sound ordinary – after all, dating applications around the world have more boys than girls – to me, this is utterly refreshing. I spent weeks at marriage bureaus across the country researching my book, and discovered that the power of refusal almost always lies in the hands of the boys. Marriage brokers are flooded with profiles of girls whose parents are desperate to marry them off and are hot in pursuit of marriageable boys. On the dating apps, the balance of power has shifted.

I go into the Truly Madly office one afternoon to speak to the employees, fresh-faced and young. There are more girls than boys – a rare statistic in most Indian offices. I tell them about a depressing piece I have just written about honour killings, in which I recounted the story of a young couple's murder, master-minded by her family because the couple had married out of caste. These atrocities are commonplace in India, and this particular incident took place less than 300 kilometres away from the offices of Truly Madly. I tell these employees that what they are doing is no light-hearted thing, even if their parents or families think otherwise. What they are doing is breaking India's archaic caste laws which marriage has bound for centuries on end.

For India's women, the journey towards personal freedom is a long and arduous one. Yet change is happening – perhaps not at cyber speed, but slowly, one swipe at a time.

S/HE GENERIS: SHAPE-SHIFTING OUR WAY ACROSS THE RIVER OF DESIRE

MARGARET MASCARENHAS

'Identities, identifications and desires cannot be untangled from one another. We become ourselves through others, and the self is a porous thing, not a sealed container.'
– Siri Hustvedt, 'My Father Myself'

Aeroplanes and lace

In the photograph on the dressing table, the man's expression suggests that he is even more excited about opening the Christmas presents than she is, although he is thirty-five, and she is only three. He is slimly debonair in a Noël Coward kind of way, though a shade darker. The blur to the left is her mother, who has not had time to take position in the frame before the camera, set to automatic, clicks.

At this stage, she is still an only child. Her father is from Goa, a former Portuguese colony in India. There is no hard evidence that he would have preferred she be a boy, even though boys are better appreciated in traditional Goan families. But this is not a traditional Goan family, and they are in Ann Arbor, Michigan, U.S.A. Her father met her mother – of French, Dutch and Native American stock – at a Thanksgiving dinner held annually for foreign students at the University of Michigan and decided to stay. He is a part of the Goan diaspora.

The first Christmas present the child opens is from her father – a toy helicopter. She is fascinated by its metallic sheen, its twirling blade. Her father excitedly commandeers the helicopter while she squeals with delight. She reaches greedily for its seductive silver, but her father is not prepared to relinquish control of the toy, saying, 'Wait. Here, let Daddy show you.'

The next present is from her American grandparents, Bess and John. A composite gift wrapped in gigantic boxes containing a child-size kitchen set, replete with pretend stove, pretend refrigerator and assorted pretend Betty Crockerish cooking implements.

The toy refrigerator, which is about three feet high, stored in her attic playroom, is where she hides her father's socks. After stowing the socks – brown, black and grey fruit that will only be discovered by her bewildered mother a month later – she strips off her clothes and dons her white and pink lace Easter hat. Digging into her mother's closet, she finds a pair of lemon satin heels and puts them on, staggering down the stairs, clinging to the railing, but determined. She sits at the foot of the stairs, facing the front door of the small house on Henry Street, waiting for her father to walk through it. This is her routine on most days. Her father is not bothered by the fact that a three-year-old refuses to wear clothes in the house and will strip at the first opportunity, but he doesn't care for little girls in pants.

It is her father, not her mother, who decides on her clothes – pastel fairy-ballerina dresses, patent leather shoes, socks of lace, made by nuns, that tie just above her chubby knees. Her mother thinks children, irrespective of gender, should have pets, climb trees and wear comfortable, sturdy play clothes. No, says her father, she should wear only dresses. In winter, tights and leggings are allowed. (What would a full-grown female helicopter pilot, raised in this manner, wear? she wonders now. Would there be some hidden remnant of childhood? Lace lingerie?)

She is five when she starts kindergarten, with her father's dress rule still in force. It remains in force even when, in first grade, she becomes the fastest runner in her class and all the boys want her on their teams at recess. Through first grade, second, third, even though she has to hold down her dress when she runs, she remains the fastest.

When Christmas rolls around, her father gets her an aeroplane.

She has a crush on her first grade teacher, Mrs Callaway. She has an even bigger crush on Robert Kennedy, whom she watches on the news with her parents. She cries inconsolably when he is killed. Robert Kennedy defines the kind of fine-featured boys she will like when she is in her teens, and the boyish-looking men she will date when she is in her twenties. Hardly unusual, given that her father is Peter Pan. Having Peter Pan as a father is not only is fun but also teaches a girl total self-reliance.

Her twenties' boy crushes will be followed by a penchant for 'manly' men, ten years her senior. At no time will she have the desire to procreate with them, however. As for marriage, she is against it on principle. Only in her forties will she discover that she can also be attracted to women – well, one woman – while simultaneously maintaining a sexual relationship with a man.

Age has a way of androgenising; when she regards her father as an old man, parchment skin stretched across fine facial bone, he almost looks like a woman.

I was raised by storytelling lit-witches

I am mildly dyslexic and also ambidextrous. I've been known to take up to ten minutes to figure out the difference between words such as 'tree' and 'moon'. Without looking at the yellow diamond ring on my left hand (an inheritance from my Indian grandfather and the only piece of real jewellery I ever wear), I can't tell right from left. It does not surprise me that I might be predisposed to the scrambling of gender eggs. Though I am biologically female and identify as such, I continue to question what it means to be female.

The role of my parents in my development becomes hazy in my memory beyond secondary school; they are, for the most part, cameos. My thinking on sexuality and gender roles evolved predominantly through reading pioneering, and often gender-bending, literary witches. Alcott, Woolf, the Brontës, Plath, Elliot, Sand, Shelley, Wollstonecraft, Hurston, Le Guin, Atwood, de Beauvoir, and so on. In my case, reading literature appears to have trumped my environment, long before intellectual knowledge was transformed by experience and feeling, long before I read any comprehensive gender studies that made it clear that while sexuality was only one aspect of gender fluidity, gender was an endlessly evolving and complex subject.

Beginning with my time as a student of comparative literature at Berkeley, several of Alice Walker's novels and essays had a most profound effect on me, compelling me to question what it means to be a woman, as well as the political rigidity and militancy of the word 'feminist' and its appropriation by privileged white women. The militant aspect of 1980s feminism was first brought home to me in junior college, when anyone wearing heels and lipstick was made to feel unwelcome at the campus Women's Lounge by the white lesbians in hiking boots who had staked a claim. I responded by staging a coup with daily sit-ins, with women who dressed as they pleased and slept with boys and men.

In my late twenties, I moved to India. I fell in love for a time with a male motorcycle-driving Bombay poet. That fizzled out when I met a charming Lebanese businessman on a trip to Dubai, an affair that overlapped with another: with a New York–based Yugoslavian art dealer, considerably older than I, whom I always suspected of being a spy. I had always had, and continued to have, intense crushes on the brains of assorted women, but no desire for sleepovers. My Indian grandmother repeatedly tried to fix me up with assorted 'nice Goan boys from good backgrounds', but not too hard; I believe that she secretly applauded my independence.

I was already in my thirties and contemplating writing my first novel in what was still known as Bombay, when I came across Jeanette Winterson's novel *Written on the Body*, in which the narrator is genderless, and Githa Hariharan's novel *The Thousand Faces of Night*, in which the retelling of Hindu myths about women from a feminist perspective serves as a subversive survival tactic. These novels, among others, propelled me towards an exploration of gender identity and gender roles, though it was still theoretical for me at the time, and was confined mostly to the relevance of gender to writing and writers.

During this period, I read with fascination studies that differentiated between sexual orientation identity and gender identity, but none of this found clear articulation in my writing. It would be another decade before theoretical began to merge with personal; this, too, in India. India, home of the most ancient sculptures of Hindu and Jain temples, where a veritable orgy of inter-loving between male and female is depicted in all its erotic splendour. India, where it has become cool for elite viewers of English-language television to watch *Orange Is the New Black*, the Emmy Award–winning series in which many of the characters, and some of the actors, are sexually fluid, and which also stars Australian gender-bender Ruby Rose. India, where I have more openly gay and gender-nonconforming friends than I ever had in the U.S. India, which has been extraordinarily progressive in legalising transgender as a third gender, but which continues to uphold laws built from colonial Victorian prudishness, laws asserting, among other incongruities, that the missionary position should be the only legally sanctioned sexual position. India, where a disturbingly rigid

Hindu conservatism, with its narrow interpretations, is on the rise, in dissonance with the Hindu pantheon's open experimentation with gender and other binaries, as described in Vedic and Puranic literature and as depicted on the walls of Khajuraho.

It is in India, country of my paternal bloodline, where I live, and where I have come to espouse the notion that gender can be fluid, that at any point in a life one could fall in love with a person, irrespective of gender, that it is possible for an individual to be simultaneously sexually oriented one way, gender oriented another way, and romantically inclined in multiple ways, and that these orientations can remain in flux.

In one of the Drexler interviews available on YouTube, Camille Paglia, self-proclaimed reigning public intellectual, and author of *Sexual Personae*, who identifies as lesbian, deplores what she considers the gender smorgasbord in open societies today, referring to it as a kind of debauchery. To me, this position is representative of another kind of straitjacket: a gender phobia of another kind. Many people make the mistake of assuming that being homosexual goes hand in hand with being progressive or liberal, but this is not the case; our sexual proclivities do not necessarily define our politics in the mainstream. In fact, some of the most politically conservative and rigid people I know identify as gay.

Personally, I applaud the explosion of gender diversity that we see today in all its Ruby Rosean glory, and view its acknowledgement as an evolutionary imperative. My bedmate of choice these days is *The Argonauts* by the extraordinary Maggie Nelson, an astonishing memoir of her life and partnership with transgender artist Harry Dodge, with table-turningly fresh thinking on gender, love and desire. I am also intrigued by the original, edgy, binary and taboo-breaking work of Indian artist Tejal Shah, who is based in Goa and self-describes as 'feminist, queer and political'. But what I hold true today – that gender and sexuality are too complex to pin down, much less legislate, that they can and do cross cultures and geographies, and might morph at any moment – is a radical departure from the ideas and ideologies I internalised while growing up.

Gender pride and prejudice as a transnational phenomenon

In 1966 my Indian grandfather became very unwell, and was suspected of having stomach cancer. We flew from the U.S. to Goa. It turned out to be a peptic ulcer and he recovered, but we continued to visit Goa nearly every year thereafter. In 1974 my parents divorced. My Goan family openly and vocally commiserated with my father, reinforcing patriarchal notions in my psyche about male/female roles. I would say that, during my formative years, I was programmed not to question my father's authoritarian way of doing things. Even for many years after, I embraced my Goan family's view of my mother as the problematic parent, bad wife, bad mother – a view that saw her only in relation to my father, rather than as a person with her own identity.

Besides female bias, gay bias (especially against boys and men by straight boys and men) was full blown in my Goan family during my formative years. Effeminate behaviour in men was a subject of derision and a trigger for verbal abuse. Similarly, women who did not outwardly represent the cultural norms of 'femininity' were frowned upon. Women who did not meet cultural standards of beauty were criticised. Bitchy women just needed to get laid. Men were the designated drivers and breadwinners and, most significantly, men controlled property. Four hundred and fifty years of Portuguese rule likely infused Goan culture with its own version of machismo.

In the late seventies, at an official dinner for Mother Teresa, while talking animatedly to my father, a wispy Indian diplomat kept placing his hand on my father's knee. Touching while talking is not unusual among Indian men. My father did not attribute it to anything out of the ordinary, certainly not anything sexual. However, his considerably younger and more savvy brother did. He went up to my father and whispered to him in Konkani – Goa's mother tongue and a language the diplomat, being from North India, was unlikely to understand. My father suddenly looked disgusted. 'Let's go,' he said. And we did. Later, I asked my uncle what he had said to my father at the dinner. 'Heh,' my uncle laughed, 'I told him the man with a hand on his knee was *bonk an so munis.*' An arse man.

Only one time did I myself express gender bias in a way that shocked and shamed me. I was in my thirties, visiting the U.S. from India, and planning to spend a few days with the retired principal of one of my primary schools. She informed me that her daughter Sarah would be picking me up at the airport. 'By the way,' she said, 'Sarah is now Steve.'

'Sex change?' I asked, impressed with my own ability to process this news without missing a beat.

'Yes,' she said, 'but in transition. Don't worry, you'll recognise him.'

Although I was perfectly fine with the *idea* of Sarah becoming Steve, this would be the first person I had known as a woman actually in the process of migration to physical manhood. On the flight from New York to Miami I became inexplicably anxious. Upon arrival, when Steve, a more manly version of Sarah, approached me, smiling, I became confused. Should I hug? Kiss? Shake hands? I settled for a kind of patting on the shoulder. 'Excuse me,' I said, 'would you know where the ladies' room is?' Steve pointed, laughing too jovially. I almost ran to it, bursting into a stall, and promptly threw up.

Disturbed by my incapacity to reconcile my progressive gender politics with the visceral reactions of my body, I willed myself to behave in a way that was consonant with my belief system. By the time I left I was able to hold extended conversations with Steve on new literature without stammering or blushing. But I never asked him about the transition, which surely he would have expected and appreciated from a friend. And, for a long while afterwards, I continued to have ambivalent, uneasy feelings about the encounter, and avoided reconnecting. If I knew where Steve was now, I would apologise profusely for my lunatic behaviour.

In contrast, I've had no problem with male friends or acquaintances transitioning to female. With them my mind and body have stayed in harmony. I myself have always floated between girlishness and tomboyishness, but I've never wanted to be a boy. The idea of losing or changing any of my female body parts is repugnant to me. Perhaps this has something to do with my reaction to Sarah/Steve.

For about twenty years now I have managed my father's inherited estate in Goa – much to the disapproval of many male members of my father's land-rich family. In the tourist brochures Goa has often been presented as a hedonistic paradise. But that is a different Goa. Goans are a fairly conservative lot, including many members of my family. To them, though I spent nearly every summer holiday in Goa, I am somewhat of an alien, my 'otherness' excused because I am (a) a hybrid and (b) an artist and writer. They have rationalised me as 'eccentric'. I have survived with some felicity on this eccentricity clause. Family members on my father's side who never left Goa to study or work continue to have a narrow and, in some cases, downright feudal outlook on caste and race, to say nothing of gender. But I seem to have missed the memo about genitalia playing a part in one's ability to be a better estate manager. Perhaps I owe this fortuitous lapse to my interest in my Hindu ancestry and my understanding of duality in Hindu mythology.

Musings on shape-shifting in Hindu mythology

Four hundred and fifty years of Portuguese rule could not entirely erase the strong influence of Hinduism, to which the Roman Catholic Church and the Portuguese eventually relented, allowing even

174

converted Hindu Brahmins to retain their caste identities, which is why those Goan Brahmins who converted from Hinduism centuries ago can trace their Hindu ancestry and the temples to which they belong. My own ancestral temples, which I make a point to visit from time to time out of pure fascination, are dedicated to Mangueshi – an incarnation of Shiva, a gender-bending deity – on my grandmother's side, and to Shantadurga – the peacemaking avatar of Durga, but still a superpower – on my grandfather's side. The Mangueshi temple also contains a subsidiary shrine to the androgenous Lakshminarayana.

Hinduism has had centuries of foreplay with the notion of transgenderism and female agency, going by their frequent appearances in Vedic and Puranic literature. The impetus towards gender-bending among the deities most often manifests in men desiring to use female power in some manner, rather than the other way around. However, frequent morphing of deities, or their merging into one entity encompassing both male and female principles, tends to be far less about sexuality or desire than about expedience, the balancing of scales and the resolving of conflicts.

Books 5 and 6 of the *Adi Parva* in *The Mahabharata* contain the story of Amba. Here is a summary: Princess Amba is abducted by the celibate warrior Bhishma as a war trophy, but he later returns her to her betrothed, Shalva. In most versions, Shalva rejects her out of a petty sense of pride, and she returns to Bhishma demanding that he correct the wrong done to her by marrying her. When he refuses, she performs intense penance for many years until the god Shiva promises she will be reborn as male so she can exact her revenge. Then Amba commits suicide by throwing herself into a fire. Shiva's promise takes a detour: instead of being directly reborn as a boy, she is reborn as a girl with the name Shikandhini, but raised as a boy known as Shikandhi. She is later unmasked as a woman when her father marries her off to another woman (surprise!). Publicly shamed, she goes into exile in the forest where she meets a forest deity, Stunakarna, who offers to exchange genders with her so that she may have her revenge on Bhishma, who claims he would never fight a woman. Shikandhi, now endowed with the all-powerful penis, becomes the warrior Arjuna's charioteer in the battle of Kurukshetra. As the chariot approaches Bhishma, Arjuna hides behind Shikandhi. Bhishma recognises Shikandhi as the reincarnated Amba and lowers his weapons. Arjuna then slays him with a volley of arrows. Shikandhi has his/her revenge but is also killed in battle. Case closed.

In another story Arjuna himself is cursed by Urvashi to become a hijra, or person of the third sex, for a year. Arjuna makes the best of it: '... wearing brilliant rings on my ears and conch bangles on my wrists and causing a braid to hand down from my head, I shall appear as one of the third sex, Vrihannala by name'[1]. Vishnu assumes the form of the enchantress Mohini in order to trick the Asuras into returning the elixir of immortality. The Lord Shiva falls madly in love and lust with Mohini, and, in several versions of the story, he impregnates her during some violent coupling, resulting in a son, Ayyappa.

Evidently, there is a great deal of both awe and ambivalence connected with female power in Hindu mythology – a blurring that often enough manifests in contemporary Indian culture on many levels, one of them being degrees of transgenderism.

A man with whom I have long shared a largely platonic relationship is named Devi (goddess). He identifies as a heterosexual male, and claims to experience revulsion at the idea of gay sex, though he has no problem interacting socially with gay or trans people. Yet his persona carries many so feminine qualities that I completely forget he is a man when sharing confidences. Many of his married women friends also see in him a confidant, and some might even be a little smitten by his boyish looks, yet none of the husbands experience this

---

1. Book 5 of *The Mahabharata*

friendship with their wives as a threat. One of them told me that even though he, Devi, is a heterosexual male, he is not 'that kind'.

When a woman loves a woman

Some years ago, while researching a paper examining the contemporary contributions of women in creative fields to gender politics, I watched two independent Charlie Rose interviews – one with the late Susan Sontag (considered first an icon and later an arch rival by Paglia) and the other with her partner, Annie Leibovitz, after Sontag's death. From them, I derived a sense of partnership where the whole was greater than the sum of its parts, which I would consider the entire point of life partnership, irrespective of gender. I had to rely on this sense when, in my mid-forties I found myself not only in love with, but sexually attracted to, and in bed with, a woman artist. A straight woman. Two women who think of themselves as straight are possibly at a disadvantage – we had nothing to compare our experience to on the female spectrum – we had to figure it out.

About time, said my bisexual friend Deepika, you've both been missing half the population in the dipping well.

Mohini's painting work, influenced by the abstract action painters, notably Franz Kline, manifested a muscular masculinity and, since she never signed her canvases, viewers in galleries usually assumed the works were by a man. It was this very forceful quality of her art that was attractive, but also other gender-related incongruities of the painter herself, whom she met when she purchased a painting. Mohini's abundant hair was bound in an enormous bun held together by a hairclip fitted with massive cloth flowers. She wore tight-fitting jeans, a kurta and closed, boot-like shoes – unusual footwear for tropical Goa. Her facial features were fine and feminine, her voice husky. She spoke in an oddly sophisticated, yet antiquated language. The overall effect: a hot, but slightly dikey librarian type. They met a few times after that for coffee or a meal. They discussed painting, ideas, books. They discovered they had almost identical bookshelves. They talked for hours on the phone; it was mostly Mohini who initiated the calls.

She was surprised when she discovered Mohini's high level of dependency on the men in her life: her father, her husband, a lover in a political power position, a youngish man with an obvious mother complex. Mohini had never balanced her own chequebook. Her husband, with whom she hadn't shared a sexual relationship in decades, travelled extensively on business, and during one of those trips Mohini asked her new woman friend to spend the night. They talked late, well beyond the witching hour. Finally, they fell asleep in the same room on separate mattresses which they had spread on the floor. Early in the morning Mohini reached out, kissed her hands, and said, 'I've never met anyone like you. May I touch you?' It was not the first time a woman had asked, but it was the first time she had said yes. And she continued to say yes for a year.

During that period, slowly, without her being fully conscious of it, she began to take over the roles of the men in Mohini's life: protector, interlocutor, financial and legal manager. Six months into the relationship, Mohini began a process of triangulation, flirting at random with men or women whenever they went out. If she objected, Mohini, smiling, would tell her she was imagining it, and display an affection that seemed confusingly out of sync with her earlier detachment.

About a year into the relationship she stood in Mohini's bedroom. She was naked before the full-length mirror, silently examining her body, still moist, glistening from the shower, her face flushed, made younger and vulnerable from being in love. This is what happens to women, no matter whom they are with, she thought: we see ourselves through the eyes of the patriarchs. We still seek outside approval, wondering, do I look good enough?

On cue, Mohini, who was watching her, said, 'Baby, you have a perfect body.' As if seeing it for the first time. Mohini had never commented on her physical attributes before, other than to say 'You look lovely' when they dressed to go out together.

Her stomach clenched as she saw Mohini's face turn sullen, forecasting a storm ahead.

That night began with a mechanical circular licking of her eyelids, which she found slightly unpleasant. It was not that she didn't know the words to tell Mohini that this wasn't doing it for her. It was that the words were caught in her throat, stuck in limbo between not wanting to upset the feelings of her female friend/lover and what she would surely have demanded from a man. But she also realised she didn't care that much. It was enough for her to feel Mohini's breath and fingers on her to experience pleasure and joy. She did not feel the need to compare, to wonder whether they were 'doing it' right. Besides, they had both agreed that Mohini would stay with her husband, and that they would not abandon their existing male lovers, so man love was always an available option for both. Meanwhile, Mohini insisted that they keep their relationship hidden. People can be cruel, Mohini said. Yes, she agreed, they can.

In the morning Mohini came into the TV room, where she was watching an art film, handed her a breakfast plate of eggs and toast, and said, 'I don't want to sleep with you anymore. It's not working for me, this intimacy.'

She stared at Mohini incredulously. 'But you are still responding to me sexually,' she said.

'That's just the proximity,' Mohini said.

She: 'Can't we discuss it?'

'It's not working for me,' Mohini kept repeating, like John Malkovich in Dangerous Liaisons, *telling Michelle Pfeiffer, over and over, It's beyond my control.*

The levelling of the gender playing field: just as with the end of any other love affair, when the beloved withdraws love, the world is shattered for the one rejected. Mohini admitted that, aside from being polyamorous, she had never been able to sustain any sexual or even any intensely emotional relationship for more than a year. Which would have been a good thing to know before the fact, she observed in retrospect.

She left Goa for Europe, and it fell to her long-time, long-distance male lover and her oldest friends to pick up the pieces. It took a long time to put herself back together. She does not know what this means in terms of her future with women as sexual partners. Other than the seemingly higher voltage and intensity of women's relationships, both as friends and as lovers, she doesn't believe that gender played a starring role in the dissolution. It was a bad breakup, resulting from the end of desire, like many others. Quite ordinary in retrospect. You think you won't get over it but, mostly, people do.

These days, she regards Mohini with an extra dose of fondness. They have discussed a potential committed relationship that would involve owning a property together with separate houses. They both agree that sex is not a necessary component of commitment, or of love. It is clear to them that a person to whom they might be sexually attracted might not necessarily be the best life partner. They both continue to have male lovers and to love each other, but in a different way. Occasionally they still sleep together, their arms and legs entwined: intimacy without desire. She no longer experiences any degree of sexual attraction and cannot even imagine a sexual relationship with Mohini now; whatever transpired earlier feels unreal. It is as though she has crossed a river as one animal and returned as another.

Who knows how this mythology will end?

'My love is the color of seashells
The shape of an egg
Try not to confuse it with breakfast'
– *Triage: Casualties of Love and Sex*, Margaret Mascarenhas

Note: some names have been changed in the interest of privacy.

KARAIKAL AMMAIYAR AND HER CLOSET OF ADORNMENTS

SHARANYA MANIVANNAN

Shortly after I first moved to Chennai from Malaysia, in late 2007, I attended a job interview wearing a knee-length skirt. Some months later, I found out from one of my colleagues that a rumour had been spread that I had said during the interview, 'I like to dress provocatively. I hope that won't be a problem.'

This incident was what first informed my functional professional aesthetic. Along the way, there were more: everything from roving eyes, which were better teeth-grittingly ignored than called out at risk, to overtures and statements that were outright sexual harassment, to other women who found it prudent to send me text messages letting me know my bra strap had been visible. Constant scrutiny is the wrong kind of attention, and I learned that I could deflect it by being neither pleasing nor provocative.

I call this aesthetic, with its slight edge of unkemptness, my Karaikal Ammaiyar approach. Karaikal Ammaiyar was a sixth-century mystic who asked for a boon that her lovely young self be transformed into a wraith so that her time could be dedicated to her vocation, undisturbed. In a male-dominated industry, in a conservative city, for any woman who needs to earn her living, she is a viable fashion icon. In order to be taken seriously, in order to be left alone, in order to be perceived as neither desirable nor desirous, I twist my uncombed hair into a bun and leave my face bare and bespectacled, throw a loose tunic over pants and slip into pre-distressed chappals. Make no mistake about it: it is a cultivated look. It is a form of armour.

◆ ◆ ◆

Vanity is at once discouraged and encouraged in women. Among the conflicting social messages we receive, we are told that to care too much about one's appearance denotes shallowness of character or lack of intellectual gravitas, but that to not appear pleasing is to be lacking in social graces or emotional stability. There are women who seem to be smitten by trends; there are women who establish a more individualistic style; there are women who seem to have no clear taste; there are women who frankly seem to not have an aesthetic sense – and each of them is perceived and pegged in a different way. Our wardrobes speak volumes for us. In the long history of female silencing, the wardrobe was an instrument long before the pen, which did not find its way into the majority of our hands until rather recent centuries. Little tells us more about the power of this instrument than the moral and cultural policing of women's attire.

'Pleasing' – denoting acceptable attention that puts other people at ease. In India, a sari in most contexts is 'pleasing'. It speaks of the woman's urge to please, to appear serious, shy, subordinate, unchalleng-ing. So why then did I find myself lodging a complaint at a Chennai hotel a few years ago because the management had assumed I was soliciting, based entirely on the fact that I had been sitting alone in the lobby in a sari? I had been waiting for my friends for a night of partying. The sari in that context was not pleasing. It was subversive. The undertone was this: women who go clubbing don't wear saris when they do because doing so would be to insult the garment and corrupt its inherent morality by bringing it into an immoral sphere. Their lifestyles were acceptable so long as they were compartmentalised. To not compartmentalise – to confuse the decorum of the sari with the abandon of the pub – was to be profoundly lacking in morality, i.e. a whore.

◆ ◆ ◆

When I moved to Chennai at the end of 2007, I left behind (in Kuala Lumpur) almost everything that I owned. Any such statement carries with it an undercurrent of tragedy. This is true – I moved to India under tragic circumstances, replete with personal losses, traduced by a brush with political dissidence. But when I think of the other leavers I know and the things they have left behind – photographs, title deeds, beloveds buried in cordoned soil – I feel guilty. How much can a person own, by way of material possessions, at age twenty-two? In my case it was mostly this: clothes, jewellery, shoes, bags and more clothes, clothes, clothes. These were what I left behind. They do not tell the story of all that I lost, but in their deceptive frivolity, they do harbour its most poignant parts.

I had gone from politically curious to politicised during my last few years in Malaysia. I had grown up there – and lived there roughly from the age of five to twenty-two, excluding a furlough of several months in my late teens when I made my first attempt to live in India (and failed, fortunate to be able to then go back to Kuala Lumpur). The short version of events is this: my student life over, I was living on a tourist visa in the country that was my home, and, unable to take the stress of having to border-run to Singapore to renew it once a month, I had come to India (the country of my citizenship), thinking I would lay low, find a permanent way back 'home', and return. But this was at the end of 2007, when the Hindu Rights Action Force was protesting the illegal demolition of temples in Malaysia. The mainstream Malaysian press was not reporting these incidents; I had been maintaining a blog on which I collected information about this very issue for two years, and was contacted by the Indian media about it. I wrote an editorial during this time about race and race-based policies in Malaysia (specifically, that any nation that operated on a system of racial supremacy and inferiority was under apartheid), which caught the attention of its government, to my immediate personal detriment. This is why I left my things there – I had not expected that I would never go back. Malaysia closed its doors to me. I stayed on in India because there was simply nowhere else to go.

◆ ◆ ◆

I no longer live in the Chennai I moved to in 2007. That city was one in which wearing jeans or sleeveless tops was considered provocative, low-rise panties did not exist to be purchased anywhere, and if one were to ask for the top with spaghetti straps from the mannequin, the sales assistant would openly tell all her colleagues, who would join her in gawking at you. These were not isolated incidents. The city shamed me into hiding my body, and, by extension, hiding my heart. The clothing-based moral shaming I experienced came from strangers and acquaintances alike. The whisper of a young man walking by me on the sidewalk: 'Why is it you don't want to wear decent clothes?' The request from a lecturer that I, clad in jeans, not sit on a stoop outside a women's college in case passers-by mistook me for one of their students. The way a former friend pointedly remarked, as I sat beside her combing my hair in an auto-rickshaw, that she had heard it said that 'only prostitutes groom their hair in public'. The subtexts may have been varied, but the cumulative effect of the shaming was the same, and so was the message: peacocks are weighted by their own plumages. Discard it or be discarded.

In 2015, none of the above applies any longer. This city, *this* Chennai, has a far greater aesthetic tolerance and diversity than could have been imagined possible. More and more, we have begun to see it: hints of skin, bright colours on the face, so many titivations that could only be dismissed as 'shallow' by someone who has never been denied the pleasure of the self-expression they provide. If a red lipstick is wonderful anywhere in the world, it is most wonderful of all on the mouth of a woman who has claimed her own voice.

Two factors influenced this change, which feels sudden, not gradual. The first was economic liberalisation. Literally speaking, once the mall culture came to the city, exposure to variety created demand for it, which in turn created a demand for tolerance. The city was forced to adapt to women's desires to look as they wanted to, not vice versa. The process is incomplete: we still play out inherited norms and expectations, some of which appear under the guise of choices, and as we do so we also play into the broader negative effects of style-consciousness, including mental and physical health-related issues, such as body dysphoria and anorexia. The second, very interesting, element that led to this change was the rise of e-commerce. Internet shopping made everything more affordable and accessible, thus diversifying our tastes, our options and what was available to us. Now we can shop without having to negotiate moral policing, body shaming or other forms of coercion.

And yet, just a month or so before I wrote this, the front cover of a popular Tamil magazine featured what its editors thought to be a great social blight: women wearing tight leggings. As many outraged people pointed out on social media, the women in the photographs were considered obscene, but not the photographer who waited for the moment the wind might flip their tunics up to reveal the shape of their bottoms.

So, still, we carry shawls to cover ourselves with when we come home late at night, because we know: the city has changed only her visage. Her nature, however, is not so easily pegged.

◆ ◆ ◆

As I write this, I am thirty years old and single. Not single suddenly or single incidentally, but single in a sustained way, the way of a person who because of committing to integrity to self, art and world simply did not commit to a mistake. You understand what I mean, though: by saying this, I have chosen to present the trajectory of my life so far in a dignified manner, shorn of its heartbreaks. One can be glad not to have committed *to* a mistake. That does not mean one hasn't made many.

Women everywhere are socialised to dress for their beholders: partners, prospective partners, the judgemental eyes of society, the critical gazes of in-laws. In India, marriage brings with it certain aesthetic requirements and rewards. These vary from community to community, but a married woman may wear some or many of these: nuptial chain, nuptial toe-rings, nose ornament, prominent bindi, wedding ring, vermilion in the parting of her hair. All of them are signifiers: she has been accepted into another household. She has been accepted. To not marry, or to no longer be married, is to be excluded in ways both subtle and obvious.

When a woman is widowed – and again this varies from community to community – she may have her bangles broken, her nuptial chain removed, her head shaved, her wardrobe changed to one of pure white, her forehead and the parting of her hair rubbed clean of vermilion.

So who does a woman dress up for when the elegant partition of marriage has not dropped its opaque curtain somewhere in her twenties? 'For myself' is a dishonest answer. I dress up so I can represent my art – which itself is a response to being a woman in my time and place, and the causatum of my choices and circumstances – and I dress up so that I do not shame it. I dress up so I can engage with the world and command attention. I dress up for the compliments. I dress up in order to feel sensuality, and in doing so to transmit it, to attract its natural corollary. 'For myself'? If not outrightly dishonest, that answer is at best inadequate.

In my mid-twenties, swollen with sad love, I bought my own *metti* – matrimonial toe-rings that are a part of the Hindu wedding ceremony, slipped onto a woman's second toes by her husband. I bought them for beauty, but I also bought them for symbolism. I was married to my art, and I meant it. My nose has been pierced since I was fourteen years old, and I currently wear a large bespoke piece of ruby, zircon and gold, considered old-fashioned and highly unusual in my generation. I made the large red bindi a part of my look sometime in my teens, and my spiritual journey eventually led to my replacing the sticker variety with holy vermilion. I look, in short, like 'a married Tamil Hindu woman'. It is not, for me, an aspirational look.

I removed my *metti* a year ago. Someone told me that I was sending out the wrong signal. Not morally or socially but emotionally. The toe-rings, too, were armour. I listened. On some days, I miss their weight. I have nothing against wearing them, or anything else, when I am moved to.

But most of all, I dress up for my friends. My friends are my significant others, and for them I conduct all the rituals that we are socialised to think belong only to the sphere of dating. For my friend who thinks my rose and cardamom perfume smells like chewed betel nut, I wear the vanilla one. For my friend who visits once a year from afar, I wear my long hair in a braid. For my fiercely intelligent friend with whom I write, who wears dresses every day, I shave my legs. Let me paint a picture: two women in sundresses in a garden cafe, earphones in, pounding away at keyboards, stopping for cake and conversation.

Romance is ambient. Night rain is romantic. Music in languages one doesn't know is romantic. Religious talismans – that kind of devotion known as *bhakti* – are romantic. Romance is a woman who spritzes her wrists with something that gives her pleasure before she sits down at her desk to write a poem about the way long loneliness caramelises the way one sees the world. You will not be surprised to know that I frequently buy myself flowers.

◆ ◆ ◆

With one of my closest friends, however, I do not usually make a conscious effort at embellishment. This is an act of solidarity. My friend is a transwoman who is out to a few people, but who, for professional and familial reasons, maintains two visages. Most of the time, she wears unisex kurtas and nothing but a touch of lip balm. Some of the time, and seldom in public, she is in skirts and lipstick, her recently pierced earlobes sparkling with baubles.

To compare the pain of her subterfuge with the daily battles ciswomen wage with regards to their appearances is to trivialise the former. And yet, there is solidarity. There is deep empathy – I, who was taken out of my skirts and not yet allowed into my jeans, *know* her, she who makes bespoke shoes in 'men's' sizes that she does not wear and has a Pinterest board full of desires.

Transwomen occupy interesting spaces in India, culturally accepted yet socially unwelcome. Traditionally, transwomen as a community have some measure of societal legitimacy, and were ascribed roles and professions including blessing newborns and dancing at weddings.

This means that, in groups, they may be able to roam freely in public spaces such as streets or beaches dressed in saris and other normatively feminine ornaments, but, with the exception of a few transgendered people who enjoy celebrity status, I have never seen a transwoman in her wardrobe of choice in a restaurant. Class divisions also remain rigid, and elite and middle-class spaces remain unfriendly. Every time we meet, my transwoman friend – cross-dressing as a man – suffers the indignity of being called 'sir' by strangers.

◆ ◆ ◆

A woman can wear a war for a very long time.

◆ ◆ ◆

I could never forget my Indianness while living in Malaysia, and so I not only embraced it but made it an act of defiance against the state-sanctioned and socially enforced racism. How I did this was, among other ways, through my appearance: this was when I began to wear the sari to readings and public events. I wore tube tops as blouses under them sometimes, and enormous spools of jasmine around my chignon at other times. Sexy, traditional – I don't even know the difference, although I am made mischievous by the knowledge that other people think they do. Even after I moved to India, when the sari should have bored me, I didn't stop. The sari does things for me that no other outfit can. When I was commissioned to perform at Westminster Abbey in front of an audience that included the British Royal Family for the 2015 Commonwealth Day Observance, my friends and family asked me – what will you wear? For me, it was never a question.

I stood there on the Sacrarium Steps, the site of a thousand years of coronations, as a brown woman in the twenty-first century, a happenstance of empire. And I did so in a soft chiffon sari in a deep red, with a brocade border of black and gold. The colours and ciphers of *Shakti*, the divine feminine principle, herself.

When I wear a sari, it is never just culturally quaint. It is with awareness and aliveness. It is a powerful garment and, like all power, one must wield it with grace or not at all.

♦ ♦ ♦

The memory of the things I left behind when I moved to India haunted me for several years. I had not been wealthy, but I had great taste and, more than that, great luck. In Tamil there is a word, *kairaasi*, that captures it. It means that I could source amazing deals with the talent of a water diviner. Most of what I owned cost no more than ten ringgit each, but all of it was beautiful. All of it I wore. I thrived in that beautiful wardrobe of mine. There was one semester in college when I was told that a small group of girls would wait by the gate to check out my outfit for the day. I was wild, vivacious, sensual – I was cowboy hats and jacquard jackets and thigh-high leopard-print boots. I was bohemian paisley and chunky necklaces and cascades of filigree, tassels and fishtail hems.

And then, for a long time, I couldn't be.

In my first few years in the city, I maintained a collection of clothing that I joked were for 'eventual migration'. I would buy things that I knew I could never safely wear in Chennai – not just because they were pretty things, but because my body longed for them, even if there was a paucity of safe spaces or reasons to wear them. What happens between a woman and a dress can be sheer choreography. We dismiss that desire too easily as vanity. Vanity that is a cardinal sin, linked to narcissism, superficiality, the inability to connect to others. But who's to say that it's all about attention or other people? Who's to say it isn't about, in fact, intangible things: the fabric of life, literal and otherwise? It's the necklace one buys for oneself on the day of an old love's wedding. It's the satin slip one sleeps in alone. It's what happens behind my transwoman friend's locked door when only the mirror is her audience, her admirer, her witness.

So I would buy these beautiful things, and simply keep them safe. For the first time in my life, I wore pants every single day. Even a long skirt would register femininity, a dangerous thing. I wore ill-fitting *kurtas* half on purpose and half out of shame, that emotion that was the sum effect of both lascivious gazes and moral reprimand-ing. I didn't have a choice: I didn't know the city, didn't understand its codes, belonged to no cliques. So, each day, as I caught auto-rickshaws and walked down busy streets and conversed with strangers and col-leagues and attempted to make friends, I donned this shamed and shabby skin with all the effort of a person learning a new dialect. Not coincidentally perhaps, I was also doing this literally – trying to scrape the sweet native patois from my tongue in exchange for the Madras *bashai* that would allow me to negotiate the city with a little less difficulty. I closeted my true self, with all her many accoutrements, in order to be safer. Until – strangely – I became safe.

♦ ♦ ♦

Fashion is about far more than vanity, or morality for that matter. It is about identity, memory and emotion. It is a background score to every interaction, conveying ambience, setting the scene, foreshadow-ing, foregrounding. Every mood-lifting ensemble is a victory. Every garment touched longingly and placed wistfully back on the shelf is a compromise – resignation that sometimes means 'not yet' and sometimes means 'never'.

I don't know how else to put it, but at some point, either the city became safe enough or I became strong enough. I stopped thinking twice about whether a sleeveless tunic would be read as a comment on my sexual availability. I paired saris with spaghetti-strap blouses and tube tops to formal events. I wore a miniskirt to a poetry reading once and posed cheekily in front of a jackfruit tree in the courtyard and learned to enjoy – and not be shamed by – some people's reactions.

Half Karaikal Ammaiyar, half cynosure.

♦ ♦ ♦

In astrology, there is the concept of the rising sign (known in the Vedic system as the *lagna*), the zodiac sign in which one's ascendant – the division between the recondite twelfth house and the public first house of one's chart – falls. The ascendant is thus liminal, the point at which the inner self is presented to the outer world. In simplest terms, the ascendant is one's appearance – the first thing another person encounters as they form their impression of you. There's no way around it, not even in metaphysical terms – one's visage is one's calling card, one's conduit, one's key.

♦ ♦ ♦

The truth is that even if I retrieved the wardrobe I left behind, I would no longer be able to fit into most of it. The body changes. Only one's nature is a constant, through vagaries of influence, catalogues of choices, seasons of taste.

The wardrobe, you understand, was only ever a metaphor.

CAST AWAY

TISCA CHOPRA

'Life is a play that does not allow testing. So sing, cry, dance, laugh and live intensely, before the curtain closes and the piece ends with no applause.' – Charlie Chaplin

I landed my first acting role at the age of two. By default. At the boarding school where my parents taught, they had no one that young to play the baby Lord Krishna. So I was cast. All I had to do was walk across the stage looking cute in a loose white *chaddi-baniyaan*. I walked to the centre of the stage, stopped at the footlights, gazed happily at the audience and refused to budge. The girl playing Yashodhara had to be sent to fetch me. I was carried off the stage, literally kicking and screaming.

My parents should have known then.

♦ ♦ ♦

The first reason I became an actor was that my mother didn't give me a sibling in time. We lived in Kabul, Afghanistan, and on snowy winter evenings my parents would go out for Embassy parties. I was left to my own devices. Second-hand fairytale books from the American thrift shop, with stunning illustrations on glossy pages, and All India Radio ki Urdu Service became my dearest friends. I would read and act out the songs on the radio to our Afghan maids. They loved Hindi films more than any Indian ever could. Dressed in my mother's curlers and brand new Fab India bedcovers, I would do my own interpretation of '*Bhool gaya sab kuch*' on the kitchen table. If I fussed about eating my supper, the maids would give me a pinch of *naswar*, a version of marijuana popular in the mountains. That made the food go down *a lot* faster – and then we could all get down to the real business of song and story. We were a happy lot indeed.

My brother came along when I was six. By that time, I was addicted to acting out stories with music. He was a ready audience – and also a very malleable one. I would act out half a story and, for what came post-interval, he had to cover my notebooks for me. Or clean my study table. In one morbid phase, I remember telling him the saddest tales of separation and pain. Weeping copiously, he would follow me around, sobbing for the second half. I discovered that in this state I could get him to do pretty much anything that I wanted. When my parents caught on, I was forbidden from telling him any more stories. I don't know who was more upset – my brother or me.

The second reason I became an actor was my deep loathing for mathematics.

I was a school principal's daughter. My father, also my maths teacher, was famous not just in his school but across campuses for his adherence to discipline. There was huge pressure on me to succeed academically. In fact it was just 'not okay' to *not* stand first. What possible reason could there be for *that*? The rest of the subjects were well under my control, but maths gave me a high fever that went away the second the maths exam was over. My fever became a regular feature, yet I had to find a way to shine and be worthy of being 'principal sir's daughter'.

Extracurricular activities were encouraged, but only by way of building a 'well-rounded personality' that should naturally progress to having a well-rounded C.V., allowing one to get a straight-laced job. For me, however, school plays, debates, poetry-reading sessions and the like were always the main thing, while the school study curriculum was a necessary evil. Happily, my English teacher had insight into my situation and was able to articulate it: 'Maths and physics are not her scene. Clearly. Then again, that is understandable. She is very culturally inclined. Maybe she is an artist.'

I was in every school play and won every debate. By the time I was fourteen, I was hosting music shows on All India Radio (AIR) and writing for a local magazine, and I stole away whenever I could to watch the latest hit Hindi films. Their impact was explosive. I came home and shut my room and did all the scenes one by one – love scenes, crying scenes and even dying scenes. I played queens, vaga-bonds and spies, dressed in costumes made from shiny nylon fabric sourced from the roadside Thursday flea bazaar. My parents, who could hear me faintly, had no real idea what went on behind those closed doors. They put it down to teenage insanity.

Since I was topping my class, no one really cared. I spread my wings, and co-wrote and acted in a play for our college fest which was probably the most sorry piece of writing ever, but the fact that we could actually write and put something up for people to see was a huge high. Once I had tasted that little lick of fame, I was never the same.

But life really turned around when a friend's mum asked me to model her Angora sweaters. She paid me 5000 rupees (equivalent to roughly US$100 at the time). My parents were aghast. They thought I would go crazy with the cash. They promptly opened a bank account for me so that I, like all good Indians, could start 'saving'. They started to think this might be an excellent way of funding my education abroad – the cherished dream of every middle-class Indian.

For this reason, and this reason alone, my parents allowed me to continue modelling. But when I left home every morning for college, my face had to be scrubbed clean as a baby's bottom. If any traces of perfume were detected on me, I was made to change. Kajal (kohl) was allowed on the college Annual Day only. My professional beauty kit consisted of two lipsticks and a blush bought by K-Mart-loving aunts travelling through North America.

As I started getting more and more serious about being an actor, dreams of moving to Mumbai, the Mecca of entertainment in India, started to form in my young head. Given my family background, Harvard and Yale were closer than Film City, Mumbai. There was no love of film in my family. We saw one film every six months, as a family outing. These were kosher films like *Gandhi*, *Hatari* and *Star Wars*. According to Dad, Hindi films were a 'bad influence'. It was very 'chee-chee'. He wanted me to become a war reporter along the lines of Christiane Amanpour, to somehow change the world. Or at least be there to report the change. Dad could not understand why I would want to do something as 'silly' as acting, when I could just as easily get through the best B-schools or the I.F.S./I.A.S. (Indian Foreign/Administrative Service). But when a few film offers started coming in from Mumbai as a result of the modelling work in Delhi, Mum and I were allowed to visit Mumbai, just to confirm how scandalous the world of films really was and how completely unsuited I was to it.

♦ ♦ ♦

As soon as we got back from Mumbai, we got some devastating news. My dad had refused the son of the local M.L.A. (Member of the Legislative Assembly) admission to his school. The boy had scored zero in the entrance exam. So Mr M.L.A. sent goons with hockey sticks and rifles to my father's office. My father had been beaten within an inch of his life. He had twenty-four multiple compound fractures.

To see my hero, my dad, in multiple traction, all limbs in casts, killed something within me forever. I realised then that I would have to look after myself in this world, because no one was infallible. And that there is a huge price to pay for being principled. I decided then that I would stick with my principles, but always be tactful, and not unbending in attitude.

Our home was sealed because it was on the school premises. We never went back to that house again. Not even to take our things. All schools in Delhi were closed for two days in protest. I started to hate Delhi; in my mind, I was already living in Mumbai. A special security force was sent to get my books from our now sealed home as I was supposed to sit my final-year exams in ten days. I took my final-year exams with two bodyguards waiting outside my examination hall.

Then came further bad news: I had done exceedingly well in my final year. The principal of my college called Dad in for a meeting. A principal-to-principal chat ensued. Dad was advised that I must pursue 'further education', do my Master's in English and finally come back and teach at my alma mater. Upon hearing this, I indulged in detailed fantasies of running away. I could see myself living the life of the impoverished artist, surviving on a single meal a day, in a ramshackle but aesthetic loft. Only the idea of seeing a picture of myself in the missing people's column kept me at home. The turmoil inside me was reflected outside. The danger from the M.L.A. was apparently not over. We lived in various places – friends' homes and guesthouses – but never long enough for anyone to find out. Dad was certainly not returning to that school or that office. So we didn't have a home, and college was over.

At this opportune moment, a random application that a couple of friends and I had sent to St Xavier's College in Mumbai, for a diploma in Advertising and Marketing, got through. I finally left Delhi. Though I was home almost every weekend and I really missed my parents, I knew I had flown the nest. Mumbai was waiting for me.

♦ ♦ ♦

As chance would have it, I landed at the doorstep of Mrs Kohli of Church View Apartments, Bandra, who was looking for a 'decent' paying guest. She was a hard-of-hearing, rajma-chawal-loving[1], good Panju-Sikh landlady, whose son had taken all her money and moved to Pune after her husband passed away. So Kohli aunty had to take a Paying Guest and the P.G. had to take the burden of her son's betrayal. She didn't want an actress or model to be her P.G. under any circumstances. Her last P.G. had had bit parts in films and when the roles ran out, she had become a semi-escort. When Kohli aunty went out of town, the young lady had used her home to meet her men friends. The building society found out and aunty was put in a very embarrassing situation. '*Badi kharaab kudiyan hondiyan ne. Raati late andiyaan ne. Aadmiyan naal hans hans ke galla kardiyan ne ...*' ('They are bad, bad girls, who come home late at night and laugh when they talk to men.') I understood why she felt this way, but this did not make my life easy.

I had to have lunch with Mrs Kohli every Sunday and watch TV with her every evening from 7 pm to 9 pm. It wouldn't have been so bad except she had very bad taste in television viewing. And she was partially deaf, so everything was watched at a very high volume. She was okay if I had to stay back for extra class at college. But, if I stayed back to have a snack or beer with my classmates and came back a second later than 9.45 pm, I wouldn't hear the last of it. *Padhai-likhai* (pursuit of higher learning), all Indians get. I think she had the train timetable for the Churchgate-Bandra local trains pasted on the inside of her toiletries cabinet.

Mumbai never lets anyone go to bed hungry, goes the saying. I must admit, Mumbai opened its arms very wide for me: I was working almost from the day I landed. Television commercials, print

---

1. A kind of red bean curry with rice

advertisements and live events were aplenty. I was meeting more and more people, being invited to film previews and getting a chance to meet people I had only seen on screen. Then there was Kohli aunty with a watch in one hand and the door chain in the other. With a 9.45 pm deadline. Things reached a head the day she locked me out and I spent the night on the stairs. I had been twenty minutes late.

Even so, all was well until she realised I wanted to act in films and that the advertising course at Xavier's was just a decoy for my parents. The neighbours came out when they heard her screaming, '*To filmach kam karna chaandi hen? Maay nahi rakhna tennu.*'('You want to work in the movies? I will not allow you to stay a minute longer!')

But somehow she figured at some point that I was not going to murder her, or take possession of her flat and turn it into a dance bar. In her own suspicious way, Mrs Kohli had become fond of me. She tried to convince me how bad the world of films was.

Absurdly enough, she was quite proud of my advertising work. '*Company de loki cahnge honde ne*' ('People who work in corporates are decent') was her logic. Kaka, her Pune-based fraudster son, got to hear, '*Ohh kudi jedi Maggi di ad vich andi hai, ohh itthe raindi ey. Main unnu dasya Maggi changi company ey.*' ('That girl who you see in the Maggi commercial on TV, she stays here. I told her to do the commercial, I told her Maggi is a decent company to work for.')

But the very mention of films got her screaming. She wanted me to be her permanent paying guest. And I wanted to be a film star. Problem. No film star stays as a P.G. They have villas with swimming pools.

Then suddenly a huge fight erupted between her and Kaka's wife, her daughter-in-law. Overnight, aunty developed huge blood pressure issues and had to be hospitalised. I had to rush between college and an ad film shoot to sit with her. Her son didn't come to meet her. I called him several times. Mrs Kohli was convinced she was going to die. The doctors were sure she would live to a hundred. At least.

She looked at me for the truth. I told her. I told her to enjoy her life, meet her friends at the Gurudwara, walk in the park or see a film on her video-cassette player.

After that episode she stopped bullying me. I could come and go as I pleased and she never locked me out again. Finally, I signed my first film in her home and with her blessings. The producers had to come home, meet her and promise I would not shoot after 9 pm. They got her a Punjabi *salwar kurta* set (a long shirt with a loose trouser worn by Punjabi women) and a box of *ladoos*[2] and I was on my way. The day-to-day goings-on of my film set were at the top of the gossip charts at the Khar Gurudwara for weeks.

Kohli aunty was my lucky break, but those were more innocent times. Most building societies now will not allow the lease or sale of flats to singles. Especially to singles in the film and television business. Many actors and directors who are big names in the business have spent nights at VT station[3] and in youth hostels, sometimes six or eight to a room. Only three are allowed at a maximum and it's illegal to have more, but who cares. This is Mumbai, *meri jaan.*

♦ ♦ ♦

While I was able to survive on account of television commercials and live events, a film, my heart's deepest desire, was nowhere on the horizon. Finally I signed my first film which, on paper, seemed to have all the qualities needed for a hit film. It turned out to be a sorry piece of work and flopped miserably.

Post this, I was virtually cast aside by the business, and all manner of new challenges arose. Not getting any work was the main

---

2. A popular Indian confection, typically made from flour and sugar, and shaped into a ball
3. Victoria Terminus, Mumbai

one. The other was that many a cheapskate assumed you were now desperate and therefore fair game for their salacious advances.

So I had to go back to auditioning for television commercials and realised that the only way forward was to succeed at these auditions. A few actor friends, who were also new to the city and waiting in the wings, got together and worked out a plan. We did mock auditions with each other. The actual audition rooms often have people going in and out, and that can be hugely distracting. So we did our mock auditions at coffee shops, restaurants or public parks.

In the middle of our mock audition, waiters took orders, friends from other tables came over and we just had to keep going with our lines. It was an amazing exercise that built an inner focus. Our focus became razor sharp. Also, we lost any feelings of self-consciousness. This practice helps me even today.

Our task each week was to redo the auditions we had messed up in the previous seven days. We sat in a circle and watched, commented and directed the person redoing an audition. We gave ourselves homework each week, too. We had to stand in front of a mirror and see what we looked like doing certain actions and figure out all the bizarre things about ourselves. We spent hours finding out who we really were. I discovered that I could make my lower lip tremble at will. It is a great build-up for weeping scenes. I look like I am about to burst into a big boo-hoo. I have used it rather effectively (and not just on film).

We did every audition we could get our hands on. We did up to six auditions a day: from famous studios to small tests at Andheri, we did them all. The more we auditioned, the easier it became. We did so many that it did not matter anymore. And in that thin line between caring madly and not giving a damn lay the key to a success-ful audition. We met people and made friends. A lot of those young assistant directors are now prolific directors making feature films, and they do remember their friends from the early days. We got so good at it that soon, between the six of us, we had cornered the ad film market. We had succeeded in making it fun and not such a 'test'.

♦ ♦ ♦

I was getting used to the feast-or-famine scenario of an actor's professional life but this time around my diary was looking as barren as a brick. I was beginning to worry. I had visited my surprised family twice, taken the not-yet-needed break in Goa, met all my friends several times over and had been massaged to within an inch of my life. I was virtually dying of relaxation.

And then suddenly, out of nowhere, a rather famous producer cum director (who we'll call R.R. – Rapacious Rascal) called, saying he wanted to meet. Full of hope, I walked into his office, all a-splendour with dangling earrings and four-inch heels.

As I entered his office, R.R. gave me an eyeful. He then went on to describe how he had launched this female actor and that she owed her place in the film firmament to him. As he gave me a very thorough scrutiny, he told me I needed to learn how to walk in heels, lose weight and get spa treatment to make my hair glossy.

I was caught off-guard but was happy to work with someone with such interest in his actors. I promised him I would look into each of the things he had suggested.

He seemed to be impressed by my zeal and finally he described the role, which was small but had the potential to make an impact. Given my work situation, it was like James Cameron had offered me Kate Winslet's part in *Titanic*. I was ecstatic.

When I told my actor friends I was part of R.R.'s big budget extravaganza, there was a visible shock reaction from most. Yes, R.R. had made many successful films, but he was also known to be a monster womaniser, I found out. He spared no one, I was warned. Working with him was the equivalent of agreeing to be his pet squeeze for the duration of the filming.

Why is it that when you don't want to hear a particular thing, nearly everyone wants to talk about that very thing? Any actor friend I met mentioned R.R. and his philandering ways. Everyone poured out their tales of woe pertaining to being cast by someone who was in power and a womaniser. An actress friend who was just getting into the movies offered me her horror story. She had been called to Chennai (the other big hub of filmmaking in India) by a casting director for a Tamil film, to meet one Mr Raja, a new director. He began calling her far too frequently in Mumbai, ostensibly to discuss the script. She was getting annoyed because these phone calls were adding no value to the script or to her life.

Mr Raja finally asked her to accompany him to the very scenic Pondicherry and Kodaikanal to go location scouting. He told her he 'wanted the script to penetrate every inch of her body'. Needless to say, she stopped taking his calls. He went on to sign two different girls one after another, who both went 'location scouting' with him. (I need not tell you but can't resist ... no film was ever made and Mr Raja is currently twenty crores[4] in debt.)

Another actress friend from a small town, who had been approached for the same role that R.R. had offered me, had been propositioned by him. She said, 'He tried to psych me. He said I needed a personality development course, diction classes, a stylist, a new portfolio, high heels and a godfather.' He went on to tell her she needed to have ten lakhs[5] (roughly US$15,000) spent on her and he was ready to 'support and groom' her. R.R. asked her to 'compromise'. When my friend, the greenhorn, did not understand what he was trying to say, he sat her down in his large corporate office and explained thus, 'So what will I get when you become a star? What will you do for me for the "support and grooming"?'

---

4. One crore is a unit of measurement equal to 10,000,000.
5. One lakh is a unit of measurement equal to 100,000.

The penny dropped and the actress got up to leave. R.R. then told her this was the 'basic' rule of the film industry. 'If you have joined this business, you should be ready for all this,' he said. As a parting shot he added that that's why he did not let his daughter join the business, but if she had, she would have had to 'compromise' too.

I lay awake nights thinking. While the film was crucial for me at that point, my moral compass pointed strictly north. There was no way I was going to 'compromise'. Every possible scenario floated through my addled brain. Should I handle the situation when it cropped up? Maybe I should have a chat with R.R. *before* the shoot? But then why should I put an idea in his head if he hadn't thought of it? Should I carry some sleeping tablets with me and drug the man, if he decided to get too close? Shall I call R.R.'s wife and get really friendly with her? R.R.'s son was an assistant director on the unit, so could he be my confidant and dissuade his dad? Should I do the film at all? I reached a decision.

Filming began with the traditional coconut being broken to mark the auspicious start of the venture. I was made to feel very welcome on the set and everyone treated me with kid gloves. I kept wondering if it was because I was liked for myself or because R.R. had given instructions to the unit to 'look after' me.

R.R. kept talking about how lucky I was to be a part of his film. I knew I was lucky to be part of the film, but I was a good casting choice too. So when he mentioned my being lucky one time too many, I told him I thought I was a good actress and so it was more than just luck that had got me the part. For a brief second R.R. looked taken aback but then he gave me an approving nod.

My guard was constantly up, alert for any sign of over-friendliness. We started the film with a few days of work in Mumbai. Friends called and checked up on me and I was happy to tell them that, as yet, there were no inappropriate overtures from his side.

But the big test lay ahead. We had a long schedule of filming in the U.S.A. The lead cast was put up at a ritzy hotel downtown. Sure enough, I was in the same hotel as the big man. And on the same floor, our rooms a few feet apart. My antenna started bristling.

The film needed me to be the romantic vixen whom the hero turns down for the more saccharine and pious heroine. When filming started, R.R. went out of his way to shoot my scenes with a lot of care, taking his time to explain every nuance with meticulous detail. We shot a song sequence that makes Hindi movies what they are. The diaphanous clothes my character wore were blown about by a storm fan angled at the appropriate degree. A special light called the 'softy' was called for to give my face that screen goddess glow, and most of my shots were tight close-ups. R.R. gave me even more time than the leading man, which *never* happens in Hindi films. We were shooting some romantic scenes which required me to be in close proximity to the lead actor. Normally, the leading man gets first dibs with the leading lady – this was a hide-bound tradition in films that are still very much a male bastion. If the lady was willing, it would be the hero who would get the first go at wooing her at the outdoor location. Using the scenic setting as his personal backdrop for a romantic date, he would start an affair with the leading lady before his wife and kids showed up at the end of the filming schedule. At this point the affair would end and all order be restored.

But the leading man was much taken with the young, attractive make-up assistant at the shoot; he was quite happy to let R.R. spend time with me and simply went through the motions.

For some shots R.R. would lean close to me and demonstrate how he wanted the lead actor to touch me or be more romantic. It was left to me to bring sizzle to the scene, so I fairly outdid my brief.

It was clear to the unit that R.R. had grown very fond of me. The younger crew members were getting quite a laugh out of it. There was many a nudge-nudge, wink-wink and I was becoming self-conscious. With R.R.'s son on set, it was getting to be an oddly embarrassing situation. I had to concentrate hard to stay focused. I listened carefully to his direction and followed with my whole heart. Regardless of the other details, this was still an opportunity for me to show my chops and I was not about to let any self-consciousness get in my way. 'Sir' was very happy and the work was turning out to be quite excellent.

Towards the end of the day's shoot, very casually, when no one else was within earshot, R.R. asked me to meet him for dinner in his room. To 'discuss the script'. It was hard to say a straight no; very awkward. Thanks to the intimacy of the scenes we had shot we had developed a certain speed-dial closeness. Heart thudding loudly, I nodded. I wondered what R.R.'s son would think of his dad hitting on a girl his age. Or maybe he knew and was hoping for the same privileges when he made director.

Sometime during the day, before R.R. had mentioned the 'script/ dinner', I had made plans with the assistant directors, including R.R.'s son, and the rest of the crew to go out that evening. I knew I had to think fast and clear. And suddenly I had a thought. It was tricky but it could work. Or I'd be on the plane back home later tonight.

When it was time to meet the director in his room to 'read the script', I requested that the hotel operator transfer all my calls to R.R.'s room. I reached his suite to find him alone, reclining on one of the chaise longes in a silky maroon *lungi-kurta* (a type of shirt and wraparound skirt that men wear). It looked so straight out of a film seduction scene that had I not been the fly walking straight into the spider's web, I would have burst out laughing at the triteness of the situation.

I had arrived with a box of luxurious chocolates and a giant bunch of flowers from the hotel's expensive boutique flower shop. I gave him a tight hug and thanked him for the extra pains he had taken over my shots. Barely had I finished my sentence when the phone rang.

It was the crew (including R.R.'s son and the good-looking make-up assistant, who was escaping the drunk hero of the film) waiting for me in the lobby. I told them to give me ten minutes to figure out the next day's work with 'Sir'. I put my hand over the receiver and asked him if ten to fifteen minutes would be enough to 'discuss the script'?

Needless to say, the whole unit knew I was in 'Sir's' room. Sir lost all his 'desire' to discuss the script. I gave him another bear hug, said a truly meant thank you and dashed down to party with people my age. 'Sir' never asked me to discuss the script again, except on set. We became dear friends and today he is the one I call if ever I need any advice.

♦ ♦ ♦

I have been asked, plenty of times – by actors, directors and producers. I play dumb. Smile and pretend I don't get the hint. Yet, somehow, many men from the film business think it is their right to ask.

Outdoor shoots are where much of the alleged 'action' takes place. Female actors are often alone on location, without 'mummy-ji' or boyfriend. The hero or the director gets a chance to cosy up to the women in the cast. An interesting thing actresses in the 1960s and '70s used to do to avoid the 'pressure' of being chased was pretend to be in a relationship with another person on the same unit. Often, the unsuspecting object of an actress's affection, the decoy, would fall head over heels in love with her. Only to find himself left out in the cold once they returned to Mumbai.

Anyone who is an artist must go in with all vulnerability. It is an occupational hazard that cannot be avoided. One cannot be safe and a good actor. Yet one needs some mechanism of self-defence to stay sane.

MATAJI

DEEPTI KAPOOR

A visit to the apartment my grandmother shares with my mother in the Delhi satellite city of Greater Noida gives little indication of the life she has led. Ninety years old now, senile, withdrawn, often disobedient (prone to grinning like a naughty child when caught hiding the vegetables on her plate), she is hardly the fearsome woman of memory.

She won't talk much unless prompted. Even then it's hard to get words out of her, unless we're returning to her childhood, the region of her brain that fires as the rest fades. Secondary evidence is hard to come by too; there are no photos of her working life on the walls, no souvenirs, no memorabilia, no certificates. She has carried nothing with her.

But she's the head of our family. The last one standing.

The men in my family have a habit of dying.

My grandfather, my father, uncles, their children too – they've all died too young. My first boyfriend also died; he fell from a moving train trying to film the sunrise. For a long time death haunted me. I saw it everywhere when it wasn't there. And even now I think my husband will die every time he goes out alone to the shops. As if it's inevitable.

◆ ◆ ◆

My grandmother, Prakash Patney, was born in British Lahore – modern-day Pakistan – in 1925. Her father, Lalji, was a confident, thick-set man with a remarkable square face, piercing eyes and a grand moustache. Self-made, very practical, he had trained to be a doctor in his youth and was sent by his older brother to England for higher studies in preventive medicine. When he came back to Uttar Pradesh, he took up a government job doing the same.

Lalji had two other daughters, Pushpa and Kailash, and, after them, three sons, but Prakash, fair-skinned, thin and beautiful, was his first and favourite. A music student, she had an exceptional voice, remarked upon by everyone. What's more, she was obedient, diligent and highly respectful to her elders. Pushpa and Kailash, on the other hand, were always very naughty, and Lalji didn't much favour Kailash, despite her intelligence, on account of her dark skin.

It should be pointed out here that Prakash is a boy's name. Why did she have a boy's name? Quite simply, because Lalji was expecting a boy; when the son turned out to be a daughter, he saw no need to change the chosen name.

Soon enough Prakash was sent away to the Annie Besant School in Varanasi. Just as she was the favourite of her father, she was of her teachers too. She was the star of the debating team and the drama class, and because of her otherworldly voice she always got the best singing parts. She had a friend there, Uma Singh, who was so exceptionally thin that she had to wear two petticoats to fill herself out. Jealous and determined, Prakash trained herself to do 1000 skips in one go, in order to be as thin as Uma Singh.

Life for Prakash here was good – not a care in the world. So when Lalji came to take her out of school, the teachers were terribly upset.

Married at sixteen: nothing remarkable in that. A matrimonial ad had been placed in the papers. Prakash's future mother-in-law came to examine her. The woman didn't care for the child's oiled hair, but Prakash was told to sing for her, and by her voice she was sold.

Married at sixteen: ripped from a blissful life. Now she was thrown into a house to be a wife. There had been cooks in her old home; she'd never made a meal in her life. In her new home she was put to work. Her mother-in-law was aghast at her inability to prepare a meal, and told her she was useless.

Her husband, Lala Babu, was a policeman, a feared agent of the law, well loved in the community, well respected, famous for his mastery of disguise while hunting criminals and his penchant for reckless driving. There's still a school near Meerut named in his honour, for his role in eradicating banditry in the area. A good husband, too, all told; he didn't beat his wife. But Prakash's days were spent with the mother-in-law, in the kitchen, being told how ungrateful she was, how worthless, how badly behaved.

Prakash bore Lala Babu a son in the first year of marriage. This did nothing to help her. Her mother-in-law, in her irrational anger, began to starve the girl; she stopped producing milk and Prakash's son almost died. Disaster was only averted when Lalji ordered Prakash back to the family home to be fattened up again, before sending her back when the milk began to flow.

Prakash gave birth to three more children – my aunt, my mother and another son, who died of cancer aged two. My aunt was born in 1944 – fair and beautiful. My mother, the last to be born – in Haridwar in 1950, in the middle of the *Kumbh Mela* – was deemed dark-skinned and unattractive.

Between my aunt's birth and my mother's birth, the British Empire left India, the nightmare of Partition took place and the country celebrated its independence. On 15 August 1947, the modern nation was born. Prakash recalled the torments of those years, the torture she suffered under her mother-in-law. She told my mother once, 'I thought in those days, either she has to die, or I do.'

But Lala Babu was the one to die, in 1952, chasing a robber in his jeep. The brakes failed, he crashed into a tree, and smashed his head into the steering wheel. His family blamed Prakash – she was bad luck, a witch. They threw her out, though not before claiming her son. It was only through the intervention of the courts that he was returned.

Suddenly, terribly free. A widow in India. The end of a life.

But Lalji was having none of it. After the traditional thirteen days of mourning he said to his daughter, 'Now it's time to get up; if you don't, you'll die hungry.'

He gave her two options. The easy one: to become a teacher. The hard: to become a doctor like him. She had already decided she wanted her children to have the same status they would have had if their father were alive. So she decided to become a doctor.

Her father's friends and colleagues called it absurd. 'She's a music student with no grounding in the sciences, how can she become a doctor?'

Lalji said, 'My daughter has chosen, she will do it.'

But the schools didn't want to take her; Lalji had to convince them. He said, 'Just let her sit the exams. If she does well, take her, if not, let it be.'

He coached her intensively, and she took to it with an equal ferocity. Like father, like daughter. She was fascinated by the sciences. As soon as she began studying she said, 'So this is how the world works! What have I been doing all this time?'

Art and music were cast aside. Physics was her new love. The most dreadful circumstances had allowed her to be free. She went through the junior science syllabus in three months, and when she sat the exams that enabled her to join the final two years of high school, she came top.

But as Lalji coached her, her children were handed over to servants, kept out of sight. When my infant mother cried, the servants removed her, so as not to disturb the student. Later, Prakash said it was a sacrifice worth making in order to improve her children's lives.

Two years of high school, eight years of medical school: study, sleep, repeat. A life sacrificed with no conception of pleasure or joy. The carefree young girl had vanished. In medical school, the student body respected this tough, widowed woman unconditionally. Those in classes far advanced referred to her, in deference, as '*didi*' – sister.

She passed through medical school with flying colours and, after another few years of internship, officially became a doctor, graduating into government service, electing to become a gynaecologist.

She had been inspired by the doctor who delivered her first son; she remembered at the time thinking, what a lovely lady, what a great profession, bringing life into the world. So much more respected than a teacher-ji.

◆ ◆ ◆

From the sixties to the eighties, Prakash worked in government hospitals, establishing a reputation as a tireless, resolute doctor with a steely constitution and an unbreakable will. The young, determined '*didi*' – sister – vanished, replaced by '*Mataji*' – mother.

Mataji reigned supreme. She would brook no dissent, commanding unwavering devotion from the men and women beneath her. She rose up the ranks, eventually becoming superintendent of the hospital in Moradabad, a dusty, unforgiving Uttar Pradesh town known for brass and gangsters.

It was the pinnacle of her service.

But it was a hard service. U.P. was, and remains, a very tough, often lawless place. Many rape cases were sent to her. Often young girls. She was unflinching: examining the vaginal discharge, checking for semen or for signs of force and violence. When, in her opinion, rape was confirmed, she would go to court with the evidence, talking coldly and openly about the circumstances of the case. Lawyers would try to intimidate her with their questions; they would use crude language, expect the embarrassed female doctor to break down. But she could be cruder and colder and more intimidating than them all. She pursued justice relentlessly; she never let a case go. The accused and their families often came to her with big money, trying to make her change her testimony, but she refused every time.

For the educated in India, it was a time of expanding horizons. America beckoned the country's bright young things. Those who could escape for a better life did, and families sent their children away with hope and blessings. But Prakash wanted to keep her children close. My uncle took after his mother in perseverance and dedication. Seeing the sacrifices she had made, he was always at the top of his class, and wanted to succeed for her. But he also wanted to go abroad. A friend offered him a job in the U.S., which had the potential to make him rich – in fact, some of these friends went on to become millionaires and even billionaires. But Prakash forbade him to go; she wanted to keep him close.

My aunt too. When her husband, who worked in the railways, found a lucrative job in the U.S., Prakash told him: 'I would never have got my daughter married to you if I'd known you were going to take her away from me.' They went anyway.

My mother, though, she knew she could never leave. To this day she laments the fact that, unlike Lalji to Prakash, no one ever said to her 'Get up, or you'll go hungry and die.' Instead she was encouraged to marry in India.

◆ ◆ ◆

My father was an intelligent man, with a God-given flair for maths and physics. But his family came from a different place from my mother's. They were freedom fighters, risen out of poverty at a confluence of religion and mental illness: his father was a Godman – at various times in his life he gave away all their possessions, abandoned his family and took to wandering barefoot across the plains, giving religious discourses to the gathering crowds. The match almost fell apart when Prakash learned of this, but she had taken a liking to my father by then, and so, in her capricious way, she let it be.

My parents ended up being deeply in love. My father passed the entrance exams for the government civil service, but failed the interview because of poor English. Next he passed the entrance exam to the police force but, on the understanding he would be posted to Nagaland in the middle of a bloody insurgency, his application was withdrawn. He began to work for the State Bank of India instead. A safe and steady job, later to give material success when the economy opened up in the 1990s.

They were living in Kanpur in Eastern Uttar Pradesh in 1980, when I was born. My mother travelled to Moradabad for my birth, and Prakash, the superintendent of the hospital, delivered me herself. Already having a son, my father wanted a girl. My grandmother was disappointed when this turned out to be the case. She held me in the air with unconcealed contempt and said: 'Here's your *kali bhavani*.' Here's your black storm-raiser.

◆ ◆ ◆

My father was posted many places for his work – we had a nomadic life. Kanpur, Bombay, Bhopal. Some of my earliest memories were of Juhu Beach. We lived in an apartment block there, when the beaches of Bombay were as quiet as Goa's. I was a shy, secretive girl, inheriting my mother's meekness and my father's fire, internalising the latter so that it only raged inside. Before the outbreak of the First Gulf War, my father was posted to Bahrain with the State Bank of India. My lasting memory there is of a huge billboard outside my window, an image of the Sheikh that covered the entire building opposite, staring at me. We lived in an apartment in the business district, in Manama, one of the smallest cities in the world. The streetlights were always on. I became obsessed with closing the curtains so tightly that not a single chink of light came through, and I would not be seen by the Sheikh.

My father adored and spoilt me, my mother kept me close. But while we were there, Saddam Hussein invaded Kuwait. Fearing for my safety, my parents decided to send me back to India, to a boarding school in Dehradun called Welham Girls'. Prakash, with her growing wealth, helped pay for this.

Taken from the tender home, thrown in with other girls who would bully and mock, you developed a thick skin, learned how to scrap and take care of yourself, fight for friends, food, small freedoms. You played politics to survive.

Immensely privileged in the scheme of things, I received a first-class education. But boarding school was a place without love. The lasting consequence of this, one my parents could not foresee, was a detachment, and a wilful independence. Before I left, I had clung to my family, a scared and obedient little girl. By the end of school I didn't need anyone. I had lost my shyness, but I was unmoored. Family, tradition, obedience … I had no care for them at all.

◆ ◆ ◆

In 1985, before we moved to Bahrain, Prakash retired from government service. She was sixty years old – by then a terrifying and formidable woman, in no mood to lay down her stethoscope. So she went to Firozabad, another dusty U.P. gangster town, famous for bangles, glasswork, fireworks and child labour, where she had once been posted. There she claimed some of her family's old ancestral land, with the intention of building a private hospital.

It was a huge plot, prime land on the main road from Agra, right at the start of town before the houses bunched in and the lanes narrowed. It was no surprise that a crooked businessman, one you'd call 'transport mafia', was already squatting on the land. First she filed a case in the courts to take it back, and then approached the chief of police, invoking her dead husband's good name. The chief, upon hearing she was the widow of the famous Lala Babu, told her, '*Mataji*, we will protect you.' Just to be sure, she went to the Transport Minister and persuaded him to threaten the squatter. This did the trick. She built her hospital, and the message went out: don't mess with this woman.

Soon the local tough guys were bringing their wives to her and she was delivering their babies. In no time she was famous. Hardened men would fall at her feet. One night a wanted man came into the hospital to see his newborn son. At the side of the crib, he removed his gun and placed it in the boy's hand. The boy gripped it, as babies do, and the gangster declared proudly, 'This is my son.'

We came to visit on summer holidays. She was not a grandmother who would tell stories and give you hugs. She'd be working while you slept and, when you woke, she'd be working some more. She had an assistant named Ram Pyari, a fierce local woman who started out as a cleaner, then became a cook, and then was trained as a midwife. By the end she could assist her in operations, administer stitches and deliver babies. But she would always cook chicken curry for us.

I watched during those holidays, looking down into the maternity ward through the grille from the apartment above. The desperate sounds of wailing mothers and howling babies, day and night – this is how I remember my grandmother's home. A place without laughter and joy, and with a sense of impending doom hanging over it.

It was her kingdom, her domain. She controlled everything and everyone here. Ram Pyari was her enforcer. If anyone tried anything with her, Ram Pyari would say, 'You speak to me.' And she'd use her crude village dialect with them.

But it wasn't as if Prakash shied away. She treated her staff with contempt, and used all kinds of abusive language if they didn't work properly.

Always, though, she fought for women and their right to live. She refused to perform sex determination tests on expectant mothers. Lots of doctors in town did, and when a baby was discovered to be a girl, the foetus was quietly aborted. But she was adamant. No girl would die because of her. One time a rich family in the jewellery trade came to her with an ultrasound from elsewhere; it showed their daughter was going to have a girl. They wanted her to abort it. She refused, and she begged them not to go elsewhere. Begged them to wait and see. And behold! The woman gave birth to a son. They treated her like a saint for that one.

At the hospital, she also ran an off-the-books adoption service. Unwed mothers, mostly young girls, would leave their babies with her, and she'd find families to take them in. Once a very young girl came in with her family, complaining of a stomachache. It was confirmed that she was eight months pregnant. The pregnancy was kept a secret. When it was delivered, Prakash told the girl and her family that the baby had died, and then gave it to a childless couple.

How strange, then, in all of this, that Prakash maintained that being born a woman was the greatest curse of all. It would be better, she often said, if a woman was not born at all.

She always had to be vigilant. Over the course of the years, other gangsters and goons would try to take her hospital away from her. Mulayam Singh Yadav, Samajwadi Party boss and ex-chief minister of Uttar Pradesh, famous for fielding criminal politicians and saying of gang rapists 'boys will be boys', had land next to hers. He wanted to expand, so he used to send men with guns to threaten her. Four of Mulayam's men came with guns, to try to get rid of her. They pointed their weapons at her head, said they would shoot. She held their gaze and refused to move, and her workers, led by Ram Pyari, formed a circle around her, until the men left.

The Agra Medical Association called her the Iron Lady, in recognition of the challenges she faced, and defeated, in her work.

◆ ◆ ◆

I finished school and moved back to Delhi in 1998. I lived with my parents begrudgingly, studying journalism at a prestigious all-girls college in Delhi. My parents, delighted to have me back, still thought of me as their little girl. But inside their home, I only felt suffocation.

But in India it was an exciting time. The India I knew was going through a great upheaval. The economy was flourishing, people were no longer fleeing abroad for a life, jobs were abundant, the arts were vibrant. Social relations were changing too; life was loosening in the cities. I worked with a Human Rights N.G.O.; I worked for newspapers and news magazines. I was the first generation of my family not looking to the government for work.

While my grandmother was ruling her hospital in the badlands of U.P., I had many potential futures – TV newsreader, human rights advocate, wife to a wealthy banker, post-grad student at an Ivy League college. It was my decision to make. It was a time of optimism and opportunity and hope. I couldn't wait to get on in the world.

Then, as I completed my first-year exams, as my parents were about to leave for a holiday in Korea, my father was diagnosed with a brain tumour. They called him to a hospital in Mumbai for exploratory surgery. When he came out he was paralysed and his speech was irreversibly impaired. Over the next year we nursed him, my brother and mother and I, until the tumour killed him. Two deaths, all told.

By the end of it, after a year of holding on, his passing was a release. But it sent me on a different path. What you might call going off the rails.

◆ ◆ ◆

This coincided with Prakash coming to live with us. In 2000, when she was seventy-five, her hands had begun to shake. Realising she was too old to carry on, and seeing my father's death as a sign, she sold the hospital and moved to Delhi to live with her widowed daughter and wayward granddaughter.

The three of us together in an apartment. A painful thing. Grief consumed. My mother, who had invested everything in my father, who had never been made to work in her life, now left alone. And Prakash, with her powers lost overnight. In Firozabad she was all-powerful. But here in Delhi, with no empire, no loyal subjects and no adversaries, she fell apart. My mother suggested she help out at a local medical charity, volunteer in some capacity to keep busy, but she stubbornly refused; if she could not have power, she wanted nothing.

For all her money, all her success, all that she had done in her life, she took pleasure from nothing, and brought nothing of it with her.

She was stranded in a new India. One opened up to the West. And then there was me. My behaviour, the hours I kept, the language I used, my clothes, my ideas about personal freedom, happiness, desire, ambition, choice, duty and sacrifice: all of this made no sense to her.

She tried to interfere, to tell me what I should do. But her sudden presence only irritated me. I resented her living with us, judging, misunderstanding, trying to assert an authority she didn't have, telling me I couldn't go out to meet people, forcing me to change my clothes, lecturing me on my life. My father had just died, and now the freedoms I had learned were being curtailed. I looked back at all their lives and saw only the damage that she had caused by insisting she knew what was best, by insisting on taking the most pragmatic approach to all situations. Get married, work. There had never been any joy in her life. Now there was sadness in mine, but I was determined never to go the same way.

Soon after, my boyfriend also died. When this happened, I decided I must live as hard as I could, be reckless and experience all that life had before it was snatched away. I rebelled; I lived a secret life, and ignored all they had to say about marriage, stability, respectability, responsibility.

All the while, Prakash slowly but clearly fell apart. Not knowing what to do with herself, she took to wandering the apartment with her stethoscope, cutting a forlorn figure, a doctor without a patient.

Only occasionally she found one.

Once, a girl in our building came to see her about her missed periods. Prakash took this to mean only one thing: the girl was pregnant and needed a discreet way out. She handed out abortion pills from her private stash. The girl, not being pregnant, having a good relationship with her family, and having nothing to hide, showed the pills to her mother.

It caused an almighty ruckus.

'What does she think she's doing,' the mother screamed, 'giving pills like this to my daughter?'

My mother was embarrassed and contrite. But, not unreasonably, she also asked: What did you think *you* were doing, sending your daughter to an elderly and senile ex-gynaecologist for medical advice in the first place?

◆ ◆ ◆

Now, when she is forced to look back, Prakash maintains the death of her husband was the beginning of her life. Without his loss, she admits, she would never have become her own person. The tragedy is how the road to this place left her blind and blinkered. Suffering so much pain, she could not see a way to live, or let others live. She could never see how happiness was a choice as much as a circumstance, nor could she see the way in which the power she developed as a woman could have been the gift she had for her daughters. She saved girls from abortions, but still believed they were a curse. For all her achievements, her fundamental belief in the conservative and patriarchal social structures of India remained.

BAMBOO BASKETS AND BROCADE SARIS: LIFE AND STORIES OF DALIT WOMEN

C.S. LAKSHMI

When I was young, I once spread the world map on the floor and decided that I would go and live in that country where no discrimination existed in terms of colour, birth, race, gender, language or knowledge. I kept crossing out one country after another, and finally the entire map was filled with cross marks except for the oceans. That discrimination, prejudice and segregation exist in all countries is the truth of the world we live in.

In 1988 I set up the Sound & Picture Archives for Research on Women (SPARROW) along with two academic friends, Dr Neera Desai and Dr Maithreyi Krishna Raj. We wanted to document women's lives and women's history, for the three of us strongly believed that positive change is possible only when we understand women's lives, history and struggles for self-respect and human dignity.

In the last twenty-five years of documenting and archiving, our anchor project has been oral history documentation. Recording the oral narratives of women from various walks of life – artists, writers, feminists, environmentalists, freedom fighters, educationists, political activists and scientists – has been an important part of our work.

We have recorded and documented the narratives of more than one hundred women writers. One such writer is Urmila Pawar, a Marathi writer whose writings reflect Dalit experiences of living and working. In India, there are four primary castes: the Brahmins (priests), Kshatriya (warriors and princes), Vaisya (farmers, traders and artisans) and Shudra (tenant farmers and servants). Those who were known as untouchables, and treated as untouchables, were considered below the caste system and had the lowest social status, because they were expected to do the menial work of the society. 'Dalit' has now become the term that defines them completely, for it carries with it not only the weight of years of oppression but also years of resistance of oppression. The language to write about their lives and politics has also changed. In all the Indian languages they are no more referred to as lower castes but *lowered* castes.

In Urmila's narration of her life one can see many stories, and in her stories one can see her life.

I come from the Dalit community [in Konkan]. My mother did not study; she was illiterate. My father had studied up to the sixth standard. Everybody in the village would think he had studied a lot. In those days it was possible to get a job after the sixth standard. So he was a teacher.

I was in the third standard when my father passed away. But since he was a teacher, he knew that a person needs education to progress. He had built a small house, like a hut, in Ratnagiri town and he brought us there [from the village Phansawale]. That is how we started to go to school. He had told my mother,

'Do whatever you can, but don't stop the children from going to school. Let them study.' So the one thing my mother understood was that we had to study. If we did not study she would beat us. She knew how to beat very well. When my father died, she had us six brothers and sisters to take care of. One of our brothers had already passed away, so there were [actually] five of us ...

We did not have enough to eat. My mother would therefore weave baskets; that was her work – to sit and weave.

My brother passed his S.S.C. [Secondary School Certificate] exams and then he caught typhoid and died. The pain of his death and the death of my father made her cry often. She only remembered how to cry and weave. She was concerned only about our studies. We would eat really low-quality food and wear poor clothes. I would not even bathe for four or five days. I would play in the dust and I would have plenty of lice in my hair. Water would be boiled hot and then a little washing soda would be mixed with it and rubbed into our hair, and then [she] washed [our hair] with this boiling water. Mother would then comb hard to pick out lice. When she poured hot water and combed through my hair, I could see stars before my eyes like flashing lightning.

There were those belonging to Maratha[1], Brahmin and other castes living around us. These people would ask mother to weave baskets [for them] and since I was the youngest, she would always ask me to go to such and such person's house to deliver the baskets. I would go, but they would make me stand outside their house. They would sprinkle water over the basket. They would drop the money from above into my hands. I would feel really hurt. So I would tell my mother that I would not go.

... I would bunk school. Because I did not go to school, the teacher would beat me. The teacher would also practise caste discrimination. He would make me sit in the last row.

---

1. Shudras who are cultivators, but have been seen as a warrior race

One good thing was that our father had brought us to a town. We benefited from that. We could see and learn the rituals, traditions and customs, ways of behaviour, ways of eating, and how we should keep our clothes clean, from the Brahmin and Maratha children in our class. And we began to behave like them. We did not have that kind of food at home. We did not have the recipes. We ate roti and *machli* [fish] because we were from Konkan and the *machli* that we ate was also of low quality. We did not know of big fish like halwa and pomfret. We went to their houses and learned how to make *ladoos* and other things for Diwali. If I tried to make these at home, my mother would scold me because it would need a lot of oil, a lot of flour. So she would not let me do it. And because she was unhappy, she would cry.

... During those days people were very backward. They would not get good food to eat, so the life expectancy of women was also very low. A woman would get very old by the time she was fifty. Thirty-five- or forty-year-old women would be called old. 'That old hag', they would call her. Now, even if we turn seventy, eighty, we do not feel like calling someone 'old woman'. We don't even think about being old women. But it was like this earlier ... Even when they got pregnant, they would be in a bad state. Nobody would attend to them ...

When women deliver today, we talk about stitches, how many stitches are needed and so on. What they would do those days was, if someone's body would tear during delivery, they would take a cloth, put a lot of salt water and a little bit of oil over it, fold the cloth over and give it to her and she had to bear it. They would give the salt-fold because salt has some protective qualities. They would give a hot fomentation. They would put burning coals in a *sigri* [charcoal stove] and let her breathe the smoke. She should sleep above it. Otherwise they would say, 'The body will ring out,' meaning she would pass wind and it would make a noise [and she is not supposed to make any kind of noise]. They would pour the hottest water possible on [the women's] hips. This meant that the task of giving birth to a child was [very difficult] for a woman. Some women would have the child's leg coming out, some would have the hand, there would be no doctor and the woman would die. The condition of women was very backward.

When I grew older, from among my relatives, all the women had shorter life expectancy. My maternal aunt was dead. Mostly they would catch TB, or [have] asthma. Other diseases like cholera or chicken pox would spread and a lot of women would fall victim to these. The women would die and then there was the [inevitable] second marriage. There are a lot of my relatives who have married twice or thrice. These women were not even aware of hygiene. They would wipe their nose and give roti with the same hand. My sister's mother-in-law would scratch her foot and then serve the roti with the same hand. When I would say, 'No, there could be germs,' she would say, 'What germs? Where can you see germs?'

Women worked very hard and often died early because poverty made it impossible to ward off diseases and deaths; however, it was not as if there were no tender moments in this life of poverty and oppression. Urmila spoke about an aunt who used to visit them, and how her mother expressed love for her:

I remember, there was this *chachi* [aunt] of my mother's, she loved my mother a lot. When she would come over, even my mother would [show her affection]. She lived alone. When she would come, bathing was a ritual. She would be bathed and given good clothes; good as in my mother's sense of the term. They were just clothes [washed] with a little soap. We would give her good clothes. And how was she bathed? There would be love in it, a lot of love. She would be made to sit, water would be heated, and *khopra* [coconut] – no soap, only coconut [was used] – Mummy would cut a piece of it, chew it and spit it on her hands and she would rub it on Chachi's arms and her body. We were young, we would not understand it – about the coconut. The *chachi*, she would go to her village and say, 'I had gone to my niece. She bathed me with chewed coconut.'

We did not use sugar in tea. We used jaggery. We did not know the use of milk at all. Our tea was without milk. We stayed in the city, so we would get a little sugar. She was given tea with sugar. She would be overwhelmed.

Often Urmila is criticised for writing about Dalit men who do injustice to their women. Dalit male writers sometimes ask her why she does not write the way they do and speak in general about the life of Dalits and the oppression they face without being gender-specific. Why does she write about her community the way she does? Urmila was also told that writing about the Dalit community may be used as a weapon by the upper castes against them, especially against Dalit men. The critics saw it as a kind of betrayal.

Urmila has dismissed the criticism, saying that it need not be seen as a weapon, and that such criticism cannot be used as a weapon against women either. In her own life, Urmila would like to straddle Dalit and feminist identities. She does not think that they are mutually exclusive.

The women from our village would come to the town to sell grass that they had cut, or wood. Our house was next to the road. My father had dug a well in our house. No one would give these women water to drink in the bazaar. They would suffer a lot. They would start from their homes at four in the morning. They would walk eight or ten miles barefoot. Their feet would be chapped, they would gather dust, their hair would be knotted and they would not have good clothes. They had no water.

My father had given my mother good advice that this well should be kept open for women. The rope and the bucket that was needed to pull out the water would also be there for those women. But my mother was very poor and miserly. She would not feel like leaving the rope there because [constant use] would easily break it. She would have to buy it again. So she would remove it and keep it aside. My father would get angry with her.

The women who would come to drink water would sit and eat their roti and chatni. I would steal onions from home and give [the onions] to them. Mummy would get very angry with me for that. When they would come, they would tell my mother all the village gossip. As she would weave, she would listen.

There was one thing about my mother – if she heard anything from someone she would not tell another person. It's like a newspaper press. Everything comes to the press but it does not get published! This is how she carried on. They all would come there – 'My husband did this,' 'My mother-in-law does this,' they would gesticulate, eat *paan*, spit it around and tell stories. My mother would sit in our courtyard under a small tree and weave. Sometimes I feel, if I had those baskets woven by my mother, we could place the needle on it [like in a gramophone] and spin it and they would tell us stories of all those people. We could have heard them.

She would record all the news, collect them. The mother-in-law would come and talk about the daughter-in-law: 'She is a burden, she is useless, she has done this, she has done that.' And she would go. Then the daughter-in-law would come and she would ask, 'Did my mother-in-law come here?' My mother would say, 'No. Why, what happened?' 'Last night she did this,' [she would say and add,] 'My husband beat me. Because of her such and such a thing happened.' My mummy wouldn't say anything to her. They would tell my mother whatever was going on in their minds. They would all come and tell my mother, [they would] cry, all this would go on.

I would be very interested to listen. But my mother would take a stick and tell me, 'Go to school.' She would be after me. But I would also bunk school and come and sit down to listen to them.

There was this funny family. The husband would beat his wife, but he would never tell her why he was beating her. He would come into the house, look around, pick up a stick and beat her. If the woman would ask him, 'Why are you beating me?' he would not tell her why. He would not speak. So what she would do is, when he would get angry, when she would feel that he was going to beat her, she would run to our house. She would come and tell my mother, 'This has happened. He has lost his temper,' and so on. So what my mother would do was this. We had a loft. She would get a ladder and make the woman sit in the loft. She would then remove the ladder and tell us, 'Go on children, go to the backyard, go behind the tree.' We would hide there. Then he would come [and ask], 'Has my wife come here?' [My mother would ask,]' No, why, what happened?' Then he would say why he was angry. She would say, 'Why did you get angry? You fight almost every day.' He would say, 'She did this. I had gone to take a bath; the water was very cold. I wanted warm water.' [My mother would say,] 'So, you should have told her. What is this you do?' The woman would be listening from above.

He would come, look around in the house in the corners. But he would not think that she would be sitting above. So he would leave. He would leave after my mother had calmed him a little, saying, 'You should tell your wife what you want and what do you do instead? You should not be doing this.' He would leave when he had cooled down. Then the woman would leave after him. This drama would go on at our place. This kind of a mess would go on in women's lives, but they would not feel that they were being oppressed by their caste.

Urmila and her friend Meenakshi Moon wrote a book on the contributions of Dalit women to the Dalit movement titled *Amhihi Ithihaas Gadawala* (We Also Made History). It has remained a groundbreaking work: the Dalit women's contribution to the Dalit movement had remained unspoken and unwritten. Urmila looks upon her own autobiography as a social document, for every person's life, she feels, is a social document. She adds that she is now ready to face life stoically, as that is what her life has taught her.

It would be difficult to end this piece without a poem by Jyoti Lanjewar, who passed away recently and with whom I had the fortune to associate and interact. Jyoti was one of the foremost Marathi writers, widely acclaimed and much anthologised, and also a pioneering Dalit woman poet. Her poem on her mother is an oft-quoted one and it is also a favourite of mine. It would complete this piece like nothing else can, as it combines the images of many uneducated but wise and stoic Dalit mothers and the educated daughters they stood by.

I Have Never Seen You
I have never seen you
In a brocaded new
Nine-yard *Ilkali* sari[2]
With a gold necklace around your neck
Or gold bangles worn on your hands
Not even rubber sandals on your feet

2. *Ilkali* is a special brocaded sari worn in Northern Karnataka and Maharashtra.

Burning your soles in the scorching heat
Bundling the tender one of your womb and
Hanging the bundle on the acacia tree
Working with the road construction workers
Carrying barrels of tar
I have seen you.

Your feet bound in rags
Planting a sweaty kiss on the naked child
Coming tottering towards you
Bearing the hunger knotting your entrails
And lips parched for water
Working to build a dam on the lake
On daily wages
Slaving hard
I have seen you

Deluge of tears in your eyes
Eternal summer heat in your life
When the burning sun got off your head
Picking cotton
Keeping it in your sari fold
Pushing behind the plough
Building the future of your children
I have seen you

In crowded streets balancing
The basket load on your head
Wrapping your tattered sari around your body
To guard your honour
Raising your sandal at anyone leering at you
I have seen you.

For a dream of four mud plastered walls
Your feet heavy with pregnancy
Carefully stepping on the scaffolding
Of skyscrapers
Carrying on your head
Scuttles of wet cement
I have seen you

In the late evenings
Untying the end of your sari for coins
To buy oil and salt for cooking
Placing a five paise coin
On your little one's hand
And saying ...
'Eat whatever goodies you want
But go to school'
Lifting the little bundle from the cradle
Tenderly holding it to your breast
And saying ...
'At least, you study, become like Ambedkar[3],
And relieve me of this basket load.'
I have seen you

Dragging your feet to your house
Skeletal body ... the heat of life
Debts to the moneylender ... a ploughshare
Half fed from sunset to dawn
Still refusing to accept charity

---

3. Dr Bhimrao Ramji Ambedkar, affectionately known as Babasaheb, was an Indian
economist, jurist, politician and social reformer who inspired the Modern Buddhist
Movement. He campaigned against social discrimination against Dalits, and supported
the rights of women and labour. He is also the architect of the Indian Constitution.

Retaining your self-respect
I have seen you.

Marching ahead in the Long March[4]
Shouting 'Change the name'
Braving the police batons
Going to jail with head held high
Seeing your only son
Falling martyr to police bullets
Consoling him...
'You died for Bhim, your life now has its meaning.'
Telling the police officer defiantly ...
'If I had two, three or four more sons, how good it would have been,
They would have fought as well.'
I have seen you.

On your death bed in the hospital
Donating the money you earned rag-picking
To the Diksha Bhoomi[5]
Gathering the precious last moments of life
And reiterating...
'All of you live in unity
Build a memorial

---

4. The Long March was part of the Namantar Andolan (Name Change Movement), which was a Dalit movement to change the name of Marathwada University in Aurangabad, Maharashtra, India to Dr B.R. Ambedkar University. This sixteen-year-long Dalit campaign began in 1978 and ended in 1994. It achieved some success in 1994 when the compromise name of Dr Babasaheb Ambedkar Marathwada University was accepted. This protest movement was notable for the violence against Dalits by the authorities. The Long March was notable for the large numbers of people who participated in it, especially women.
5. Diksha Bhoomi is a sacred monument of Buddhism. It is located where the architect of the Indian Constitution, Dr Babasaheb Ambedkar, converted to Buddhism on 14 October 1956, along with about 600,000 of his followers.

Fight in the name of Baba.'
And with your dying breath saying
'Jai Bhim'[6]
I have seen you.

I have never seen you
In a brocaded new
Nine-yard *Ilkali* sari

Translated by C. S. Lakshmi and Sharmila Sontakke from the original Marathi *Tu Kadhich Disli Nahis* in *Ajoon Wadal Uthale Nahi* (The Storm is Yet to Come)[7]

---

6. *Jai Bhim* is a greeting phrase used by Dalit Buddhists, especially Buddhists who converted with, or because they were inspired by, Dr Bhimrao Ramji Ambedkar. The phrase literally means 'Victory to Bhim' (i.e. to Dr Ambedkar). It was coined by Babu L.N. Hardas who was a staunch follower of Dr Ambedkar. The term is not religious in origin or meaning, even though it is mostly used by Dalit converts to Buddhism. It has been used by converts from the long-exploited and downtrodden classes as a mark of respect towards their ideologue Dr Ambedkar.
7. This translation is based on the English translation of the same poem by Jyoti Lanjewar's daughter Dr Aparna Lanjewar Bose in *Red Slogans on the Green Grass*, Scion Publications Private Ltd, Pune, 2008, pp. 30–35

TWO SISTERS, TWO LIVES

NIRUPAMA DUTT

Devi and I were sired twenty-eight years apart by a grand, but tragic, patriarch. The decades separating her birth from mine were eventful ones: India was freed from British rule, and the country was partitioned. Devi learned many a bitter lesson of life – lessons that I, so vastly her junior, was spared.

Despite the great love we had for one another, somewhere in Devi was the regret that she never got the chances in life that I did.

♦ ♦ ♦

There she stands by a table spread outside the Lahore house; perhaps the photographer wanted some natural light. On the table is her baby brother, wearing a hand-knitted coat and booties. She is posing by the table looking into the camera with innocence, too shy even to smile. She is wearing a dark georgette sari and a pale blouse with puff sleeves, like cine-heroines of the thirties. Her thick hair is pulled back into a bun. She is petite, pretty and only thirteen. The year is 1940.

The child Devi is posing with is her stepmother's first born; in other words, my brother. It would be fifteen years until I would come along, the last child in a family of eight children. Devi and I were the only girls.

♦ ♦ ♦

Devi was born when our father returned from a seven-year stay across the seas, studying history and philosophy at Cambridge and law in Dublin. He returned to India after his father's death to support his mother and siblings, in addition to his own wife and first child. He was not a happy man: there was no time to start a legal practice, and he had not made it in the coveted Indian Civil Services. The next best choice was the Provincial Service; he appeared for the examination and the results came after the birth of Devi in 1927. He was selected to an influential administrative post and he held his baby daughter in his arms saying, 'Devi is my lucky one. She has brought her father a good job. God bless her!'

But Devi's tall, fair and beautiful mother, Ramrakhi, died young. Ramrakhi was just a year over thirty, pregnant again and miserably sick. She died one night of severe infection. Devi was left a motherless child, and slightly cranky at that. She was only six, and a burden on the aunts.

Our father decided that she be sent to her maternal grandmother in another town for better care. The grandmother had many grievances against our father for leaving Ramrakhi for seven long years to pursue his studies abroad. Pained by the death of her own daughter, she had little patience with her granddaughter. So when this grandmother tired, Devi was packed off to her paternal grandmother, who lived a frugal, unhappy life of a widow in the village. That's how Devi spent four years, with interrupted education, being tossed from one grandmother to another, imbibing the values of the two, and at ten she revolted and returned to her father's home in Lahore.

When Devi was twelve, our father took the decision to remarry. This infuriated Devi's oldest brother, who could not bear the idea of someone replacing his dead mother, but Devi was quiet, for she had learned not to display her emotions even to herself. She was curious nevertheless about the new entrant, and awaited her with eager anticipation even as her aunts warned, 'Just you wait, you stubborn one! Your stepmother will soon be here to fix you well and proper.'

When the car arrived, the bride, all veiled in gold-embroidered red silk, saw a little girl with a long plait standing still at the end of the driveway. When the bride got out of the car, Devi stepped forward, solemn and serious, folding her hands and saying in the chaste Hindi that she had learned at school: 'Greetings to you, Mummy-ji.' Just twenty-three, although considered over-age in her clan for marriage, the bride – who was to become my mother – was wedded to a man seventeen years her senior with three children, and she felt a little awkward being addressed as Mummy-ji. But she embraced the girl and whispered, 'Call me Biji.' '*Biji*' was the commonly used word for 'mother' in Punjab. Devi nodded in acceptance, and the bride took on the role of *Biji* from then on. Biji was to recall this later and say, 'My heart went out to the little girl. I had lost my mother when but a child, and I knew the pain of being motherless.'

♦ ♦ ♦

In spite of all his years abroad, our father felt that girls had to be kept away from Western education and should grow up bearing the heavy burden of tradition and religion. So Devi was Daddy's dutiful and good little Hindu girl, one who would make her Mohyal Brahmin clan proud by later being an equally good daughter-in-law and wife.

If Devi had been considered the lucky one, I was the perhaps the 'unlucky one'. I was born to Biji when she was forty and my father had already retired from service; he considered me to be the harbinger of sinking fortune and hard times.

I was told that my father was very anxious that his eighth living child should not be a girl. Biji told me later, 'He would fold his hands and say that I should not spoil his old age by bringing him a daughter at this stage.' He would ward off his worries during the pregnancy, saying, 'An astrologer has told me that I will have seven sons.' Perhaps he did not want to suffer the pain that had come his way because of his daughter Devi; Devi's life had already turned out to be a sad one by that point. But Biji, on the other hand, had always wanted a girl child who would achieve all that she had not been able to achieve. In fact when Biji gave birth to her third son, she was so disappointed that she kept him dressed like a girl until he was three.

♦ ♦ ♦

My first memory of Devi dates back to the time when I was three or four years old. I remember her as a slim girl in a plain *salwar kameez* with a thick, long plait hanging down the nape of her neck. She would cycle every day to college, trying to fill the gap of a disrupted education. Our brothers, barring the oldest, called her '*Behan-ji*', a respectful way of addressing an older sister, but I decided to call her 'Mummy'. Our mother was Biji to all anyway, and Devi seemed to fill the bill of a mummy. She was not firm and authoritative like Biji, but soft and indulgent. Biji insisted that I was now big enough to walk on my own, but 'Mummy' would still carry me if I complained that I was too tired to walk. She would give her share of sweets to me. I often played the make-up expert with her. I would open her plait and comb her lovely hair and then tie it into a ponytail with one of my bright red ribbons. At times I would even get bolder and powder her cheeks.

She would bear it all with utmost patience. I asked her if she would be my 'Mummy' and I could be her daughter, and she said a smiling yes.

One day, however, Devi betrayed me. She took me to her college on her bicycle to show me a crafts exhibition; one of her college mates asked her who I was, and she replied, 'My younger sister.' I came home and created quite a row. Biji asked me how Devi could have told her friend that I was her daughter, when they had not even mentioned in the college that Devi was married. That's when I learned for the first time that my dear 'Mummy' was married, and that her marriage was related to the picture in the cupboard.

◆ ◆ ◆

There was a framed picture that I would see in Devi's cupboard, placed prominently but shut away from others' eyes. In it she was dressed like a bride wearing a huge nose-ring, with a vermilion mark on her forehead, and by her side was a handsome boy with a shock of wavy hair. The picture was tinted in pastel colours by a Shimla photo studio and dated back to the year 1949. As I was to learn, the boy was the notorious Satinder, and he had wrecked Devi's life.

Our brilliant but eccentric father had met Satinder on a train journey when Devi was just thirteen. Taken with the looks and manner of the boy, who belonged to a well-respected family of our clan, my father decided that he was just the right match for his dear daughter. Satinder had only just started his career as a clerk, but my father felt that he would be able to use his influence and get him a better job. The two families conferred and Satinder and Devi were engaged, although the marriage was to take place only after she turned eighteen.

Much happened in those six years between Devi's engagement and her wedding. The country gained independence from British colonial rule, it was partitioned, and our family was among the millions displaced. The family moved from Lahore to Shimla, where the Punjab government for India was shifted, after losing much by way of movable and immovable property. No one from the extended family died, no woman was raped or displaced, as had happened in the bitter communal frenzy of those times on both sides of the new border, and our father's job was intact, but the family members were refugees nevertheless. The Garden Town house in Lahore was looted and burned down a few days after our father came to this side of the border to join the family at Shimla, in the blood-drenched August of 1947.

Life began again and preparations started for Devi's wedding. It was a grand marriage and she went with a huge trousseau.

However, she never got to use that trousseau. She saw maybe two months of happiness before wedded life became a saga of torment. Devi was maltreated and emotionally tortured, because her husband was romantically entangled with his older brother's wife. While Satinder was working in Delhi, Devi was made to live in Kanpur with her sister-in-law, who was furious when she came to know that Devi had conceived in the second month of marriage. When Satinder came to Kanpur, the sister-in-law would rarely allow the two to be alone. Once or twice she barged into the room when Devi and her husband were sharing an intimate moment. Satinder was under the spell of his voluptuous sister-in-law, who was known to have a way with men.

Next, the sister-in-law started a tirade, spreading rumours that Devi was of licentious nature: who knew who was the father of her baby girl? Devi bore all this silently, although broken in spirit, because the traditional advice to a Hindu girl at the time of her marriage was that she was being sent away from her father's home and only her corpse should return.

♦ ♦ ♦

When Devi's daughter was eleven days old, Devi's sister-in-law made one desperate and final attempt to finish the bond between Devi and her husband. She took the baby and held her under a cold-water tap – this, during a biting cold November in North India. She then dropped the baby into Devi's lap with the words, 'Warm her up, now.'

Within three days, the baby was dead. She died of pneumonia.

Devi was to lament all her life, 'How could I have warmed her up?'

The child's death and her husband's growing indifference made Devi smuggle a letter to her parents, saying that if they did not come to fetch her she would have no choice but to commit suicide. Devi's parents rushed to Kanpur, and she returned home alive in what she was wearing. The rich trousseau of gold, silver, Persian carpets, cut glass, Royal Doulton crockery, teak furniture, clothes and much else was left behind.

Devi had only been married for a year, and she returned home deeply injured in her heart and soul. Unable to get over the trauma, she refused to give herself a second chance. This became a point of dispute between the parents. There were marriage offers from other boys, but our father said that Satinder would come round. He declared, with patriarchal orthodoxy, 'I will not take my daughter's personal life to the court.'

Devi supported this, for she felt that she would win Satinder over with her love and sincerity. Later, she accounted for why she did not move on, even though she was only nineteen at the time, with the fatalistic words: 'If things were going to work out, they would have worked out. I went there pure and unblemished, but returned with a blemish.'

I was six, I think, when Devi left the Chandigarh home. I still remember her sad and quiet in her inexpensive khadi shirt, walking out with our father, with only a small bag and a few other belongings. I wept and went running towards her, crying, 'Stop her, Biji! Devi is going away!' Biji did nothing of the sort; she told me in a flat voice, 'Let her go. She is going to her husband. Maybe she will find peace there.'

Devi went away to give her husband a second chance, but by then he had found another paramour.

All Devi got was violence.

◆ ◆ ◆

By the time Devi left for the second time, things were not good at home: the fortunes had fallen. The huge unplanned family, our father's retirement, the grand house he had built and the unsettled younger children had all led to a kind of unhappiness. There was no money; there were fights all the time.

But Biji was a woman of rare courage and resilience. Although she had been born into a wealthy home, and then married well, she took the hard times that came her way in her stride.

◆ ◆ ◆

If Devi had been her father's daughter, I was my mama's darling all the way: she invested all her unfulfilled dreams in me, even if this meant becoming overprotective, because I was born an underweight baby with a chronic bronchial problem. If there was no money to buy me a new dress for my birthday, she would tear up a sari and stitch me a party frock. It was Biji who took me to be admitted to my first school in Chandigarh when I was five, and she saw to it that I went to the best convent in town: Carmel Convent.

I remember in Class 8, my fees were invariably delayed as the remittance that came every month from my older brothers was often late. The names of the defaulters were read out loud in class and I would feel humbled in front of all my classmates. One day, returning home from school, I made a decision and prepared myself to tell Biji to pull me out of this school and send me to the government girls' school where my cousins went. But Biji ruled it out, saying: 'You will

study where you are studying. Times may be hard but we will manage.'
And we did manage.

Biji encouraged me in almost every activity, from singing to
dancing, from cooking to swimming, but I didn't seem to have any
great talent. It was only in the last three years of school when we were
away in the hill town of Shillong in North-East India that my flair for
drawing and languages surfaced. This blossomed further in college, at
Chandigarh, and I topped English language and literature.

My excellent final results at school saw me earning merit in the
university: I could do my Master's in English literature on a scholarship. The expected path for me was to do my Master's and then
teach in a college. All my cousins were in academia, but I wanted to
study journalism. I pleaded with Biji to let me do a one-year journalism course and if it led nowhere, I assured her I would return to the
Master's. No decision could be taken without my big brother Raj's
approval, but Biji let me go my way. Raj was furious when he heard it:
'So, she thinks she will be a writer? All we have seen are her letters full
of spelling mistakes.'

Devi said, 'The gift of writing comes to you from our father.' I felt
it came from my mother, who was well schooled in Indian literature
and enjoyed reading poetry; but perhaps our father had saved this gift
for his seventh son and it had come my way.

♦ ♦ ♦

Comparing the two of us, Biji would say, 'When I found Devi a bit
slow at completing tasks or making decisions, I would wish for a
daughter who was a fast mover, but little did I know that she would
be too fast!' I dared to do all that Devi had not done by way of taking
risks, making quick decisions, speaking my mind, and generally reject-
ing a victim identity dictated by my gender. Unlike Devi, who put
her faith in patriarchy and took great pride in saying that she always

did what her father and brothers expected of her, I took pleasure in challenging my brothers and doing what I wanted.

I became a professional writer and this brought me a clear sense of identity. But I suffered in my personal life: I fell in love not once but twice and was terribly hurt, and after these two failed romances, I made the decision to be single. I disdained the idea of an arranged marriage, common enough even then in my country. Also, I had started enjoying the independence that my single status gave me.

It really did not bother me what others thought. However, by deciding not to marry, I missed out on having a child. To remedy this, after some time, I decided I wanted to adopt a child. When I first started talking about this, my friends and family just thought of it as another whim. But I persisted, and then Biji started supporting the idea.

By this time, a cousin and her husband had helped Devi find a job at a children's home. This had made her active once again, and she nurtured the children with great love, but was upset when those she had reared were adopted. When I spoke to her of my desire to adopt, Devi confessed: 'Mine was a disrupted education, but had I been financially independent, I would never have married. I would have adopted a child and lived with her.'

Devi wanted me to adopt a baby boy, but I was adamant that it had to be a baby girl. I had received so much love from two mothers, Biji and Devi, and I wanted to pass it on to another uncertain girl child. My little girl came to me from the children's home where my sister worked.

I did not choose the baby, because the idea of doing so was unpleasant. I just asked for the youngest girl child, and was given the second-youngest because the youngest was frail and ill. Devi had already given my daughter the name of Upasna. She was ten months old when I got her.

I always took Upasna to be a gift to me from Devi.

◆ ◆ ◆

Devi's greatest loss came when our father died, less than two years after she had moved away. 'God knows how many other heart attacks he suffered, bearing the burden of so large a family,' Devi wailed. 'We just made demands on him, but never thought of his anguish.'

I think often of Devi's own anguish, to this day. Devi's was one of the most painful and unhappy lives of the girls in our extended family. The other girls learned a lesson from Devi's misfortune: there was no way they were going into marriage without being educated and economically independent. Partition and displacement played a role too: there came a growing awareness of education and employment opportunities for women. Women were studying, working and achieving, they were marrying, yes, and some stayed on in the institution of marriage holding on to their own identities, while others walked out of it with few regrets.

I include myself here, along with the other women in my extended family. Because of the life Devi lived and what I learned from her, I achieved economic independence, and I made my own choices – even that of staying single and adopting a girl child.

◆ ◆ ◆

One day, when Devi caught me alone in the living room she walked up to me and said, 'She would have been fifty-four now.'

'Who?' I asked.

'My daughter,' she said.

I was silent, for I knew my sister must be feeling very alone. She rarely mentioned her lost child. 'You know she died of pneumonia, the third day after she was placed under the running tap in the cold of November,' said Devi, though of course I knew this story well. 'Had she lived, she would have been fifty-four.'

In her last exchange with me, during the illness that would lead to her passing, Devi said, 'Remember, you have to write my story.' Devi, dear sister of mine, your story is so poignantly alive in my heart as I put it to paper, but tell me: where does your story end, and where does mine begin?

THE SCIMITAR OF WORDS

CHITRA BANERJEE DIVAKARUNI

I stood on the corner of the dusty street, next to a couple of goats that were busily foraging for food in a pile of garbage. The sun glared down on me and my heart beat unevenly, a mix of nervousness and anticipation. I was waiting for my guide, a woman I did not know. All I had was her name: Nafisa. I would travel with her into the heart of the Baiganwadi slums of Mumbai, and visit one of the Pratham *balwadis* (preschools), a library and a vocational centre that taught computer usage to teenagers. For the last six years, halfway across the world in America, I had worked with a group of Pratham volunteers, raising money to support the organisation's endeavours to fund such programs for underprivileged children and youth. I had created many stories in my head, pieced together from photographs the Pratham India team had sent us, at once heartwarming and heartbreaking; I had imagined what it would feel like to step into a school or centre, and who might people them. Finally, my dreams were about to collide with reality. Would I be pleased? Disappointed? Amazed? I did not know.

A cheery '*Salaamalaikum*' pulled me back to the present. A diminutive young woman stood in front of me, clad in the burqa that traditional Muslim women of the area wore but, unlike them, she was not the least bit shy. She gave me a dazzling smile, informed me that there was no time to lose because there was so much to see, and took me firmly by the hand and led me down a narrow path bordered by open drains. Such was her enthusiasm as she pointed out the local landmarks and said a friendly hello to the shopkeepers that within a few minutes I began to view the place differently. Behind the squalor there were people who were working hard to get by from day to day, who hadn't given up, and who were able to preserve a unique dignity in the midst of dirt. Already my journey was beginning to transform me, just as Pratham had transformed the lives of over 7.7 million children in the last twenty years.

'So what got you interested in Pratham?' Nafisa asked as she dexterously manoeuvred us around a man carrying an enormous basket of vegetables on his head.

It wasn't an unexpected question. I already had an answer prepared. 'I'm a writer, so I'm particularly aware of the power of reading and writing, and how much you need them to get ahead in life,' I said. 'I wanted to help children who might not have access to them otherwise.'

◆ ◆ ◆

But the true genesis of my passion for literacy, especially for girls – my obsession, almost, with this – is far more complicated. It goes way back into my childhood, and it involves a woman named Sarita.

Sarita worked for my family for about six months when I was five years old. My father had been recently transferred to Kolkata, and my mother needed a live-in maid. Somehow word travelled, as it does in India, and one day Sarita knocked on our door. At first my mother was reluctant to hire her because she did not have any references. But after speaking with her and looking into her large, unblinking eyes and her earnest face, she agreed to try her out for a month.

Sarita was a diligent worker. She would finish all her household tasks quickly and efficiently. After that, all she needed to do was to keep an eye on my younger brother, and on me when I returned from kindergarten. She was fascinated by our toys. We were not rich, and the toys were fairly rudimentary. Wooden tops, stuffed cloth dolls, alphabet blocks. But even I, young as I was, could tell that they were a great novelty to her. She was fascinated even more by our books – they were simple picture books in Bengali – and would often ask me to read some of them to her. I myself was not a great reader yet, but I had memorised all the books, so I would pretend to read them.

'What a smart girl,' she would say in wonder.

'Can't you read?' I asked Sarita once.

She shook her head, and a look of shame flashed across her face. My existence had been fairly sheltered, and I had not yet come in close contact with any adults who could not read. I remembered staring at her in surprise.

'Will you teach me?' Sarita asked.

I agreed. I thought it a great entertainment, teaching an adult. I'm afraid I was not a very good teacher. I got impatient and raised my voice if Sarita was unable to recognise a letter, or to read the simple three-letter words I wrote for her. When my mother found out what was going on, she rescued Sarita from me and began to teach her herself. Under proper guidance, Sarita blossomed. Soon she was reading as well as I was – perhaps even better because she began to read some of our books to my brother and me. At first I was jealous, but then I accepted it in the way children do. Sarita stayed up late at night after all her work was done, writing in a notebook with a pencil and eraser my mother had given her. She treasured these items dearly, and when she was done with them, she put them carefully away in the small box that held her few belongings. Seeing her enthusiasm, my mother bought more difficult books and continued teaching her. Soon Sarita could read enough of our daily newspaper to understand the gist of news articles. My mother, as delighted as any Pygmalion, began to talk of sending her to adult school in the evenings. And although my father warned her not to go overboard with educating a servant, she was determined.

It was only as an adult that I wondered how smart this young woman, deprived in her youth of all educational opportunities, must have been. And how far she might have gone if her education had been allowed to continue. But that was not to be.

One weekend morning we were awakened by a commotion at our door, someone banging on it and shouting. It was a man, and he sounded furious. Luckily, my father was home. He opened the door to see who it was. All of us clustered behind him to see what was going on. The man was burly and his face was dark with anger, particularly when his eyes fell on Sarita. She flinched and backed away into the kitchen when she saw him. He shouted obscenities at her and insisted that she go home with him. When my father asked what he meant, he said that she was his wife and that she had run away.

My father was very annoyed by all of this. His job as a tax auditor was a stressful one, and he liked his weekends to be calm and peaceful.

'Find out if this man's accusations are true,' he ordered my mother.

My mother found Sarita squeezed into a corner behind the meat safe. There was a look of terror on her face. She told my mother that yes, she was married to this man. 'I ran away because he beat me,' she whispered. 'Sometimes he brought other men home and tried to make me do bad things with them.'

What kinds of bad things? I wanted to know. But my mother shooed me away, her face grim. She went to my father and whispered in his ear, and his face, too, changed. 'Get out,' he said to the man, his voice soft but chilling. 'Otherwise I'll call the police.' The man blustered and shook his fist, saying that he had a legal right over his wife, but my father slammed the door in his face. The man shouted threats for a while, but finally he left.

That night, my parents had a huge fight. I tried to eavesdrop, but I could not make out much, except that my father thought Sarita would bring them more trouble and should be let go, while my mother thought we needed to protect the maid. In the morning, they did not speak to each other, and for the first time since I was old enough to be aware of such things, my father did not say goodbye to my mother when he left for work. Later, I found my mother crying in the bedroom.

I don't know how the matter would have ended, but Sarita took things into her own hands. She was very quiet all day. The next morning, she was gone.

My mother was worried, but my father was visibly relieved. 'That's one less worry for us to deal with,' he said. 'Make sure she hasn't stolen anything.'

My mother was very upset. 'Sarita would never steal from me,' she said.

She was right. When we looked through the house we found that not only did Sarita not take anything that did not belong to her, but she had left behind her treasured notebook, along with the eraser and pencil. It was as though she had given up on her hopes of education, of ever being able to change her life in that way.

We did not know what happened to Sarita after she left us. We never heard from her. But as a teenager and then an adult, I could not forget her. I often tried to imagine her life. I pictured her fleeing by night train to another city far away. I hoped she was working in a home where her employers were kind to her. But sometimes when I was feeling low, I was afraid her husband had found her and dragged her back to a horrifying life in the slums. In any case, I doubted that she would have been able to continue studying, and without an education what choices did she have? Though I knew that as a child I hadn't had the power to help her, I still felt guilty about it. And I promised myself that when I could, I would do something so that children, especially girls, would not end up in a position like hers.

♦ ♦ ♦

My own growing up, though I was well educated, was fraught with different challenges. They had to do with the fact that mine was a traditional Indian home, and that I was a girl.

I still remember the first time the unfairness of my situation struck me.

It was a delicious monsoon day in Kolkata, dramatically wet and windy. I was about to run out to the flooded street and float the paper boats that I was an expert at making and get soaked in the warm rain with the other children as I always had. But my mother said I couldn't. I was too old now and it wasn't proper.

I didn't understand. 'But brother's doing it,' I pointed out, 'and he's older.'

'That's different,' my mother said, her eyes sad but firm. 'You're a girl.'

I couldn't believe my ears. My mother, who always encouraged me to try harder in school, who told me I had the brains to win the first-place prize, was telling me this? It was my first experience of the prison the world constructs around women and their bodies, the prison that even my mother, whom I'd believed to be all powerful, could not break through.

I moped around for months, not knowing what to do with my newly restricted, dwindling life. I began to notice how young women from families like mine were not allowed to stay out late, even to study. The way they had to be chaperoned when they went to the houses of their girlfriends. The way they were married off halfway through college and then dropped out to have babies. I could feel the net of propriety descending upon me.

But literacy came to my rescue.

One day I found my brother's Indian history textbook lying on his desk. I flipped desultorily through the pages. It was a boring book with lots of small print and few illustrations. Then a picture stopped me.

In this picture a woman sat on a tiger skin while a man knelt nearby, offering her his scimitar. Instead of flowing veils, she wore the male attire of the time: baggy pants and a vest. Instead of daintily sniffing at a rose, like the women in my father's book of Mughal paintings, she leaned forward boldly to grasp the weapon offered to her. The caption below the picture read 'Sultana Raziyya'.

Amazed, I read and re-read the pages avidly. The Sultana was the first woman to sit on the throne of Delhi. (Later I would discover that she was the only woman to do so until Indira Gandhi came to power in the twentieth century.) In 1236 she was nominated by her father, Iltutmish, to succeed him and overcame her weak brothers to rule the volatile kingdom for a brief time.

Raziyya shocked her Muslim court by promptly dispensing with her veil and presiding over them barefaced. She passed laws on racial and religious tolerance and levied taxes to build schools and wells. She could recite the Koran but preferred to write poetry, and she made friends with a number of writers and artists.

The noblemen of the court soon revolted against Raziyya, who fought valiantly but was captured and thrown into prison. But she didn't give up. She talked her jailer, one of the nobles who had been part of the opposition, into marrying her and helping her escape. She died heroically while leading one last, superbly scandalous charge from atop a huge elephant.

Here was someone who had refused to stop when people said to her 'You can't do that! You're a girl!'

Something happened to me as I read and re-read Raziyya's story, a strange sea change. I didn't know how I would manage it, but I promised myself that, like Raziyya, I wouldn't give up. I'd do my best to slash through the taboos that bound us as tightly as mummy wrappings to show the world what a girl could do, no matter how many people stood in her way.

It was the beginning of decades of battle, much of it painful. But ultimately – thanks to the power of education, and to a mother who would not compromise on my schooling, no matter how much people pressured her – I did it. Words became my scimitar, and with them I began to help others – especially girls and women – break out of darkness into light. I wrote my books – for children as well as for adults, and I spoke up for literacy and the work Pratham was doing.

Now, here I was in Baiganwadi, to look at some of the results.

◆ ◆ ◆

The *balwadi* was a single-room preschool, its grey concrete floor scrubbed scrupulously clean. I could see that it was a home – the teacher's home, Nafisa told me. To accommodate the children, the young woman who was the teacher had pushed her meagre furnishings – a dining table and a bed – against the wall. In one corner were a stove and a sink, a few neatly stacked pots. Folded saris and pyjamas hung from a clothesline that was strung up between nails that had been hammered into the far wall. Fourteen children sat cross-legged on the floor, reading out words as the teacher pointed to a large poster that she had pinned to the windowsill. There was much excitement as we entered, and the children vied with each other to answer the math and vocabulary questions that Nafisa, who was clearly familiar with the curriculum, asked. There was even greater excitement when the teacher pointed to America on a world map that hung from another wall and told the children that I had come all the way from U.S.A. to see them – on an aeroplane!

Feeling suddenly shy under their wondering gazes, I handed out coloured pencils and American cookies that stirred much excitement and clapping. I wanted to say something inspiring to them, something about how I wished them well, and how they were off to a great start because they were learning to read and write. But the words that came to my mind – *study hard, don't give up, you can be successful* – felt clichéd and inadequate. I didn't know how to articulate what I really wanted to say: that I hoped their journey into literacy would bring them their own Raziyya, who would inspire them on to their loftiest goals. So, finally, I just hugged the children and told them how happy I was to see them. And then I followed Nafisa out, blinking in the sudden, hot Mumbai sun.

As I walked out of the slums and back into my own life, I thought again of Sarita, who must have lived in a place much like this one – and perhaps still did, if she had cheated death – and how hard she had tried to escape her fate. But my sorrow at the memory was a little less this time. I had something to balance against it: the faces of those *balwadi* children, bright with learning, and the confidence of the women who blossomed through teaching them, all of us wielding the scimitar of education.

ABOUT THE AUTHORS

Anita Agnihotri writes in Bengali. Born in Kolkata, she started writing early in her childhood, and in the 1980s, she started publishing both prose and poetry. She has authored over one hundred short stories, several volumes of poetry, and novels and stories for children. Anita also writes on issues of development, reflecting the people's perspective of reality; the lives of silent, vulnerable and marginalised people lie at the core of her thought. Now author of forty books, Anita has been translated into several Indian languages including English, and into German and Swedish. Married, with two children, Anita lives in Delhi where she also works as a member of the Indian Civil Service.

Anjum Hasan is the author of the novels *The Cosmopolitans*, *Big Girl Now* and *Lunatic in my Head*, and the short story collection *Difficult Pleasures*; the last three of these titles have been published in Australia by Brass Monkey Books. She has also published a book of poems called *Street on the Hill*. Her books have been nominated for various awards including the Man Asian Literary Prize, the DSC Prize for South Asian Literature, the Hindu Best Fiction Award and the Crossword Fiction Award. Her short stories, essays and poems are widely published including most recently in *Granta* and *Griffith Review*, as well as in *Five Dials*, *Wasafiri*,

Drawbridge, Los Angeles Review of Books, Asia Literary Review and anthologies such as *A Clutch of Indian Masterpieces: Extraordinary Short Stories from the 19th Century to the Present* and *The Bloodaxe Book of Contemporary Indian Poets.* Anjum is books editor at *The Caravan*, India's leading magazine of long-form reporting and essays.

Annie Zaidi writes fiction, non-fiction, poetry and scripts. She is the author of *Gulab, Love Stories #1 to 14* and *Known Turf: Bantering with Bandits and Other True Tales*, which was shortlisted for the prestigious Crossword prize (non-fiction). She is also the co-author of *The Good Indian Girl* and the editor of *Unbound: 2000 Years of Indian Women's Writing.* Annie's work has appeared in several anthologies including *Eat the Sky, Drink the Ocean, Mumbai Noir, Women Changing India,* and *Griffith Review 49: New Asia Now.* Her scripts 'Jaal', 'So Many Socks' and 'Compartment' have been performed in various venues in Mumbai. 'So Many Socks' was nominated in several categories including best script for the prestigious META awards for drama. She lives in Mumbai and freelances for various magazines and websites.

Chitra Banerjee Divakaruni is an award-winning author, poet, activist and teacher. Her work has been published in over 100 magazines and anthologies, including the *Atlantic Monthly, The New Yorker, The Best American Short Stories* and the *O. Henry Prize Stories.* Her books have been translated into twenty-nine languages, including Dutch, Hebrew, Bengali, Turkish and Japanese, and have been bestsellers nationally and internationally.

Photo by Krishna Giri

Her awards include: an American Book Award, a Premio Scanno award from Italy, a PEN Josephine Miles award, and a Light of India award. Two of her books, *The Mistress of Spices* and *Sister of My Heart*, have been made into movies. Divakaruni teaches in the nationally ranked Creative Writing program at the University of Houston, where she is the McDavid Professor of Creative Writing. She serves on the Advisory Boards of Maitri and Daya, organisations that help survivors of domestic violence, and on the Emeritus board of Pratham, a literacy non-profit.

C.S. Lakshmi has been an independent researcher in women's studies for the last forty years. She has a PhD from Jawaharlal Nehru University, New Delhi, and has several books and articles to her credit. She is also a creative writer who writes about love, relationships, quests and journeys in the Tamil region and elsewhere under the pseudonym Ambai. She has been writing from the age of sixteen and is a well-known writer in Tamil. Her stories have been translated in three volumes: *A Purple Sea; In a Forest, a Deer*; and *Fish in a Dwindling Lake.* The latter shared the Hutch Crossword Award 2006 for translated fiction.

She is currently the Director of SPARROW (Sound & Picture Archives for Research on Women). She lives in Mumbai with her filmmaker friend Vishnu Mathur, who also happens to be her husband, in a small third-floor flat with a view of the sea, along with her nineteen-year-old foster daughter Khintu and her two little brothers Krishna and Sonu who brighten up her life.

Deepti Kapoor was born in Moradabad, Uttar Pradesh, and grew up in various places across North and West India, studying in Dehradun and Delhi and completing degrees in Journalism and Social Psychology. She worked for a decade in print media in Delhi and Mumbai, first as a reporter and later as an editor. In 2007 she left Delhi for Mysore and later Goa, to study and teach yoga and write. Her first novel *A Bad Character* (Penguin Random House, 2015) was shortlisted for several awards in India, and was published in translation in France (Seuil, 2015), where it was shortlisted for the *prix Médicis étranger* 2015. Deepti also writes for various publications including *Granta, Condé Nast Traveller* and *The Guardian*, and reviews hotels for travel magazines and websites. She is currently writing her second novel, a multi-perspective narrative about an American yoga student travelling through India.

Ira Trivedi is the bestselling author of four books. *India in Love*, her most recent book, is a seminal work of non-fiction on India's social revolution and sexual violence. Her first novel *What Would You Do to Save the World?* was published when she was eighteen. Ira writes regularly

Photo by Catriona Mitchell

for *Foreign Affairs, Foreign Policy, Times of India, Hindustan Times, The Telegraph* and other publications. She has been called one of India's most important youth voices, and she speaks regularly to media and on forums in India and internationally. Her work on gender and culture has won several awards. Ira won a U.K. Anti-Slavery Day Media award in 2015 for her article on bride trafficking 'When a Bride-to-Be Is a Bride to Buy', and was honoured at the House of Lords in England. She holds a MBA from Columbia Business School and a BA from Wellesley College. When not writing, she is doing or teaching yoga.

Leila Seth was the first woman to top the Bar examinations in London, the first woman judge in the Delhi High Court, and the first woman to become Chief Justice of a state High Court. She was appointed as a judge in 1978 and retired as Chief Justice of Himachal Pradesh in 1992. In 1995 she was appointed as a one-member commission to examine the death in custody of Rajan Pillai and to suggest improvements in medical facilities for prisoners. She was a member of the 15th Law Commission of India (1997–2000) and also one of the three members of the committee set up after the gang rape of Nirbhaya in December 2012 (known as the Justice Verma Committee) that gave recommendations to the government on amendments to the criminal law and other matters.

She is the author of three books: *On Balance*, her autobiography; *Talking of Justice*, a collection of essays on people's rights in modern India; and *We, the Children of India*, a book for children explaining the preamble to the Constitution of India, which she believes should be read by every child in India.

Margaret Mascarenhas is a multilingual transnational writer, consulting editor and independent curator of Indo-American origin. She is the author of the diasporic novel, *Skin* (Penguin, 2001), which has been taught in colleges and universities and highlighted in numerous academic papers on post-colonial literature in India, Portugal and the U.S.A. Her second novel, *The Disappearance of Irene Dos Santos* (Hachette U.S.A. 2009), set in Venezuela where she grew up, was the recipient of a Publishers Lunch award and a Barnes and Noble Discover Pick in literary fiction. *Triage: Casualties of Love and Sex*

(HarperCollins India, 2013), is her first published collection of poetry, flash memoir and sketches. She was the founding Director of the Goa Centre for the Arts in 2011, and Convenor of its advisory board in 2015. She is the Founder-Director of the Blue Shores Prison Art Project in Goa. Margaret lives most of the year in Goa, where she has ancestral roots, and where she maintains a residency in the picturesque village of Calvim for working artists and writers.

Mitali Saran is a Delhi-based freelance writer. She has never had a shred of ambition, and therefore doesn't have what you'd call a career, but along the way she has worked full-time for the newspaper *Business Standard* and for *Outlook Traveller* magazine, and written freelance for a range of news, feature, travel, and review publications. She is constantly torn between the urge to travel and the urge to curl up with a good book. She now writes two fortnightly columns ('Stet' and 'Inter alia') for *Business Standard*, and doesn't understand why people keep asking what else she does. She thinks that a day spent with friends, playing guitar, and dancing tango is a day as meaningless and doomed as a seriously productive day, but a lot more fun. She fully intends to take the more fun road to hell.

Photo by Catriona Mitchell

Namita Gokhale is a writer, publisher and festival director. She is the author of twelve works of fiction and non-fiction. Her first novel, *Paro: Dreams of Passion*, published in 1984, created a furor due to its frank sexual humour. Her other books include: *Gods, Graves and Grandmother; A Himalayan Love Story; The Book of Shadows; Shakuntala: the Play of Memory; Priya in Incredible Indyaa; In Search of Sita: Revisiting Mythology; The Habit of Love;* and the edited anthology, *Travelling In, Travelling Out.*

Gokhale is a founder and co-director of the ZEE Jaipur Literature Festival and 'Mountain Echoes', the Bhutan Literature Festival. She is director of Yatra Books, a publishing house that specialises in translation. She has curated Kitaabnama, India's only multilingual book show for the national TV channel Doordarshan. As a literary activist, she is passionately committed to showcasing the Indian languages.

Nirupama Dutt is a poet, journalist and translator, as well as an art, literary and film critic. She writes in English, Punjabi and occasionally in Hindi. Her most recent work was an English translation of Gulzar's anthology of poetry *Pluto* (HarperCollins, 2015).

She received the Punjabi Akademi Award for her anthology of poems, *Ik Nadi Sanwali Jahi* (*A Stream Somewhat Dark*). Her anthology of poetry *The Black Woman* was published in English (Aesthetics Publications, 2009). Her other books include: *Stories of the Soil*, an English translation of forty-one stories from Punjabi (Penguin, 2011); *Poet of the Revolution*, an English translation of the memoirs and poetry of Lal Singh Dil (Penguin, 2013); and *The Ballad of Bant Singh*, the biography of a Dalit activist and singer. She is currently working on a novel.

She lives in Chandigarh with her daughter and granddaughter.

Photo by Pablo Bartholomew

Rosalyn D'Mello is a widely published freelance art writer based in New Delhi. Her first non-fiction book *A Handbook For My Lover*, an erotic memoir, was published in 2015 (HarperCollins). Her art reviews and features have been published in *Art + Auction, Modern Painters, Passages, Art India,* and *Take on Art.* She is a regular contributor to *Vogue, Open, Mint Lounge, Art Review,* and *Art Review Asia.* She was the associate editor of *The Art Critic*, a selection of the art writings of Richard Bartholomew from the fifties to the early eighties. She was among five writers nominated for Forbes' Best Emerging Art Writer Award in 2014 and was also nominated for the inaugural Prudential Eye Art Award for Best Writing on Asian Contemporary Art in 2014.

Salma is a writer of Tamil poetry and fiction. Her work speaks about the taboo areas of the traditional woman's experience. She has published two volumes of poetry: *Oru Malaiyum Innoru Malaiyum* (An Evening and Another Evening) and *Pachchai Devadhai* (Green Angel). Her novel, *Irandaam Jaamangalin Kadhai* (2004), revolving around the lives of women in a Muslim community of rural Tamil Nadu, was considered a landmark achievement in Tamil. When it was later translated into English as *The Hour Past Midnight* (2009), Salma made her mark as a writer in the rest of India and abroad. Salma also published *Saabam* (The Curse), a collection of short stories in 2012. A political activist for the cause of women's empowerment, Salma was Chairperson of Tamil Nadu Government's Social Welfare Board between 2007 and 2011. She lives and works in Chennai.

Sharanya Manivannan's first book *Witchcraft* (Bullfighter Books, 2008) was described in *The Straits Times*, Singapore, as 'sensuous and spiritual, delicate and dangerous and as full as the moon reflected in a knife'. She was specially commissioned to write and perform a poem at the 2015 Commonwealth Day Observance at Westminster Abbey, London, to an audience that included the British Royal Family. *The Altar of the Only World*, a book of poetry, and *The High Priestess Never*

Photo by Catriona Mitchell

Marries, a book of stories, are both forthcoming from HarperCollins India; a children's book is forthcoming from Lantana Publishing, U.K. Sharanya writes a personal column, 'The Venus Flytrap', which appears in *The New Indian Express*. Her essays, fiction and poetry have been widely published internationally, and she has participated at readings in the U.K., Australia, Indonesia, Germany, Malaysia, Singapore and India. She was born in 1985 in Chennai, where she now resides.

Tisca Chopra is a Bollywood actress known for her unconventional roles. She chooses to be part of stories that she feels need to be told, and has acted more than forty feature films in different languages with many eminent directors, including Aamir Khan, Prakash Jha, Madhur Bhandarkar, Abhinay Deo and Nandita Das.

Tisca got her big break in *Taare Zameen Par (Like Stars on Earth)* – India's official Academy Awards entry for Best Foreign Film in 2009 – and received several national and international awards for her performance. Tisca also starred in *Qissa*, which premiered at the Toronto Film Festival in 2013 and won the prestigious NETPAC Award for Best Asian Film. In 2012, Tisca was nominated at the New York Indian Film Festival for Best Actress for her work in *10Ml Love*, a film based on *A Midsummer Night's Dream*.

Tisca has also worked extensively in theatre with Naseeruddin Shah, Feroz Khan and Satya Dev Dubey.

She has a Bachelor's Degree in Literature from the University of Delhi. Her bestselling memoir *Acting Smart* (HarperCollins, 2014) is being translated into Hindi, and she is currently working on a film script that she plans to produce.

Photo by Catriona Mitchell

Tishani Doshi is an award-winning writer and dancer of Welsh-Gujarati descent. Born in Madras, India, in 1975, she received a Masters in Writing from Johns Hopkins University in the U.S.A. She worked in London in advertising before returning to India in 2001, where a chance encounter with the legendary choreographer Chandralekha led her to an unexpected career in dance. She has published five books of poetry and fiction, the most recent of which is *Fountainville* – a medieval Welsh tale recast among opium dens, gang wars and a surrogacy clinic. Tishani currently lives in a village by the sea in Tamil Nadu.

Photo by Catriona Mitchell

Urvashi Butalia was co-founder of Kali for Women, India's first feminist publishing house. She is now Director of Zubaan, one of the imprints founded by Kali when it shut down operations in 2003. She has had a long involvement with the women's movement in India, and writes on a range of issues relating to women and gender in India. She has spent many years teaching a professional course in publishing. Her best-known publications include an award-winning history of Partition, *The Other Side of Silence: Voices from the Partition of India* (which won the Oral History Book Association Award and the Nikkei Asia Award for Culture), *Speaking Peace: Women's Voices from Kashmir* (edited), and *Women and the Hindu Right: A Collection of Essays* (co-edited). She is currently working on a number of book projects.

ACKNOWLEDGEMENTS

My heartfelt thanks go to the contributors to this book who, without exception, agreed to be a part of it because they felt the issues addressed here were important ones. Thank you all for your willingness to take this leap, for probing into your own life experiences in ways that took courage, so that this book could become a kaleidoscope of poignant and pertinent and daring stories about the female experience. For some of you, writing 'from the self' meant exploring new terrain, and this brought with it certain vulnerabilities. I thank you for agreeing to share the hidden, the deeply felt, the intimate, the sometimes disquieting details of your lives, so that others might benefit from reading them. Your words will surely resonate with readers in India and beyond, striking universal chords with women's experiences everywhere.

Namita Gokhale, who wrote the foreword, was an invaluable guide and generously shared her knowledge of Indian language writers. Namita is an inspiration to me and many others with her dedication and belief in fore-fronting women's voices and her support of writing of all kinds in India.

A huge thanks goes to the team at Hardie Grant Books in Australia, and in particular to the book's commissioning editor, Meelee Soorkia. This book would simply not have been birthed

---

without Meelee's unwavering commitment, professional mastery and unfailing good humour. From the initial brainstorming meetings in Hardie Grant's Melbourne office, to the pulling together of the final details from different time zones, the process of working with Meelee was a joy. Thanks also to Hardie Grant Publishing Director, Fran Berry, for believing in this book.

Thank you to Manasi Subramaniam at HarperCollins India, who championed this anthology from the moment she heard about it at Sydney Writers Festival, when it was still in its infancy, and has maintained her enthusiasm throughout.

Thanks, too, to the Australia-India Council for a grant that will bring contributors from this anthology to Australia, so that their voices can be heard there and important live discussions can take place around the themes of the book.

And finally, to the mothers and grandmothers mentioned in all of these personal stories, those women who have taught their daughters to stand tall and become educated and to have a voice – yours is a precious legacy. May it be safely cherished and passed on.

ABOUT THE EDITOR

Photo by Rio Helmi

Catriona Mitchell is a writer, editor and literary events programmer who fell in love with India initially through its literature when in her teens, and later via her first actual visit in 2007. In 2009, she received an Asialink Arts Residency with Teamwork Arts and Jaipur Literature Festival (JLF) to conduct research into the work of twenty-four contemporary Indian authors. Since then, she has had an ongoing engagement with JLF (in her mind the most vivid event on the planet), which continues to fuel her deep interest in contemporary Indian literature and culture.

In 2012 Catriona co-created the Bookwallah train tour which took Indian authors, Australian authors and a portable, pop-up library of Australian books through South India by train for a month, and delivered live events at every stop along the way. Bookwallah won an Australian Federal Government arts award in 2013. Catriona directed, shot and edited a thirty-minute documentary of the Bookwallah tour, which screened in India and Australia.

Catriona has a Masters in Writing, and an M Phil in Creative Writing from Trinity College Dublin. She is a former Program Director of the Ubud Writers & Readers Festival, Bali.

Passionate about telling compelling women's stories, Catriona publishes conversations with remarkable women from around the world in an online magazine called *Brava! brave women, bright ideas*.